# Q Tips

# Q Tips

_____

*Fast, Scalable, and Maintainable Kdb+*

**Nick Psaris**

$\vec{\sigma}$

**Vector Sigma**

Hong Kong

Books may be purchased in quantity and/or special sales by contacting the publisher, Vector Sigma at sales@vector-sigma.com.

Published by: Vector Sigma, Hong Kong SAR

ISBN: 978-988-13899-0-9

10 9 8 7 6 5 4 3

For J & Z

# Contents

# List of Q Tips

# Foreword

Every q/kdb+ programmer wants to use the language safely and efficiently. The proven way to get to that point in a short time is to enlist the help of an expert colleague or friend. Nick has written a friendly book that, with careful study on your part, will do perhaps 80% of what that colleague would do for you.

He starts with the basics of loading the interpreter and proceeds all the way up to large distributed data applications. In the process he suggests ways to ensure that your code is safe and efficient. Because the text is full of worked and very well explained examples, you can start from a base of code that you understand and then build from there.

This is a book by a practitioner for practitioners. It will raise the level of discourse. Bravo!

Prof. Dennis Shasha
Department of Computer Science
Courant Institute of Mathematical Sciences

# Preface

My journey through programming languages leading to q started in 1999. At the time, I had been using Perl to import and export data from log files, configuration files and databases. I had also adopted the Perl community's preference for short and concise (though perhaps obscure) code. During a trip to Hong Kong, a colleague showed me Perl's ability to create nested arrays of hashes, hashes of arrays and hashes of hashes. Until that time, this was the most powerful data structure I had ever used. It allowed me to load multiple datasets, "join" them by their hash key, compute aggregate statistics and generate summary reports with ease. This was, by far, the most convincing reason to use Perl.

It was not until 2006 that I first encountered q. I was joining a new team and preparing to permanently move to Hong Kong. The team was rewriting their US trading system in kdb+. I was given the responsibility to customize it for Asia. My long history with procedural and object oriented programming languages did not prepare me for this head-first dive into kdb+. What did prepare me, however, was my desire to combine data from multiple sources, generate actionable reports, quickly prototype new functionality, all while writing as little code as possible. I soon discovered that although Perl excelled in each of these areas, q took things to another level. Loading, joining, and analyzing data was not only faster (and required less memory), it could also be done with far less code.

This combination of decreased memory footprint, faster execution, and quicker prototyping, opened up new business opportunities. We replaced jobs that took hours to run with ones that ran in minutes. We increased the universe of analysis from hundreds of items per day to thousands. Instead of running reports overnight, we could run them on-demand, providing semi-real-time access to previously unimaginable amounts of information.

It did not take long for me to acknowledge the power of kdb+ and the q programming language. Learning q was not easy however. The language was still evolving, documentation was cryptic and incomplete, and sample code was hard to find. I was lucky to work on a team that prized short efficient q code. Similar to the kdb+ mail groups, we would compete with each other to generate faster and shorter solutions.

In hindsight, I can see my attraction to Perl's hashes of hashes and arrays of hashes was because they were actually a poor-man's implementation of keyed and unkeyed tables. Kdb+ includes these data structures as language primitives, integrates them with the standard operators, and provides new operators for algorithms specific to tables.

Though the documentation has improved and the language is more stable, it is still hard to learn q best practices without asking another q expert. I have collected some of my best practices and included them as tips. The book is not meant to document every feature of kdb+ and the q programming language. Kx System's Wiki [wiki] [265] page is the best place for that. This book was written to take you on a journey covering the most important areas of the language. Along the way, I hope the tips provide a foundation for you to continue the journey yourself, and begin to think like a q-god.

# Chapter 1

# Introduction

Another jump in performance and productivity. With kdb+ we have merged the k and k-SQL languages into a single language for queries, time-series analysis and general programming. This means that customer programs will be smaller and faster to write.

— Arthur Whitney *An Interview with Arthur Whitney (2004)*

We live in a world filled with data. Whether it is real estate prices, website clicks, financial security prices or racetrack horse times, the amount of data only increases as time passes. An analyst often begins by storing data in a spreadsheet, only to realize the solution does not scale once they have spent many hours customizing it to their needs. What may have started as a small problem, quickly grows too big for a spreadsheet to manage. At this point a search for an appropriate database begins. There are many proprietary and open source databases to choose from - each with their own advantages.

## 1.1   Why Kdb+?

A typical database installation requires three teams: the database administrator, the schema designer, and the end user. With kdb+, all three teams can be combined into one. An analyst obtains data, records it into a kdb+ database, and later analyzes the data themselves. This is all possible because kdb+, though in name is a database, is merely a combination of the file system and the q programming language. Backups, permissions and segments are all delegated to the file system. Creating, deleting, and modifying tables are all features of the q programming language or the file system. Q allows data to start as small in-memory tables. If the tables grow or are expected to grow, they can be moved to disk. And finally, if the tables grow beyond the size of either the local file system, or the amount of data typically held simultaneously in memory, they can be segmented across multiple directories and/or file systems. None of these features requires a database administrator. Of course if the project is successful, these three roles may be split among teams, but that is an option and not a necessity.

A common data analysis work-flow consists of connecting to a database, performing a query to extract the desired dataset, and then analyzing the records. It is often the case that different scripting languages are used to extract data from the database and perform the analysis. Python and Perl, for example, are often used to extract data and R and Matlab are used for the data analysis. While nothing prevents a kdb+ database from being used as the back-end database in this example, it is also possible to use q as the scripting language for data retrieval *and* analysis. This enables seamless integration of data and analytics. Alternatively, because both the scripting language and the database are both running q programs, a q function defined in a script can be sent to the database where it is evaluated and then only the results are returned. This is a reversal of the paradigm where data is brought to the analytics. With q, analytics can be sent to the data.

The advantages of using the same scripting language to both build and query the database, go beyond using the high level algorithms provided by q for data manipulation. The synergies work both ways. You can also use tables and high level database operators in your own analytics. In addition to the standard primary data structures such as lists and maps, kdb+ also has tables.

By far the biggest selling point for kdb+ is its speed. Kdb+ is a column oriented database, which means that, unlike most databases where rows of data are stored together, data in kdb+ is stored by column. Each column is stored in contiguous memory, both in-process and on-disk, allowing computations across columns to be performed with astonishing speed. When the results of a vector operation are then used as the inputs of the next operation, all the data stored in the CPU's memory cache can be accesses immediately without needing to search in the slower/larger caches or even the slowest and largest memory store located on the motherboard. In addition, modern CPUs provide custom interfaces to accelerate vector processing. Kdb+ takes full advantage of these optimizations to achieve optimal performance. Saving data in columns instead of rows also allows each column to be mapped in and out of memory when needed, thus reducing the need for all data to be loaded simultaneously. All updates in kdb+ are performed in a single thread. This removes the need for any resource locking, and thus provides another speed enhancement.

## 1.2 What is Q?

Arthur Whitney wrote q as the most recent in a line of array programming languages. After getting his feet wet by developing implementations for Lisp and APL, Arthur developed his first new language: A (a Unix version of APL). This was followed by a quick one page interpreter [incunabulum] [267] that inspired the J programming language [jsoftware] [267]. He then developed k (the underlying language q is written on). The goal for each of these languages was to limit the extended character set of APL/A/A+ [aplus] [267] to the ASCII character set. K has gone through many iterations, each a distillation of the previous. Q itself is a layer on top of the k4 language. This last layer adds readability and database management support. K5 [kparc] [267], a smaller and faster version of k, is currently being implemented.

The complete package of the q programming language and the database management infrastructure is known as kdb+, and is owned and supported by Kx Systems. To get our first program up and running, we will first need to download the free version. Although fully compatible with the production version, it is only available for 32-bit architectures. This limits the in-process memory to 4GB. It is available on all common desktop platforms: Windows, Linux, Solaris and OS X.

The names kdb+ and q are often used interchangeably. This book, however, will make a clear distinction between the two. Q will always refer to the programming language, its syntax, and its operators. My use of kdb+ will refer to the complete environment. It includes the interpreter, Inter-Process Communication and event callbacks. Finally, although the terms "operator" and "function" are quite similar, I will reserve the term "operator" for any function that is provided by the q language. Some q operators are implemented in C and others are, in fact, q functions. Regardless of their implementation, I will refer to them all as operators.

## 1.3 Programming Paradigms

Q is an interpreted, dynamic, event-driven, functional, array programming language.

- Q is interpreted because it requires no compilation phase. All functions are compiled into bytecode at run time. Definitions are compiled at startup and are lazily resolved. They must therefore be syntactically correct at startup, but the ordering of compilation is not important.

- Q is dynamic in both function definition and variable types. Function definitions and variable types can be changed at runtime. This flexibility adds a runtime penalty as both the function definition and variable type must be checked for each function call.

- Q is an array (or vector) programming language. It generalizes operations on scalars to work for lists as well. When the datasets are large and the lists are long, the penalty for this type checking is amortized over each of the many operations performed in highly efficient compiled code. This overhead becomes important when datasets are small.

- Q exhibits characteristics of a functional language because functions are first class citizens. They can be passed as arguments to and returned by functions, saved in variables or stored in data structures. Q also allows partial application or binding of function arguments to form new functions. It is not a *pure* functional language, however, because functions may have side effects.

- Kdb+ processes can be written as event handlers. Without concurrency, all q functions run in a single main thread. To enable interaction with other processes or libraries, q implements the reactor design pattern. It demultiplexes the concurrent messages and synchronously invokes callbacks. Responding to multiple asynchronous events allows kdb+ processes to be used as a Complex Event Processor (CEP).

## 1.4 What is in This Book?

Chapter 2 [7] starts by demonstrating how to install and run the q binary, as well as configure and customize the q environment. It then gives an example of typing commands at the prompt and explains how to recover from errors caused by incorrect syntax. The chapter finishes with an overview of a few of q's unique syntax rules.

Q's forte is in data analysis. Chapter 3 [21] demonstrates many ways to generate data. It first explains how lists are stored, manipulated and inspected. It then provides examples of generating ordered data. The remainder of the chapter focuses on random data - both numeric and non-numeric.

Chapter 4 [35] explains how to write functions to manipulate and analyze data. It introduces three ways of converting uniformly distributed random numbers to normally distributed random numbers: 12 uniforms, the Box-Muller transform and the Beasley-Springer-Moro method.

Chapter 5 [51] begins by explaining how to load q libraries. It then describes how we can use namespaces and directories to better scope data and functions into logical groups. The chapter concludes by demonstrating how we can import functions between directories.

Chapter 6 [63] uses the tools introduced in the previous chapter to generate simulated financial time series data. Beginning with a function to generate a random walk, the chapter then introduces the date and time types built into kdb+. The final section builds a security price path and explains how to round prices to correctly model reality.

Q's "killer feature" is the existence of the table as a primary data structure. Chapter 7 [73] introduces three new data types: dictionaries, tables, and keyed tables. The chapter introduces the syntax used to declare these types as well as many important operators needed to manipulate them. It also emphasizes their internal memory layout.

Having covered all the tools needed to generate and manipulate datasets, you may jump to Chapter 14 [163] for an introduction to q-SQL. If you continue on to Chapter 8 [91], however, you will learn how loops are generated in q and how to optimize large kdb+ datasets for performance. The chapter discusses each of the four attributes available in kdb+ and how they can be used to increase the speed of accessing records.

Chapter 9 [109] creates utility functions to generate quote and trade tables. Useful techniques such as creating ranges of random data, using a sorted dictionary to implement a step function and rounding prices to the nearest tick are demonstrated. The functions developed will be used again when we build a working CEP engine.

Chapter 10 [121] and Chapter 11 [139] step through the process of building and running a CEP engine. Timer, logging and command line option libraries are introduced in Chapter 10 [121]. Chapter 11 [139] then demonstrates how to open a server socket, load configuration from delimited files, and finally start the CEP engine.

By default, kdb+ imposes no restrictions on client connections. Any client can modify the kdb+ server's internal state. Chapter 12 [153] covers important topics needed to secure a kdb+ server. Topics include limiting access to specific users, integrating with corporate authentication software and making the server read only. The chapter also explains how to access connection specific information such as the source IP address, ID and hostname.

Chapter 13 [159] is small, but includes important debugging techniques. It begins by explaining the debugging interface and proceeds to provide examples on debugging errors from asynchronous events. The chapter concludes with a section on conditional "breakpoints".

Either by using the tools developed in Chapter 9 [109] to build historical trade and quote tables, or by running the CEP engine from Chapter 11 [139], we now have actual data to analyze. Chapter 14 [163] introduces q-SQL which can be used to query kdb+ tables. To some, q is synonymous with q-SQL. Each of the fundamental q-SQL operators is discussed before explaining the evolution of a pivot function. More advanced queries are then covered and the chapter concludes with an introduction to each of the table join operators.

As our datasets continue to grow, we will reach a point when the amount of data exceeds the available memory on our computer. Chapter 15 [201] covers different methods of coping with the problems that big datasets introduce. The chapter discusses how data can be partitioned by columns and rows. It even discusses how kdb+ can be configured to partition the partitions to create a segmented database. The chapter finishes with a discussion on how data can be compressed on disk, mapped into memory and accessed by multiple process.

With our dataset built, Chapter 16 [225] demonstrates techniques to access kdb+ data from different environment. It begins with q's native ability to effortlessly send and receive data (and functions). The chapter then describes how q's network protocol has been implemented in other languages. We then discuss how to request data from q's builtin web server by using both text-based HTTP and binary WebSocket protocols. The chapter ends by presenting the qcon command line tool which can be used to administer kdb+ servers.

Chapter 17 [235] presents a few advanced techniques. It begins by building a profiling utility to measure the performance of CEP engines. The internal representation of functions and views are discussed. Two forms of derivative pricing are presented and the basics of multi-core processing are demonstrated. The chapter concludes with an example of how to use functional programming techniques to write a histogram library.

The last chapter, Selected Web Resources [265], lists many useful web resources. In addition to links to Kx System's sites, the chapter has a few links relating to q's history and future. This is followed by a glossary listing common terms used when discussing both q and functional programming.

Finally, Appendix A [273] contains a listing of all the source code used in the book. Used together, the code can run the CEP engine, profile its performance, price derivatives, and generate histograms of the data we generate.

## 1.5  Who is This Book For?

This book is designed for developers with experience in at least one programming language who are looking to use q to store and analyze large datasets, to develop analytic engines that subscribe and publish event streams, or to combine large datasets with stream-like functions to create a backtesting system. Q has the ability to span both the big data and high frequency domains. Applying q to either domain brings huge advantages in productivity. Using it in both domains creates revolutionary opportunities.

Learning q can be challenging for a number of reasons. For some, the terse syntax can be confusing. Regardless of your programming experience, the q syntax will take time to understand and potentially master. The effort you spend learning q will pay dividends in productivity.

Other hurdles include cryptic error messages and the concept of functional programming. Aside from reading the online manual from beginning to end many times, there are two ways to learn q faster. The first is to actually start writing programs yourself. The second is to read other people's code. Many tricks are passed from person to person, never being formally documented. This book takes you step by step through the creation of a real Complex Event Processor (CEP) engine. In the process, the code is explained and important tips are introduced. The functions developed are self contained and can be used immediately in your own projects.

Chapter 2

# Getting Started

I skimmed documentation of Python after people told me it was fundamentally similar to Lisp. My conclusion is that that is not so. "read", "eval", and "print" are all missing in Python.

— Richard Stallman *How I do my computing*

This chapter starts by describing how to install q on your own machine. This is as simple as downloading the q binary from the Kx website. We then introduce the q) REPL and cover the requisite *Hello World* example. Learning q from the command line is easy because examples are short and q provides a fully functional "read", "eval" and "print" loop (or REPL).

Before continuing to introduce the q language, we take a diversion and discuss two important items. The first is how to recover from accidental syntax errors. And the second is how to prevent the syntax errors to begin with. We discuss a few unique syntax rules that typically cause confusion when first learning q.

By the end of this book, we will have developed a fully functioning CEP engine. All the presented code is listed in Appendix A [273]. You can also download it from GitHub: https://github.com/psaris/qtips. Before installing the q binary, take a moment to download the Q Tips source.

## 2.1  Installing kdb+

The free version of the q binary can be downloaded from Kx System's website [free] [265]. This book covers features included in kdb+ 3.2. If you already have an older version installed, you will want to take this opportunity to download the latest copy. Pick the archive suited for your computer and uncompress it into a directory.

Five files will be downloaded and saved in a directory named after the platform you selected. You can now open README.txt for more specific information about the installation and a list of other kdb+ references. Coding in q is an interactive process. It is quite common to rerun the same command with slight variations to inspect the results or compare performance. To make this process easier, it is important to have an environment that can recall previous commands. Running q from a DOS prompt provides rudimentary access to historical commands by using the up arrow. The default terminal environments on *nix operating systems such as Linux, Solaris, and OS X do not provide this feature. The rlwrap utility not only enables recalling historical commands, but also allows searching and auto-completion. Follow the steps in the README.txt file to install rlwrap.

```
$ rlwrap $QHOME/m32/q
q)
```

## Configuration

There are two important files in the installation. The first file is the q binary itself. It is located in the platform specific folder with a name like w32, s32, v32 or l32. The second file, q.k, is the file that defines many of the q operators. As previously mentioned, q is implemented as a mix of C, k, and q itself. The q.k file includes the implementation for many operators defined in k and q. Over time, a few of the operators previously implemented in q.k have been rewritten directly in C to increase performance. The complete list of operators defined in C can be found in the .Q.res variable.

```
q).Q.res
`in`within`like`bin`binr`ss`if`do`while`exec`select`insert`update`delete`av..
```

The installation directory also contains another file named s.k which is used to implement an SQL interface for ODBC clients. It also provides an example of how to define other languages on top of k.

On startup, the q binary must load the q.k file to pick up the q definitions. For the q binary to find this file, you must first set the QHOME environment variable to the full path of the directory holding q.k. Once you have become more familiar with the q language, you can obtain a deeper understanding, and perhaps pick up a few coding pointers, by reading the q.k file.

## Running q

Now that the binary is installed, and the QHOME environment variable is configured, we can start the kdb+ process. Here is an example of running q on my laptop.[1]

```
$ ./m32/q
KDB+ 3.2 2015.03.04 Copyright (C) 1993-2015 Kx Systems
m32/ 4()core 2048MB nick nicks-macbook.local 192.168.1.103 NONEXPIRE
```

---

[1] If you are running on a 64-bit machine, you will also need to install 32-bit libc libraries to allow the 32-bit version of kdb+ to work.

There are few points to highlight here. On the first line of the banner, the 3.2 refers to the `kdb+` version. This is followed by the `q` binary release date. On the second line, the m32 matches the architecture used to start the binary. `4()core` indicates that `kdb+` is capable of seeing 4 cores on my machine. If you purchase a production license, the number of licensed cores would appear within the parentheses. If you do not plan on using multiple cores per `kdb+` instance, it is possible to reduce the number of cores visible to the `q` binary on *nix machines by changing the CPU affinity with the `taskset` utility. The number of available cores is followed by the system's available memory, login ID, machine name, IP address, an optional company name and license expiration date ("NONEXPIRE" in the case of the free 32-bit version).

## Customization

Once the `q` binary starts, it checks for a production license file: `k4.lic`. By default, it looks in the same directory as `q.k`. The location of the license file can be customized by setting the `QLIC` environment variable before starting `q`. `Q` then looks for a file named `q.q` in the same default location. This file is used to customize your `kdb+` installation. The name and location of this file can also be customized by setting the `QINIT` environment variable. Any code within the `QINIT` file will be executed before control is returned to the user. The free 32-bit version of `q` will start without either of these files. The production 64-bit version, however, requires a license.

`Kdb+` has a builtin web server. You can use it to view tables, download data, run custom queries, or even issue commands to modify the `kdb+` server itself. If you would like the `q` web server to return files such as a `crossdomain.xml` or `favicon.ico` file, these can be placed in an `html` directory directly below `QHOME`. Once again, the location of this directory can be customized. This is not an environment variable so its customization must be done from within `q`. By assigning a new value to the `.h.HOME` variable, either by hand or from within the `q.q` customization file, `kdb+` will search a different location for web pages. More will be discussed about interacting with the `kdb+` server in Chapter 16 [225].

---

**Q Tip 2.1** Parameterize system architecture

---

Instead of hard-coding the architecture, setting an environment variable such as `QARCH` allows you to switch platforms without having to modify your code.

```
$ export QARCH=m32
$ rlwrap $QHOME/$QARCH/q
```

You can then create two aliases. One for `q` itself.

```
$ alias q=$QHOME/$QARCH/q
```

And another for the version that uses `rlwrap`.

```
$ alias Q='rlwrap $QHOME/$QARCH/q'
```

---

## 2.2   Basics

Like many interpreted languages, q has a command line interface or REPL (read-eval-print-loop). If you start q from an interactive terminal (i.e.: shell or DOS prompt), a q) prompt is printed to indicate your input is needed (though this can be turned off with the -q command line argument).

As the name implies, a REPL reads input from the prompt, evaluates the command, prints the results, and loops around waiting for input again. This is a very powerful environment to code in, and as Richard Stallman hinted at, any language lacking a *REPL* is deficient.

### The Command Line

Let's begin with the obligatory *Hello World* program. If you type "hello world" at the q) prompt, the character vector will be echoed back.

```
q)"hello world"
hello world
```

Kdb+ detects that we are running q from an interactive environment and will not exit until we make an explicit request. This can be done in a number of ways. We can send an "end of file" (EOF) character by either typing Ctrl-d on a *nix machine or Ctrl-z on a Windows machine. This will terminate the program. Alternatively, we can type a double backslash to exit the process.

```
$ q
q)\\
$
```

To force the process to shut with a specific exit code, we can use the exit operator.

```
$ q
q)exit 2
$ echo $?
2
```

We can also save our program into a file and call it from the command line.

```
$ echo '"hello world"' > helloworld.q
$ q helloworld.q
KDB+ 3.2 2015.03.04 Copyright (C) 1993-2015 Kx Systems
m32/ 4()core 2048MB nick nicks-macbook.local 192.168.1.103 NONEXPIRE
"hello world"
q)
```

Or we may even include the path to the q binary in a shebang line. We can then call the script directly without first referencing the q binary.

```
$ echo '#!/$QHOME/$QARCH/q' > helloworld.q
$ echo '"hello world"' >> helloworld.q
$ helloworld.q
KDB+ 3.2 2015.03.04 Copyright (C) 1993-2015 Kx Systems
m32/ 4()core 2048MB nick nicks-macbook.local 192.168.1.103 NONEXPIRE
"hello world"
q)
```

When expressions are received from user input or a saved file, q evaluates each expression and prints the results. To display the results, q uses an internal function .Q.s which pretty-prints the data.

In our *Hello World* example, we asked q to evaluate the character vector "hello world", and by default it printed the results. We can suppress this default printing by appending a semicolon at the end of our line. Adding the semicolon actually returns a null value which by convention is not displayed.

```
q)"hello world";
q)
```

In some sense, then, this is not really a valid *Hello World* example. The application has only evaluated the expression "hello world". We did not actually request "hello world" to be printed. It was merely a side effect of command evaluation. To explicitly print something to STDOUT or STDERR, we must first learn about file handles.

### File Handles

Q reveals its Unix influence by exposing file handles as their integer values. On startup, three file handles exist.

- 0 STDIN (user input)

- 1 STDOUT (program output)

- 2 STDERR (error messages)

Handles created by opening files or sockets with the hopen operator are allocated an unused integer greater than 2. File and network handle operations will be discussed in more detail in the section called "File/Network Handle Operators" [55].

We can now return to the *Hello World* example and actually request the character vector "hello wo rld" to be printed to STDOUT (or even STDERR).

```
q)1 "hello world\n"
hello world
1
q)2 "hello world\n"
hello world
2
```

The return value from writing to a handle is the handle itself. We can see this value is displayed because we did not include the trailing semicolon. Adding the semicolon back allows us to print exactly the text we want, and nothing else.

```
q)1 "hello world\n";
hello world
```

---

**Q Tip 2.2** Use a negative file handle to automatically append newlines

---

To fit within the ASCII character set, q operators change their behavior based on the type and value of their operands. In the case file handles (including STDIN and STDERR), passing text to a negative file handle automatically appends a newline.

```
q)-1 "hello world";
hello world
```

When kdb+ is started interactively, input is read from the STDIN file handle which is attached to the terminal. If we redirect the output from a separate process into q's STDIN, it will accept commands from that process instead. Once EOF is reached, the process will terminate.

```
$ echo '1 "hello world\n";' | q
hello world
```

We can even close STDIN to force program termination after all expressions are evaluated.

```
$ q helloworld.q </dev/null
hello world
```

Before learning how to write our own functions, we should discuss the importance of a single backslash.

## Single Backslash

We have seen how using a double backslash "\\" exits a kdb+ process. It is possible that during your initial experimentation with q, you entered a single backslash "\" and saw the q) prompt disappear. You have actually exited the q language and descended into k. For the curious reader, you can use this mode to write and test k code. For example, we can see how to sum a list of numbers in k.

```
q) \
  +/1 2 3 4
10
```

Typing another single backslash returns the session to the q prompt. An alternate way to define code in k is to prefix the statement with a k). The following percentile function definition,

**.stat.pctile**

```
pctile:{[p;x]x iasc[x] -1+ceiling p*count x}
```

can be equivalently defined in k.[2]

```
k)pctile:{[p;x]x(<x) -1+-_-p*#x}
```

Another place the single backslash comes in handy is when q throws an exception. Q operators do their best to return the most appropriate value depending on the type and value of all parameters passed to them. For some combinations, however, there is no valid result. In these cases, an exception is thrown. When this happens, the calling function is suspended and the prompt is changed to display its directory and another layer of parentheses.

```
q)1 mod `
k){x-y*x div y}
'type
div
1
`
q.q))
```

This indicates that q has entered the debugger. If we type another invalid statement, another layer of debugging is entered and another level of parentheses is displayed at the prompt. We will talk more about directories in Section 5.3 [57] and the debugger in Chapter 13 [159]. Ctrl-c will not exit the debugger, and Ctrl-d and "\\" will quit the application. One way to return to the q) prompt is to type a single backslash "\". This will exit one layer of debugging. Remember to type a single backslash for each level. Trying to exit multiple levels by typing a double backslash will exit the program, not the debugger.

A single backslash can also be used in a q source file. Used as the only character on a line, a forward slash begins a multi-line comment. The multi-line comment continues until the end of file or a closing backslash is found. At any other location, a space followed by a forward slash comments the remainder of the line.

```
/
all text following a single forward slash
is ignored until the end of a file
or a single back slash is encountered
\
```

---

[2] This implementation uses the Nearest Rank method. Alternative implementations include the Linear Interpolation Between Closest Ranks method and the method proposed be the National Institute of Standards and Technology (NIST). A benefit of the Nearest Rank method is that it always returns an element of the list.

---

**Q Tip 2.3** Include sample code in your source files

---

A single backslash, that has not been preceded by a single forward slash, causes q to ignore all remaining text in the file. This is useful for including code or comments you want to save for later, but do not want evaluated when the file is loaded.

```
\
all text following a single back slash is ignored
```

In each of the above cases, a single backslash means *exit*. At the q prompt, it exits the q session and descends into k. At the k prompt, it exits back to q. When typed within the debugger, it exits one layer of debugging. After a single forward slash, it exits a multi-line comment. And finally, when found on a line by itself, it exits the parsing of a source file. The only thing it will not exit is the process itself. For that, you need two backslashes.

## 2.3   Syntax Rules

As with any language, q has its own syntax rules. The rules, in general, are similar enough to other languages that they can be picked up quite quickly. There are, however, a few differences with other major languages that often cause confusion. We will cover these now.

The k programming language was designed to be an APL-like language written completely with the ASCII character set. APL uses a complex character set that requires the use of a keyboard template to help enter the characters. In order to condense the extra APL characters into the limited k ASCII set, many of the operators were overloaded to perform different operations depending on the type and number of arguments. In the process of distilling the character set, some operators were dropped, and a few commonly used ASCII characters took on new meanings.

The genp function below generates a table containing a simulated security price path. We will ignore the actual implementation of the function for a minute, and instead focus on the syntax. The genp function will be formally introduced in Chapter 8 [91].

```
genp:{[id;S;s;r;dtm]
 t:abs type dtm;
 tm:("np" t in 12 14 15h)$dtm;
 p:S*path[s;r;tm%365D06];
 c:`id, `time`date[t=14h], `price;
 p:flip c!(id;dtm;p);
 p}
```

## Assignment

The definition begins with the function name followed by a colon ":". Q uses the colon for assignment instead of the equal sign "=". This allows the equal sign to be used for equality testing. Assignment is discussed further in the section called "Assignment" [25].

## Equality

A common programming mistake in some languages is to confuse a single equal sign "=" with a double equal sign "==". Instead of performing a comparison, a single equal sign silently assigns a new value. It is not possible to make this mistake in q because the assignment and equality operators are different characters. Instead of testing for equality with a double equal sign, q uses a single equal sign. The fifth line of genp creates a different list of symbols depending on whether the variable t equals 14 or not. Equality is contrasted with identity in the section called "Identity vs Equality" [53].

## Strings

Strings are stored as vectors of characters and are surrounded by double quotes. The string on the third line is treated as a vector of two characters. Character vectors are discussed in the section called "Character Vectors" [22].

## Symbols

Symbols are interned strings. That is, they have the memory efficient property that every equivalent symbol points to the same location in memory. Symbols are stored in an internal map and instead of being surrounded by quotes, are prefixed by a single backtick. We discuss symbols further in the section called "Symbols" [30].

## Characters

Q does not use single quotes to delimit characters. The single quote character is reserved for throwing exceptions (discussed in the section called "Exceptions" [43]) and looping over arguments (discussed in the section called "Minimize Calls to each" [110]). Characters are delimited by double quotes, just like character vectors. To distinguish between a single character and a character vector we must ensure the character vector is a list.

To create a list with a single element, we can use the enlist operator.

```
q)enlist "q"
,"q"
```

The `enlist` operator takes any value (atom, list, dictionary, table, etc.), and creates a list whose first and only element is the value itself. Different ways of creating a single element list are discussed in the section called "Single Element Dictionaries" [78].

## Brackets

Returning to the beginning of the function, we can see that the definition begins with a left brace and ends with a right brace. The function parameters are then enclosed with brackets. Brackets are also used for function invocation. This was done specifically to emphasize the similarities between indexing into a list and evaluating a function. In both cases, the operation performs a transformation from inputs to outputs. For example, the `path` function on the fourth line is being called with three parameters. Brackets are needed to call the `genp` function as well.

```
q).sim.genp[0;100;.3;.03;2000.01.01+til 252]
id date       price
--------------------
0  2000.01.01 100
0  2000.01.02 98.71948
0  2000.01.03 98.80453
0  2000.01.04 98.13703
0  2000.01.05 97.80133
..
```

A common mistake is to use parentheses for function invocation.

## Parentheses

In q, parentheses are used, along with semicolons, to create lists. Line 6, for example, creates a list with three items: `id`, `dtm` and `p`.

If we used parentheses for function invocation, we would actually be creating a list and passing it as a single argument to `genp`.

```
q).sim.genp(0;100;.3;.03;2000.01.01+til 252)
{[id;S;s;r;dtm]
 t:abs type dtm;
 tm:("np" t in 12 14 15h)$dtm;
 p:S*path[s;r;tm%365D06];
 c:`id,`time`date[t=14h],`price;
 p:flip c!(id;dtm;p);
 p}[(0;100;0.3;0.03;2000.01.01 2000.01.02 2000.01.03 2000.01.04 2000.01.05 ..
```

The result is a projection that can still be passed four more parameters. Projections are introduced in the section called "Projections" [71].

Parentheses can also be used to enforce operator precedence. The third line uses parentheses to ensure everything in front of the cast operator $ is executed before using the result as its left operand. This is because q has an irregular notion of operator precedence: it has none.

## Operator Precedence

Every statement in q is evaluated from right to left. The parser begins at the end of the line, and proceeds to the beginning. This considerably simplifies code because it often reduces the need for parentheses. It can also lead to some confusing errors. Although you will never need to consult an operator precedence table, you may have to reorder standard mathematical notation. Other languages, for example, would treat the following expression as multiplication followed by addition: $2*3+4$. In q, the addition occurs first because it is the right most operation. This would then be followed by the multiplication.

```
q) 2*3+4
14
```

Q allows us to insert parentheses to force evaluation order.

```
q) (2*3)+4
10
```

But a more idiomatic way is to reorder the operation.

```
q) 4+2*3
10
```

## Semicolon

We have already seen how semicolons are used to separate function arguments - both during definition and invocation. We have also seen semicolons separate list elements and end each line of a function. In summary, semicolons are used to separate blocks of evaluation. When semicolons are forgotten the resulting space between tokens is interpreted as either function invocation or indexation. In either case, the resulting error message rarely gives an indication to the actual problem.

Forgetting to include a trailing semicolon within a function definition is a common mistake that is hard to track down. Q Tip 4.6 [44] reminds you to ensure all lines within a function have a trailing semicolon. In addition, each line of a function should have leading whitespace.

## Leading Whitespace

The second line of genp begins with a single character of whitespace. When the q interpreter evaluates code, either typed at the q) prompt, or loaded from a .q source file, it continues to accumulate text for parsing until it finds another command starting flush left. This allows functions, views and SQL statements to span multiple lines. The interpreter ignores all trailing newlines between statements.

Forgetting to indent every line of a function by at least one space is a common (and hard to debug) mistake. The amount of whitespace does not matter, but it must exist. If the q parser encounters a line that is flush left, it assumes a new definition has begun. If this line is in the middle of a function definition, the parser stops defining the previous function and the function will be incomplete. The remaining lines of code will then be illogical and q will stop parsing and throw an exception after encountering any syntax errors.

## Comma

Calling a function with arguments separated by commas instead of semicolons is also a common mistake. It results in similar errors as calling a function with parentheses instead of brackets. The comma operator ", " joins elements together to form a list. The resulting list of parameters would again be a single argument passed to the function.

```
q).sim.genp[0,100,.3,.03,2000.01.01+til 252]
{[id;S;s;r;dtm]
 t:abs type dtm;
 tm:("np" t in 12 14 15h)$dtm;
 p:S*path[s;r;tm%365D06];
 c:`id,$[t=14h;`date;`time],`price;
 p:flip c!(id;dtm;p);
 p}[(0;100;0.3;0.03;2000.01.01;2000.01.02;2000.01.03;2000.01.04;2000.01.05;..
```

When switching between programming languages, remember this crucial difference.

## Division

The percent character % on the fourth line is not actually performing the modulo operation. Like the J language, q uses the percent sign for division.

```
q)1%3
0.3333333
```

Though not the perfect division symbol ÷ that APL uses, it is the best approximation using the ASCII character set. With division defined as the percent sign, the modulo operator was given a proper operator name mod, and the forward slash / was used as the comment character

```
q) /everything after a forward slash is a comment
```

and a way to modify functions to implement iteration (discussed in the section called "Over" [48]).

## Min and Max

The last two operators that can often cause confusion are "&" and "|". These operators are often known as bitwise AND and bitwise OR. Used on booleans, these operators do actually mean AND and OR.

```
q)0101b & 1111b
0101b
q)0101b | 1111b
1111b
```

But this is only a special case. The operators actually mean MIN and MAX and can be used with many other types in addition to booleans.[3]

```
q)(1;"abC";10:00) | (3;"ABc";05:00)
3
"abc"
10:00
q)(1;"abC";10:00) & (3;"ABc";05:00)
1
"ABC"
05:00
```

Think a bit longer and you'll realize that even when used with booleans, the operators still mean MIN and MAX.

Given at least one vector as an operand, the "|" and "&" operators will also return a vector. The min and max operators are different. They only accept a single operand, and return a single value as a result. Each of these functions is used in Section 17.3 [257] to generate histograms.

With a few common stumbling blocks clarified, we now turn to generating our own dataset.

---

[3] It is worth noting, however, that symbols, while having a definite lexicographical ordering, can not be used with the min, max, "|" or "&" operators.

# Chapter 3

# Generating Data

Anyone who considers arithmetical methods of producing random digits is, of course, in a state of sin. For, as has been pointed out several times, there is no such thing as a random number — there are only methods to produce random numbers, and a strict arithmetic procedure of course is not such a method.

— John von Neumann *Monte Carlo Method (1951)*

Q excels at loading, analyzing, transferring, and storing data. The best way to learn q is to have our own dataset to play with. Financial time series data is the most popular type of data stored in kdb+ databases. By the end of Chapter 11 [139] we will have built a CEP engine that generates simulated security price, quote and trade data. The first step in this process is to understand how q can generate datasets. We will first discuss lists in general, and then proceed to cover q operators that create lists of data: both ordered and random.

## 3.1 Lists

Fundamentally, q has two data types: atoms and lists. Atoms represent a single value, and can be of any type. Lists contain multiple values and can be of uniform or non-uniform type. When all the values of a list are the same type, kdb+ can store and operate on the values extremely efficiently. These lists are also referred to as vectors. Kdb+ also has other data structures such as dictionaries and tables, but as we shall see, they are actually internally represented as combinations of lists.

Uniform lists are vital to performance for a few reasons. Firstly, uniform lists can be stored as compact arrays. In addition, since kdb+ performs type checking at runtime, a uniform list only needs its type checked a single time and not for each element. Finally, once the type has been checked, performing arithmetic operations on uniform lists can be implemented in highly optimized C or assembly code. But the optimizations do not stop there. Modern CPU's provide native vector instructions to perform multiple operations in parallel. These benefits will be discussed further in the section called "Monte Carlo Simulation" [245].

## Character Vectors

In our *Hello World* example, we printed the character vector "hello world" to STDOUT. As with any list, it can be indexed,

```
q)"hello world"[0]
"h"
```

reversed,

```
q)reverse "hello world"
"dlrow olleh"
```

and joined.

```
q)"hello", " ", "world"
"hello world"
```

We can use the take operator "#" to take the first few elements of the list,

```
q)5#"hello world"
"hello"
```

or the last few elements.

```
q)-5#"hello world"
"world"
```

We can even rotate the list.

```
q)5 rotate "hello world"
" worldhello"
```

## Atomic Functions

The power of q is its ability to transparently operate on both atoms and lists. A function is called atomic if it operates on a list of values as if the function was independently applied to each of the list elements. All arithmetic operators are atomic. To add two lists of numbers, there is no need for us to explicitly loop or iterate over each element. Q efficiently performs this for us.

```
q) 1 2 3 + 4 5 6
5 7 9
```

This ability to manipulate vectors as computational units without writing explicit loops is a standard feature of array programming languages. Operations performed between an atom and a list also have logical definitions.

```
q) 1+1 2 3
2 3 4
```

In the following example, an atom is compared to a vector of numbers and a list of booleans is returned. To disambiguate the list of ones and zeros from an actual number, the type character for booleans ("b") is appended to the list.

```
q) 3>1 2 3
110b
```

This same technique of adding characters to disambiguate types is used with many other types as well. To create a list of floats instead of integers, we can add a decimal to at least one element of the list,

```
q) 1 2. 3
1 2 3f
```

append an "f" directly to the list,

```
q) 1 2 3f
1 2 3f
```

or use scientific notation.

```
q) 1 2 3e0
1 2 3f
```

## List Length

Vectors are stored in contiguous memory - both in-process and on-disk. Non-uniform lists must store more complex information, but the data is still stored in a data structure that allows random access. In all cases, the length of the list is known at all times and stored alongside the data. As a result, the count operator can return this number without having to actually count the number of items. Since all extended data structures are built on lists, we can use the count operator on all objects.

```
q) count  0 1 2
3
q) count  "hello world"
11
```

Instead of throwing an error when attempting to obtain the length of atoms, functions, and all other non-list types, q defines their length as 1.

```
q) count 0
1
```

## List Syntax

In addition to integers and characters, we can build lists of other types as well. Some uniform lists must be entered as a list of values without spaces. Boolean, character, symbol and byte lists are provided here.

```
q) 010b
010b
q) "hello world"
"hello world"
q) `hello`world
`hello`world
q) 0x010e
0x010e
```

All remaining types are entered with spaces (providing the type qualifier at the end when needed).

```
q) 1.0 2.0 3.0
1 2 3f
q) 2000.01.01D 2000.01.02D
2000.01.01D00:00:00.000000000 2000.01.02D00:00:00.000000000
```

## Mixed Lists

To create a mixed list, each item must be separated by a semicolon and the complete list surrounded by parentheses.[1]

```
q) (1i;1;2f; `3)
1i
1
2f
`3
```

Q makes it easy to enter short lists of constant data. We now turn our attention to generating longer lists.

---

[1] The default integer type in q prior to version 3.0 was the 4-byte integer. Because of this default, no trailing "i" was needed to represent a 4-byte integer. To explicitly enter an 8-byte integer, a clarifying "j" was needed after the number. Since version 3.0, however, 8-byte integers have become the default integer type and the clarifying "j" is no longer needed. In order to enter a 4-byte integer, we must now explicitly append a clarifying "i" instead. The behavior for all explicitly typed literals has never changed. Only untyped integers were affected.

## 3.2   Ordered Data

Instead of using a for loop to successively generate elements of an ordered list, the idiomatic way to build lists in q is to use the `til` operator. The `til` operator generates a list of consecutive integers starting with 0 and ending with one less than then its numerical argument.

```
q)til 10
0 1 2 3 4 5 6 7 8 9
```

We can then use vector operations to transform this list. We can, for example, generate a list of the first 10 perfect squares.

We start with the `til` operator to generate a list of integers between 0 and 9. Adding 1 obtains a list of integers between 1 and 10. The results can then be saved into the variable x with the assignment operator ":".

```
q)x:1+til 10
```

We can then multiply x by itself to obtain the list of perfect squares.

```
q)x*x
1 4 9 16 25 36 49 64 81 100
```

### Assignment

Q permits value assignment in any location we desire. This is very convenient, and is often used to make functions shorter and faster. The previous two lines can be combined into one - this time using in-place assignment.

```
q)x*x:1+til 10
1 4 9 16 25 36 49 64 81 100
```

Q also allows us to dynamically assign and access variables. Instead of using the actual variable, we can use a symbol, with the same name as the variable, to refer to it. The `set` operator dynamically assigns data to the variable named by its left operand.

```
q)`squares set x*x:1+til 10
`squares
```

We can then use the `get` operator to retrieve the stored data by again referring to a symbol with the same name.[2]

---

[2] Assigning and retrieving values through indirection only works for global variables and not variables defined within functions.

```
q)get `squares
1 4 9 16 25 36 49 64 81 100
```

This by itself does not offer an advantage over saving the data directly into the variable. It does, however, give us the flexibility to access and operate on variables dynamically created during the running of the program. Assuming the name of a variable is stored in the variable v, we can dynamically assign it a value.

```
q)v:`squares
q)v set x*x:1+til 10
`squares
```

This forms the foundation of meta-programming and is used in the section called "Instrumenting Functions" [237] to dynamically redefine the definition of functions.

## Aggregating Functions

Factorials can be computed by using the prd operator to multiply a list of integers.

```
q)prd 1+til 10
3628800
```

The prd operator is an example of an aggregating function. An aggregating function always reduces the dimension of the data supplied as its operand. Applying an aggregating function to a list, for example, produces an atom. Applying it to a list of lists, also known as a matrix, produces a list.

Ordered data is useful for replacing loops and writing structured functions. But our goal is to generate fictional price paths, so we move on to random data.

## 3.3   Numeric Random Data

Q has many numeric and temporal (time) data types. Internally, each temporal type is stored as a numeric value of the appropriate precision. Because of this mapping, random values can be obtained for both numeric and temporal types with no extra work. There are two ways to obtain random numbers: with and without replacement.

## Generate

To generate a random number we use the "?" operator. The left operand is an integer indicating how many numbers to generate, while the right operand is a numeric or temporal value indicating the upper limit of the random values. For example, we can generate 10 integer values between 0 and 9.

```
q) 10?10
5 2 3 9 6 1 9 3 4 3
```

Negative upper limits clearly have no meaning, but for the specific case where the upper limit is an integral value 0, q will generate random values across the whole range of positive and negative values (excluding null).

```
q) 10?0i
1152912151 574596 -1442020277 2129661801 1885121318 492299291 940693873 -16..
```

Temporal data types stored as integral values return values between 0 and a logical maximum.

```
q) max 10000000?00:00
23:59
q) max 10000000?00:00:00
23:59:59
q) max 10000000?00:00:00.000
23:59:59.990
q) max 10000000?0D
0D23:59:59.994146078
```

For the case of dates, an arbitrary choice of 1 leap year cycle, or 1461 days, was chosen as the upper limit.

```
q) max 10000000?2000.01.01
2003.12.31
```

For non integer types, random numbers are generated on the complete range of positive values up to, but not including, the supplied limit.

```
q) 5?10f
6.040846 3.813266 2.540645 5.162951 5.403325
```

All temporal types work as well.

```
q) 2?2036.01.01T
2031.04.25T17:48:18.651 2026.06.17T11:38:07.756
```

## Deal

To perform the same operations without replacement, we can pass a negative value for the left operand. This is often called *deal* as it is similar to dealing out cards from a deck.

```
q) -10?10
6 4 7 8 9 2 5 1 0 3
```

Logically, it is not possible to generate more than 10 random values between 0 and 9 without replacement. Q throws an error if this is attempted.

```
q)-11?10
'length
```

Q has not implemented deal for all data types however.  To generate random temporal values without replacement, we can generate standard integers, and cast the results to the type we want.

```
q)"u"$-9?10
00:04 00:05 00:00 00:01 00:06 00:07 00:02 00:08 00:09
```

Casting between types in q is very flexible.  We will discuss this in more detail in the section called "Casting Between Types" [116].

## Single Values

We can use the rand operator to generate single random values.  The next example generates a single byte.

```
q)rand 0x0
0x51
```

We can see the actual implementation of the rand operator by typing its name at the q) prompt.

```
q)rand
k){*1?x}
```

It begins with a k) so we know it is implemented in k.  Starting at the end of the function we can see that it uses the "?" operator to generate a list with one random value.  It then uses the * operator to obtain just the first element and return it as an atom.[3]  As with all monadic operators, this has been aliased to a word.  To access the first element of a list in q, we use the first operator.  Similarly, the last operator accesses the last element.  The first operator is defined in q.k, but the last operator is defined in C. This has not always been the case.  Before the last operator was added to the language, a popular (due to its terse syntax) algorithm to obtain the last element of a list was to reverse the list and then take the first element.  You can still find many instances of this technique in q.k.  Since the k operator for reverse is "|", we can obtain the last element with *|.

```
q)\
  *| 1 2 3 4
4
```

Reversing a list is of course inefficient, so the last operator is therefore preferred.

---

[3] It is interesting to note that the k operator for accessing the first element of a list is the same as that in C: "*".

## 3.4  Non-numeric Random Data

Q also allows us to generate random values for types other than numeric and temporal. Since there is no natural ordering of these types, we can not provide a maximum value. Instead, we must supply the null value.

The null character can be optionally entered as `0Nc` or `" "`.

```
q)10?0Nc
"dyqoskxdqc"
```

Q internally stores Globally Unique Identifiers (GUID)s as a vector of bytes. The null GUID also has two representations: `0Ng` and `00000000-0000-0000-0000-000000000000`.

```
q)rand 0Ng
31f9c72e-815c-3e49-c172-d104b8bb0ab3
```

### Bytes

To guarantee a number to be globally unique, GUIDs requires 16 bytes of information, or the size of two 8-byte integers. The size of the internal `K` structure is already 16 bytes, 8 of which are required to store metadata (such as its type, reference count, and attributes).[4] The other 8 bytes are used to store atoms ranging from the smallest character to the largest 8-byte integer. In order to store the 16-byte GUID, the internal `K` structure must therefore store the data as a vector of bytes. We can see these 16 bytes by using the "vector from scalar" operator `vs`.

```
q)0x0 vs rand 0Ng
0x8c6b8b64681560840a3e178401251b68
```

We can similarly obtain the byte representation of many other numeric values.

```
q)0x0 vs 2
0x0000000000000002
q)0x0 vs 2h
0x0002
q)0x0 vs " "
,0x20
```

And conversely, byte arrays can be converted to their numeric values with the "scalar from vector" operator `sv`.

```
q)0x0 sv 0x00000002
2i
```

---

[4] The complete layout of the K structure can be found in the `k.h` header file located in the Kx C repository [crepo] [266]

Every byte of a hexadecimal number is represented by two characters. If we generate 10 bytes, we actually see 20 hexadecimal characters following the hexadecimal marker 0x.

```
q) 10?0x0
0x6c104fb48ceeb4f142d8
```

But when we check the length of the byte vector, we can see it only has 10 elements.

```
q) count 10?0x0
10
```

## Symbols

Q also provides a useful syntax for generating lists of random symbols. Unlike character vectors, symbols are atoms and point to a single place in memory. Symbols begin with a backtick "`" and do not require double quotes. The backtick is a natural delimiter allowing us to create lists of symbols without spaces.

```
q) count `hello`world
2
```

Since all symbols with the same value point to a single place in memory, an equality test between two symbols is a simple pointer comparison. There is no need to compare each character.

Generating random symbols is just as easy as generating random numbers. Using a symbol representation of a number as the right operand of the "?" operator will generate random symbols of the specified length. This special case works for symbols of length 1 through 8 characters. Also, note that the characters used to generate the symbol only sample from the first 16 characters "a" through "p".

```
q) 5?`1
`c`k`c`h`c
q) 5?`8
`agpmifej`nfbcjcho`faebphdd`kliknhbb`pjljcfjj
```

## Random Selection

We can also generate a list of random items from predefined lists. Q has internal variables which include all the lower and upper case letters: .Q.a and .Q.A respectively. (There are also sets which include all numbers .Q.n, numbers with capital letters .Q.nA, alphanumeric .Q.an, and all the characters used in base 64 encoding .Q.b6. This makes it easy to generate random character vectors with the appropriate character set.

```
q) 10?.Q.A
"ZYJKZMVLUK"
q) 10?.Q.b6
"z5kZnKBZ7c"
```

Passing a negative left operand to "?" continues to generate random values without replacement. As a toy problem, we can select a few cards from a deck of cards. If we represent the card values as a list of characters "234567890JQKA" (using "0" for 10), and the suits by the characters "DCHS", we can use the cross operator to generate the **full d**eck of cards.

```
q)show fd:"234567890JQKA" cross "DCHS"
"2D"
"2C"
"2H"
"2S"
"3D"
"3C"
"3H"
..
```

We can then deal a few cards from the deck,

```
q)-7?fd
"QS"
"3H"
"4H"
"6H"
"AS"
"7D"
"5S"
```

or shuffle the whole deck.

```
q)-52?fd
"7H"
"3H"
"4D"
"6S"
"7C"
"9D"
"3C"
..
```

## 3.5  Random Seed

The random numbers produced by q are seeded with a fixed value upon system startup (the negated first 6 digits of PI: -314159). We can use the system command \S to display,

```
q)\S
-314159i
```

and set this value.

```
q)\S 100
q)\S
100i
```

To ensure reproducibility, we can reseed the random number generator and perform our test again.

```
q)\S -314159
q)10?100
12 10 1 90 73 90 43 90 84 63
q)\S -314159
q)10?100
12 10 1 90 73 90 43 90 84 63
```

There are many other system variables that can be changed using the backslash notation. Some of them can also be set to with command line arguments. The complete list can be found on the Kx Wiki [syscmd] [266].

Commands beginning with a backslash "\" are system commands. Single letter system commands are reserved for q, while longer names call out to the operating system for evaluation. These same commands can be placed in a file and executed when loading the file from a script. Sometimes, however, the arguments to these operators may depend on run-time parameters. If we create a character vector with the exact command we want to run, q provides the system operator to evaluate it. To dynamically generate a unique random number seed at system startup, for example, we can seed q with the number of milliseconds since midnight. The current time, accurate to the nearest millisecond, is obtained with the .z.T system variable. Casting the result to an integer returns the value in milliseconds.

```
q)"i"$.z.T
59428613i
```

Seeding with the number zero turns off the random number generator, and all random numbers will be 0. To prevent this from happening at midnight, we can add 1 to the current time. We can then execute a system command with variable text by using the system operator. We can leave off the leading backslash from the \S system command because the system operator prepends it for us.

```
q)system "S ",string 1+"i"$.z.T
q)\S
55538672
```

Using the system operator also allows us to manipulate the results of its operation. The result of calling the system operator on builtin kdb+ operations will be a numeric value (or values) depending on the operation performed. We can save the random seed into a variable and access the results later.

```
q)s:system"S"
q)s
-314159i
```

All other commands are returned as a list of raw character vectors. Each element corresponds to one row of the command's results.

```
q) system"pwd"
"/Users/nick/Documents/qtips"
```

Chapter 4

# Functions

Simplicity is prerequisite for reliability.

— Edsger W. Dijkstra

A function provides a way to package blocks of code for reuse. Q functions can have up to eight arguments. This may seem like a barbaric limitation, but there are positive side effects of this design choice. Each parameter passed to a function adds record-keeping overhead. Keeping parameter lists small makes the resulting bytecode smaller and the functions faster. It also promotes small and specific functions - both good practices in functional programming.

In practice, niladic (zero parameter) and monadic (one parameter) functions are implemented the same. They can both be called with either zero or one argument. In the niladic case, the single argument will be silently ignored. And calling a monadic function with no arguments results in the single parameter being assigned the generic null (::) (discussed in the section called "Generic Null" [141]). In order to pass more than eight pieces of information to a function we can use more complex data structures such as lists, dictionaries and tables which are discussed in Chapter 7 [73].

All functions return a value. A function that has no explicit return value will return (::), the generic null. In *pure* functional languages, functions accept arguments and return results without modifying any global state. Q is not a pure functional language, and functions can therefore modify global state. It is not easy to independently test functions that modify global state, so good practice would dictate that any data structure that needs to be transformed should be passed as an argument to the function, and the modified value passed as a return value. This not only makes the code easier to maintain, it also allows performance gains by permitting parallel execution of functions. The function can be run many times, without worrying about how the global state may have changed. Two or more copies can even be run simultaneously without having to worry about locking data structures to prevent data corruption. More will be mentioned on this topic in Section 17.2 [244].

Our goal is to generate price paths that follow a random walk. To do this, we must obtain normally distributed random variables. We have seen how q can generate uniform random variables with the "?" operator. To convert these to normally distributed variables, we must write our own function. This chapter will cover three different methods to do this: summing 12 uniforms, using the Box-Muller transform on two uniforms, and using the Beasley-Springer-Moro transformation on a single uniform.

## 4.1   12 Uniforms

The simplest way to generate approximately normal random variables with a mean of 0 and standard deviation of 1, is to sum 12 uniformly distributed variables and subtract 6. This is definitely a crude method as the values will only cover the range (-6,6). But the statistical properties of the distribution are in fact what we need. The math behind the transformation from uniform random variables to normal random variables is based on the central limit theorem which states that the sum of independently drawn samples from the same distribution tend to a normal distribution irrespective of the original distribution. Taking the uniform distribution as our source, the standard deviation becomes 1 when 12 samples are added. We are left to subtract 6 to ensure the average value is 0. We first test the code at the q) prompt.

```
q)-6f+sum 12?1f
-0.1734415
q)-6f+sum 12?1f
-0.2846941
```

### Operation Ordering

We could have written the code slightly differently by adding parentheses or brackets.

```
q)sum[12?1f]-6f
-0.1281373
```

---

**Q Tip 4.1** Rearrange operators to reduce the need for parentheses

---

Though the resulting code may be more intuitive, it is by far more common to rearrange the order of operations to allow your eye to travel from right to left, with a minimum of back tracking to determine the location of any closing brackets. In this case, we were able to remove the brackets and parentheses altogether.

### Lambdas

To turn this into a function, we wrap it with braces.

```
q){-6f+sum 12?1f}
{-6f+sum 12?1f}
```

This is an example of a niladic function that takes no arguments. All q functions accept a minimum of 1 argument, so this is in fact a monadic function. But since it never makes a reference to its argument, it can be called with no arguments, and the single argument, which will be passed as the generic null, is simply ignored. And even though it has no name, it is still a legitimate function. In many languages an anonymous function is called a lambda. In Section 3.2 [25] we generated the first 10 perfect squares. Instead of declaring a temporary variable,

```
q)x*x:1+til 10
1 4 9 16 25 36 49 64 81 100
```

a lambda could have been used instead.

```
q){x*x}1+til 10
1 4 9 16 25 36 49 64 81 100
```

## Function Parameters

This example also shows how q allows us to reference the first argument of a function without declaring its name. Q will allow up to three automatic function arguments: x, y, and z. We can access them simply by using their name in a function. In fact, since all functions take at least a single argument, we can always access the value, null or not, using the automatic variable x.

**Q Tip 4.2** Leave z for last

The valence of a function, or how many parameters it expects, depends on what automatic variables are referenced. If the only variable used is x, the function has valence 1 and only takes a single argument. Introducing y changes the function to valence 2. And of course referencing z makes the function valence 3. A common error is to reference z without y (or even x) and not realizing that the function is expecting three arguments. The result is actually a projection (or partially applied function) that still expects two more arguments before it is executed. Projections are discussed further in the section called "Projections" [71].

```
q){z*z}1+til 10
{z*z}[1 2 3 4 5 6 7 8 9 10]
```

Instead of using automatic variables, we can alternatively list the parameters of our function in brackets. In this example, we called the variable n instead of x.

```
q){[n]n*n}1+til 10
1 4 9 16 25 36 49 64 81 100
```

Explicitly defining function parameters prevents automatic variables from being created. Accessing an undeclared variable will generate an exception.

```
q){[n]x*x}1+til 10
{[n]x*x}
'x
q))
```

As this example shows, single argument functions can be called by placing the arguments next to the function. We also have the option of using brackets.

```
q){x*x}[1+til 10]
1 4 9 16 25 36 49 64 81 100
```

But unless we need the brackets to enforce the order of operations, there is no need for the extra characters. We have the same choice for functions that take no arguments. For example, we can either call our 12 uniform function with brackets

```
q){-6f+sum 12?1f}[]
-0.1734415
```

or with any argument we want (even thought it will not be used).

```
q){-6f+sum 12?1f}`
-0.4128298
```

When a function takes more than one argument we are required to call it with brackets and separate each argument with semicolons. Using the .stat.pctile [12] function, we can compute the first and third quartile values of any list of numbers.

```
q).stat.pctile[.25 .75;1+til 1000]
250 750
```

For the special case of q operators that accept two arguments, we can interpose the function between the first and second arguments. This is so natural for binary mathematical operators it hardly seems worth mentioning. But it also works for all builtin dyads (two-argument functions). For example, the correlation between two sets of numbers can be computed by placing the operands on either side of the operator.

```
q)x cor neg x:til 100
-1f
```

This does not work, however, for user defined dyadic functions. As we will see in the section called "Drop" [129], it is actually possible to add new builtin operators to the .q namespace and call them with in-fix notation. But this is not typically encouraged.

---

**Q Tip 4.3** Even lists and dictionaries can use juxtaposition

---

Many languages use brackets to index into lists and dictionaries. Q does as well. The fact that q also uses brackets to call functions is no coincidence. In q, calling a monadic function with brackets is syntactically the same as indexing a list or dictionary. The syntax exposes an underlying mathematical property: lists, dictionaries and monadic functions each map a single set of inputs into outputs. Q emphasizes this equivalence by also allowing lists and dictionaries to be indexed by placing or juxtaposing the index next to the list or dictionary. Just as monadic functions can be called by placing their arguments next to the function, lists and dictionaries can be indexed without brackets as well.

```
q) `hello`world 0
`hello
q) `hello`world 1
`world
```

Juxtaposition is often preferred to bracket notation because it removes the need to perform the mental gymnastics of parentheses and bracket balancing. In addition, it requires one less character: a single space instead of an opening and closing bracket. And in some cases we can even save two characters by dropping the interposing space.

## Function Names

To make our 12 uniform function reusable, we need to give it a name. We can do this by assigning the function definition to a variable.

```
q)u12:{-6f+sum 12?1f}
```

We can then call the function by name,

```
q)u12[]
0.9192507
```

copy it,

```
q)unif12:u12
```

or inspect it.

```
q)u12
{-6f+sum 12?1f}
```

Being able to access the definition of a function is quite powerful. Not only does it allow us to debug a function when an error occurs, but it also allows us to programatically redefine the function definition. Section 17.1 [235] uses this technique to profile our CEP engine.

## Reference Counts

Q copies, assigns, and passes variables by reference. All references point to the same underlying data structure until a modification is attempted. Once a modification is made, new memory is allocated and the underlying structure is copied. Any references to the original value remains unaltered. This behavior is also known as copy-on-write. Q keeps track of each variable's reference count and deletes the object once the count drops to 0. We can access this reference count by using the $-16!$ operator. In our example, both $unif12$ and $u12$ point to the same function so we should expect the reference count to be 2.

```
q)-16!u12
2i
q)-16!unif12
2i
```

If we redefine $u12$, we can see that both functions now have a single reference.

```
q)u12:{-6f+sum 12?1f}
q)-16!unif12
1i
q)-16!u12
1i
```

All operators beginning with a negative number followed by the exclamation point are internal k functions exposed to the q language. Some have been given proper q operator names: hsym, attr, parse, eval, hcount and md5. Others were only intended to be used internally by q: .Q.s1, .Q.host, . Q.addr .Q.gc. The rest have not been given function names, but can still be accessed directly by their negative numeric value followed by the exclamation point. The complete list of internal operators can be found on the Kx wiki [internal] [265].

## Cut

If we are required to call $u12$ with an argument, we might as well make the function more useful by modifying it to return multiple normal variates. We can easily change the function to accept the number of random numbers we want.

**.stat.u12**

```
u12:{-6f+sum x cut (12*x)?1f}
```

```
q).stat.u12 5
1.413652 -0.4731901 -0.1391228 -0.3146378 -0.8652832
```

Reading the function definition from right to left we first see that we are generating $12*x$ uniform variates. We then see the cut operator which converts the one dimensional list into a matrix with x rows and 12 elements per row. The `cut` operator progressively cuts its right operand at as many equal intervals as possible. Any remaining elements are returned in the last value. In our case, we know the list is equally divisible by `x`, so the result is a matrix. Continuing to `sum` the result and subtract 6 produces `x` normal variates.

We can test our random number generator by checking the mean and standard deviation of a long list of variates and confirming they are close to 0 and 1 respectively.

```
q)avg .stat.u12 1000000
0.0008539
q)sdev .stat.u12 1000000
1.00037
```

Kdb+ has always included the population deviation, variance and covariance operators: `dev`, `var` and `cov`. As of `kdb+ 3.2`, it now includes the sample deviation, variance and covariance operators: `sdev`, `svar` and `scov`. The new operators include Bessel's correction to compute a more accurate estimation of a sample's deviation and an unbiased estimate of its variance and covariance.

## Skew and Kurtosis

But what of the 3rd and 4th order central moments skewness and kurtosis? As they are more useful in theory than in practice, `q` has not defined them in the language. But we can easily define the population statistics ourselves.

**.stat.skew**

```
skew:{avg[x*x2]%sqrt m2*m2*m2:avg x2:x*x-:avg x}
```

```
q).stat.skew .stat.u12 1000000
-0.005535035
```

**.stat.kurt**

```
kurt:{-3f+avg[x2*x2]%x*x:avg x2:x*x-:avg x}
```

```
q).stat.kurt .stat.u12 1000000
-0.1004693
```

Both `skew` and `kurt` are very dense functions. To read them, it is important to begin at the right, and continue to the left. Let's take `skew` as an example. The first step in computing an nth central moment above 1 is to remove the mean. Since we no longer need the original data, we can use compound assignment to subtract the mean and assign it back to the original variable `x`.

```
x-:avg x
```

---

**Q Tip 4.4** Use compound assignment for increased efficiency

---

The following statement achieves the same results without compound assignment, but would be slower.

```
x:x-avg x
```

## Compound Assignment

Q passes arguments by reference. In most cases, they are immutable references. Attempting to extend, resize, or update a list, for example, will create a complete copy of the original data before modifying the structure. This is an inefficient process, especially if our intention is to assign the result back to the original variable. Compound assignment allows simple operators to potentially modify the original data structure, thus removing the need to create another copy. Each of the single character operators $-.\sim=!@$ $\#\$\%^\&*\_+|,<>?$ has a compound assignment variant. We will see in the section called "Index Apply" [102] that it is also possible to modify structures without creating a copy by adding a layer of indirection and passing the global variable's name instead of the variable itself.

As we continue reading the skew function from right to left, we see that it squares x and saves the result into variable x2. This is another example of using in-place assignment. This, too, will need to be squared, so we save it off before continuing on to save the average squared deviations in m2. The rest of the function is simple multiplication and division. It is worth knowing that even though q has an exponentiation function exp and a power function xexp, it is much faster to use multiplication and the sqrt operator when the exponent is a small integer or simple fraction.

The functions we have used have all been simple enough to be q 1-liners. As the algorithms become more complicated, we need the ability to span multiple lines and give our function parameters more meaningful names. Let's move on to a better generator of normal random variables.

## 4.2 Box-Muller

The Box-Muller transform[1] converts 2 uniform random variates into 2 normal random variates. The transform produces results that more accurately represent the normal distribution but requires more work (code and processing power). The first step of the Box-Muller transform is to convert two uniform random variables into the polar coordinates of a normally distributed variable. The second step transforms them back into rectangular coordinates.

**.stat.bm**

---

[1] Box, G. E. P.; Muller, Mervin E. A Note on the Generation of Random Normal Deviates. The Annals of Mathematical Statistics 29 (1958), no. 2, 610—611.

```
bm:{
 if[count[x] mod 2;'`length];
 x:2 0N#x;
 r:sqrt -2f*log x 0;
 theta:2f*acos[-1]*x 1;
 x: r*cos theta;
 x,:r*sin theta;
 x}
```

## Conditional Operations

The Box-Muller transformation always produces two normal variates. The function therefore requires an even number of uniform variates. The first line of the function throws an exception if an odd number of variates are provided.

```
q).stat.bm 1?1f
'length
```

The function begins with an `if` clause. Everything up until the first semicolon is evaluated. If the result is true (or evaluates to an integer not equal to 0), the remaining clauses until the closing bracket are executed. There are no `else` statements in q so `if` is generally used to handle special cases instead of choosing between two code paths.

**Q Tip 4.5** Limit control flow statements to a single line

Keeping `if` (and `while` and `do`) clauses limited to a single line helps keep code readable and debuggable. The only way to debug a q function is to evaluate its lines - one by one. If control flow statements span multiple lines, it is not possible to evaluate them by copying and pasting the lines. If the code block becomes too long to fit on a single line, then the body of the clause should be moved to a new function. This also helps keep function sizes manageable.

## Exceptions

In this case, the body of the `if` statement throws an exception. The single quote "'" is used to report the exception, while the symbol that follows it defines what the exception will report.

```
q)'`length
'length
```

It is also possible to report an exception with a character vector. This is useful when the message is longer than a single word.

```
q)'"not an even number of uniform variates"
'not an even number of uniform variates
```

## Multi-line Functions

After the declaration, the remaining lines of the function start with a leading space. Multi-line functions must be indented with at least one space. The definition of a function continues until the parser encounters a line with no leading whitespace. In addition, all newlines are ignored. Because of this, we must introduce semicolons to separate each logical block.[2]

**Q Tip 4.6** Make sure each line in a function ends with a semicolon

It is a common mistake to forget semicolons when moving working code from a test file into a function. The errors of such a mistake are never helpful. If your code works when run line-by-line, but not when run from within a function, make sure all your lines end with a semicolon.

## Reshape

The second line of the `.stat.bm [42]` function uses the "#" operator to reshape the one dimensional list into two equal sized lists. The basic form of the take operator "#" takes elements from the front (or back if the left operand is negative) of a list.

```
q)4#til 10
0 1 2 3
q)-4#til 10
6 7 8 9
```

If more elements are requested than exist in the list, "#" will cycle through the list enough times to complete the request.

```
q)10#1 2 3 4
1 2 3 4 1 2 3 4 1 2
```

If the left operand is a list with two integers, "#" reshapes the list into an N x M grid.

```
q)2 5 # til 10
0 1 2 3 4
5 6 7 8 9
```

---

[2] In contrast to q, k does note require semicolons at the end of each line. Newlines also act as statement separators. But this also means that k statements within a function can not span multiple lines.

For the special case where one of the dimensions in null, q will determine the missing dimension based on the number of elements in the list. This is how we used the operator in .stat.bm [42]. The usage is similar to the cut operator but in this case we know the first dimension, and want q to compute the second dimension. With cut, we specified the second dimension of the matrix and wanted q to compute the first.

```
q)2 0N # til 10
0 1 2 3 4
5 6 7 8 9
```

If the number of elements in the list can not be evenly divisible by the provided number, the matrix will have an incomplete row.

```
q)2 0N # til 9
0 1 2 3 4
5 6 7 8
```

In addition to the take "#" operator, q provides an analogous drop "_" operator. It also accepts a positive (negative) integer as the left operand, but instead of taking that many elements from the front (back), it drops them.

By providing a list of positive integers for the left operand, drop "_" can *cut* a one dimensional list into two dimensions. The list of indices provided to the drop "_" operator are used to cut the list like a pair of scissors, throwing away any elements before the first cut.

```
q)3 5 8 _ til 10
3 4
5 6 7
8 9
```

In the case we want to keep the first elements, we must ensure our list of cuts begins with 0.

```
q)0 3 5 8 _ til 10
0 1 2
3 4
5 6 7
8 9
```

The remaining lines of .stat.bm [42] implement the Box-Muller algorithm.

## Return Values

The last line of the function returns the values stored in x.

```
x}
```

**Q Tip 4.7** Use the closing brace to document a function's return value

Ending a function with the returned variable on its own line helps document the function. In functions that return nothing, the closing brace can be used on a line by itself.

```
}
```

In this case the returned value will be null.

The colon ":" operator can be used to return values before the end of a function. I find the use of this operator limited to cases where an `if` clause has determined an exceptional case. If, for example, an empty list was passed as an argument, there would be no need to do any further computation. In this case, we could return the empty list back as the result. This is discussed further in Q Tip 11.2 [142].

```
if[not count x;:x];
```

### Loading Code

To define this function which is over one line long, we must load it from a saved file. I have included this function in a file called `stat.q`. Passing a file as the first argument to q causes the script to be loaded before control is returned to the user.

```
$ q stat.q
KDB+ 3.2 2015.03.04 Copyright (C) 1993-2015 Kx Systems
m32/ 4()core 2048MB nick nicks-macbook.local 192.168.1.103 NONEXPIRE
```

Once the function has been loaded, we can generate an even number of normal variates.

```
q).stat.bm 6?1f
0.05194905 -0.3839414 -0.01888353 0.461822 0.374629 -0.07562953
```

The Box-Muller transform is popular for its speed. To further investigate q syntax and build our tool box, we now move to a slower generator of normal random variables that only requires a single uniform variable as input.

## 4.3  Beasley-Springer-Moro

The Beasley-Springer-Moro method[3] takes a single uniform random number and uses a polynomial approximation to compute the inverse cumulative normal function. It also uses Horner's method to reduce the number of multiplications. To make the values as accurate as possible, the transformation is divided into two regions: the central region, which uses the Beasley-Springer approximation, and the tail region which uses a Chebyshev approximation proposed by Boris Moro.

---

[3] Moro, B. (1995): The Full Monte. *Risk* **8**, 57-58.

## Central Region

We start with the normal inverse approximation for the central region.

**.stat.cnorminv**

```
cnorminv:{
 a:-25.44106049637 41.39119773534 -18.61500062529 2.50662823884;
 b: 3.13082909833 -21.06224101826 23.08336743743
   -8.47351093090 1;
 x*:horner[a;s]%horner[b] s:x*x-:.5;
 x}
```

The first two lines define the polynomial coefficients a and b. The definition of b wraps across multiple lines without a semicolon. There is no need for a line continuation character because the q interpreter keeps reading until it encounters a semicolon or an unindented line.

## Horner's Method

The fifth line uses Horner's method[4] to compute the results of two polynomial approximations. We will use Horner's method multiple times, so it is worth defining it as a function.

**.stat.horner**

```
horner:{{z+y*x}[y]/[x]}
```

The horner function accepts two parameters: the list of polynomials and an initial value to apply the approximation to. The function then iteratively applies the anonymous function {z+y*x} to the initial value using each of coefficients. Using the horner function allows us to simplify a long list of additions and multiplications

```
a[3]+s*a[2]+s*a[1]+s*a[0]
```

to a single iterative call.

```
horner[a;s]
```

The "scalar from vector" operator sv has also been designed to compute Horner's rule.

```
q)a:1 2 3 4 5f
q).stat.horner[a] 2f
57f
q)2f sv a
57f
```

---

[4] Knuth, D. E. *The Art of Computer Programming, Vol. 2: Seminumerical Algorithms*, 3rd ed. Reading, MA: Addison-Wesley, pp. 467-469, 1998.

But to compute simulated security prices, we need to use it on many values.

```
q).stat.horner[a] 3?1f
7.169644 5.345855 13.79351
```

And `sv` only works for single values.

```
q)(3?1f) sv a
k){{z+y*x}/[0;x;y]}
'length
q))
```

## Over

The looping in both `horner` and `sv` is controlled by the `over` adverb "/" which changes a dyadic (two parameter) function into a monadic function that takes a single list of values. An adverb is an operator that changes the behavior of a function that appears directly before it. Each call to the modified function will take the previous value as the first argument and the second argument will be the next value from the list. This process continues until all values from the list are used and only the final value is returned. Other languages refer to this process as fold, reduce or accumulate.

If we had used the `scan` adverb "\" instead, each of the intermediate values would have been returned. Though these values are not useful for our purposes, modifying the code to return all intermediate values is useful for debugging new functions. One very popular place to use the `scan` adverb is when computing exponentially weighted moving averages. Given a decay factor x and a list of observations y, an exponentially weighted moving average can be computed using the `scan` operator.

```
ewma:{{(y*1-x)+z*x}[x]\[y]}
```

```
q)ewma[.25] 1 2 3 4 5f
1 1.25 1.6875 2.265625 2.949219
```

This example, however, shows a function with three parameters: x, y, and z. The first parameter, x is fixed, or bound, and the resulting dyadic projection is used with the `over` adverb.

This is a nice first cut, but it can be improved. We can reduce the number of operations by rearranging terms.

```
ewma:{{y+x*z-y}[x]\[y]}
```

Every time through the inner function, x is multiplied by z. Atomic operations like this are slow and should be removed from the iteration. Because both of these values are known outside the inner function, the value can be computed before we perform the `scan` operation.

```
ewma:{{z+y*x}\[first y;1-x;x*y]}
```

This is the first time we have seen the `over` adverb called with more than one argument. In this case, the first argument (`first y`) is used as the starting value for the inner function's `x`. The function's result will be used as the next iteration's `x` value, and so on. The number of iterations will depend on how many elements are in the remaining arguments. They will be passed to the inner function one at a time.

We can demonstrate how the inner function would work if we were to compute the exponentially weighted moving average of the numbers from 0 to 4, with a decay factor of .1;

```
q).stat.ewma[.1;til 5]
0 0.1 0.29 0.561 0.9049
q){z+y*x}\[0;.9;.1*til 5]
0 0.1 0.29 0.561 0.9049
```

Computing the exponentially weighted moving average is so common that kdb+ 3.1 augmented the `scan` operator to permit an even shorter and faster computation. We can actually use the decay factor as if it were a function.

```
q)0 (.9)\ til 5
0 1 2.9 5.61 9.049
```

Parentheses were needed to prevent the `0 .9` from being interpreted as a vector of floats. We can now rewrite `ewma` one last time.

**.stat.ewma**

```
ewma:{first[y](1f-x)\x*y}
```

## Tail Region

Returning to the `norminv` approximation, we can use the `.stat.horner` [47] function again to implement the tail approximation.

**.stat.tnorminv**

```
tnorminv:{
 a:0.0000003960315187 0.0000002888167364 0.0000321767881768
   0.0003951896511919 0.0038405729373609 0.0276438810333863
   0.1607979714918209 0.9761690190917186 0.3374754822726147;
 x:horner[a] log neg log 1f-x;
 x}
```

## Vector Conditional

To help writing functions that operate on atoms and lists, q provides a vector conditional operator that is special cased to also work on atoms. The `?[;;]` operator accepts a boolean or a list of booleans as the first parameter. For all true values 1b, the corresponding item from the second operand will be returned. And for all false values 0b, the returned value will be picked from the corresponding index in the third operand. We can pass atoms as any of the operands and q will treat the value like a list of appropriate length.

```
q)?[10101010b;"z";"abcdefgh"]
"zbzdzfzh"
```

This comes in handy because we do not know if the caller of our function will pass a single value or a list of values. Using the ?[;;] operator allows us to write code that handles either case. The downside of using vector conditional is that both true and false code blocks are evaluated. Q Tip 5.4 [61] introduces the scalar conditional operator which allows lazy evaluation for each block.

We can now use the vector conditional operator to dispatch between the central and the tail approximations.

### .stat.norminv

```
norminv:{
 i:x<.5;
 x:?[i;1f-x;x];
 x:?[x<.92;cnorminv x;tnorminv x];
 x:?[i;neg x;x];
 x}
```

And the resulting function can be called with both single values and lists.

```
q).stat.norminv .5
0f
q).stat.norminv .25 .75
-0.6744897 0.6744897
```

We have now accumulated a few useful functions. To make them reusable, we must save them in a location that can be loaded again later. The next chapter introduces how to create reusable libraries and partition our code and data.

Chapter 5

# Code Organization

> We will encourage you to develop the three great virtues of a programmer: laziness, impatience, and hubris.
>
> — Larry Wall *Programming Perl (1st Edition)*

I must admit, the best q developers I have ever met have been lazy, impatient and hubristic. The first two come easily enough. After experiencing the speed at which new algorithms can be written, and the code executed, all q developers become lazy and impatient. Coding in any other language suddenly becomes a waste of your time. The hubris comes later. It is not easy to write q programs that others will not want to say bad things about. The first step towards that goal is to write short reusable algorithms. These short algorithms invariably come with short names as well. To prevent them from conflicting with each other, we need to use namespaces. This chapter begins by demonstrating how to load libraries. After introducing namespaces and directories, and the distinction between the two, the chapter concludes by providing a utility to import functions between directories.

## 5.1  Libraries

Just as q has provided us a list of functions we can use, q allows us to package our own functions for reuse. The \l system command evaluates all the code in a file. If we start q without passing stat.q on the command line, for example, we can load it on demand.

```
q)\l stat.q
q).stat.bm 2?1f
-0.2139312 0.6133312
```

The Kx q repository [qrepo] [266] has many libraries, including Arthur Whitney's own `stat.q`. In addition, the Kx Subversion repository [svn] [266] provides access to libraries that other developers have contributed to the `kdb+` community.

## File Paths

Quite often the path to a q library may not be known when writing your code. It may depend on runtime configuration. In these cases, we need to load the library by constructing the path as a character vector and then use the `system` operator to execute the `\l` command. There are many ways to construct file paths. For example, to load a library located in *tmp* we can build the path by explicitly joining the directory and file name with a hard coded path delimiter.

```
q)path:"/tmp"
q)system "l ",path,"/stat.q"
```

We can also build the path by using the q "scalar from vector" operator `sv`.

```
q)"/" sv (path;"stat.q")
"/tmp/stat.q"
```

---

**Q Tip 5.1** Build path names by joining symbols, not character vectors

---

Manipulating file paths is so common that q provides a syntax to split and join files on both the platform specific path separator and also the period "`.`" for file extensions. When a list of symbols are joined using the null symbol "`` ` ``" as the delimiter, the resulting symbol is joined with a period "`.`". This is a nice way to add file extensions.

```
q)` sv `stat`q
`stat.q
```

Symbols with a leading colon are also known as handles. They are the same as normal symbols, but q treats these symbols as file or network paths. Joining a list of symbols whose first element is a handle creates a single file path with platform specific path separators automatically inserted. This reduces mistakes and increases code clarity.

```
q)path:`:/tmp
q)` sv path,`stat.q
`:/tmp/stat.q
```

The same operations work in reverse as well. Using `vs` to split a symbol breaks it on each period "`.`".

```
q)` vs `file.ext.ext2
`file`ext`ext2
```

Splitting a handle, merely splits the symbol into two pieces: the directory and trailing file (or sub-directory).

```
q)` vs `:/tmp/stat.q
`:/tmp`stat.q
```

## File Existence

Attempting to load a file that does not exist will throw an exception. For more control of our application's behavior, we can first test for the file's existence. The `key` operator can be used for this purpose. If the file exists, the file's name will be returned. If the path is a directory, the list of files in the directory will be returned. And if the path does not exist, the empty list will be returned.

```
q)key `:stat.q
`:stat.q
q)key `:stat
q)
```

Knowing this, we can test for the existence of the file before attempting to load the library by either comparing against the empty list or the file name itself.

```
q)f:`:/tmp/stat.q
q)if[not ()~key f;system "l ", 1_string f]
q)if[f~key f;system "l ", 1_string f]
```

It is important to note that we used the match operator "~" instead of the equality operator "=".

## Identity vs Equality

The match operator "~" always returns a boolean indicating if the two operands are exactly the same. For atoms, the match operator and the equality operator "=" have the same behavior. When one value is a list (or dictionary or table), the equality operator returns a list (or dictionary or table) with a member by member comparison. Using the equality operator to check the results of `key` will therefore return an atom if the file is found, or a list if the path is a directory or is not found. Since a list can not be used as the condition statement in an `if` block, this will throw an exception. We can see the difference between equality and identity with an example.

```
q)()=`a
q)()~`a
0b
```

In addition, although the equality operator is tolerant when comparing types,

```
q)0=0f
1b
```

the match operator is not.

```
q)0~0f
0b
```

The match operator "~" is also useful when comparing the results of two different function implementations. There was once a discussion on the `k4` discussion group [listbox] [266] about how to best implement an autocorrelation function.

The initial proposal `ac1`, created a very large intermediate matrix of data. The implementation uses a composition and the *each-right* operator - both of which will be introduced in the section called "Minimize Calls to `each`" [110].

```
q)ac1:{c%first c:(sum x*)@/:xprev[;x] each til count x:x-avg x}
```

Using the "time and space" system command `\ts` we can time the execution of the function over a long list and also see how much memory (in bytes) was allocated during its execution.

```
q)x:til 5000
q)\ts ac1 x
688 327956848
```

The final proposal operated on the data row by row, and used the "$" operator with float vectors as both parameters to compute the dot product. It is much faster and uses less memory.

```
q)ac2:{x%first x:x{(y#x)$neg[y]#x}/:c-til c:count x-:avg x}
q)\ts ac2 x
73 309632
```

We can compare the results of both functions with the match operator "~" to confirm that both implementations produce the same results.

```
q)ac1[x]~ac2[x]
1b
```

The second implementation is shorter and faster. Let's add it to our statistic library.

**.stat.ac**

```
ac:{x%first x:x{(y#x)$neg[y]#x}/:c-til c:count x-:avg x}
```

## Environment Variables

We return now to our goal of loading libraries based on a dynamically generated path. Instead of hard-coding library paths into the application, it is possible to use an environment variable to construct the path. A simple, but not robust, example would be to load libraries from my home directory.

```
q)libdir:hsym `$getenv`HOME
q)system "l ", 1_string ` sv libdir,`stat.q
```

The `getenv` operator returns the value of the environment variable as a character vector. There is a complementary `setenv` operator that will set or change the value of an environment variable. For example, we can change the value of the *HOME* environment variable and the preceding lines of code would source the `stat.q` library from */tmp* instead of my home directory.[1]

```
q)`HOME setenv "/tmp"
q)getenv`HOME
"/tmp"
```

To cast the character vector to a symbol we can use the cast operator "$" with a null symbol as the left operand.

```
q)`$getenv`HOME
`/tmp
```

## File/Network Handle Operators

Q provides the `hsym` operator to perform the common operation of prepending a colon ":" to the path. Operators relating to file and network handles all start with a leading "h". Other examples are the `hopen` and `hclose` operators which open and close files and network connections as well as the `hdel` operator which deletes files and the `hcount` operator which counts the number of bytes in a file. Using the `hsym` operator we can convert the *HOME* environment variable into a file handle.

```
q)hsym `$getenv`HOME
`:/tmp
```

After loading a library, it is useful to inspect the q session to see what functions were added to the workspace. The `\v` system command lists all the variables, while the `\f` system command lists the functions.

```
$ q stat.q
q)\v
`symbol$()
q)\f
`symbol$()
```

---

[1] Neither of these locations are suggested for use in production systems.

It looks like we have not defined any variables or functions. But that is because we inspected the global namespace, and the functions were declared within the `.stat` namespace.

## 5.2  Namespaces

The global namespace is good for testing new functionality. But when the code is ready to be shared with others, leaving it in the global namespace risks name clashes with other parts of the system. Scoping variables becomes necessary when the size of the project begins to grow.

Namespaces are used to partition code to prevent variable name clashes. By default, the system commands act on the root namespace. In our example, this returned no variables or functions. But if we check the `.stat` namespace we will see all the functions defined within `.stat.q`.

```
q)\f .stat
`ac`bm`cnorm`cnorminv`erf`ewma`gbm`horner`invert`iqr`kurt`norminv`nr`ohlc`p..
```

There are so many functions in `stat.q` that q was forced to truncate the display.

---

**Q Tip 5.2** Customize your q experience

---

When `kdb+` runs out of horizontal or vertical space to display the remaining text, it appends two periods to signify that some text has been truncated. To change the number of rows and columns displayed, we can use the `\c` system command. The following line, extends the display to 20 rows long and 1000 characters wide

```
\c 20 1000
```

It is possible to automatically set the column width of our q session to match that of our UNIX terminal by using the `COLUMNS` environment variable. As we discussed in the section called "Environment Variables" [55], the `getenv` operator allows us to obtain any environment variable as a character vector. We can then use the `system` operator to dynamically set the q display size.

```
q)system "c 20 ",getenv`COLUMNS
```

Querying the system variable shows us the new value.

```
q)\c
20 179i
```

Since this is a personal preference, it is a good item to place in your own `q.q` file. After loading all q function definitions and before returning control to the user, q loads the contents of the file located in the `QINIT` environment variable. If this variable is not defined, it attempts to open a file named `q.q`.

To create a namespace we use the dot `"."` character within our variable name. For example, to place a few variables into the `qtips` namespace we would type the following.

```
q)qtips.a:1
q)qtips.b:2
```

We can then get the list of variables in the `qtips` namespace by passing `qtips` to the `\v` system command.

```
q)\v qtips
`a`b
```

Or, we can inspect the namespace directly.

```
q)qtips
 | ::
a| 1
b| 2
```

Notice how there are three fields in the namespace even though we only defined two. A namespace is actually just a mapping from a list of symbols to a list of values. To ensure that any value type can be stored in a namespace, q automatically starts the namespace with a null key mapped to the generic null value (`::`). If q determines that all elements of a list are of the same type, it collapses the mixed list to a vector. This is normally a good feature, as it makes future operations more efficient. But namespaces must hold all types. Including a null value as the first element prevents q from collapsing the list to vector.

The root namespace has no name, making it tricky to inspect. To see the contents of the root namespace we can not just call it by name. We need to use its symbol representation and ask for its value.

```
q)value `.
timer | ``job!(::;+`name`func`time!(`dump`updp`updp`updp`updp`updq`up..
ref   | (+(,`id)!,`u#0 1 2 3 4)!+`px`ts`qs`vol`rfr!(110 80 10 5 2f;0.05 0.0..
prices| +`id`px`time!(`g#`long$();`float$();`timestamp$())
price | (+(,`id)!,`u#0 1 2 3 4)!+`px`time!(110 80 10 5 2f;2015.03.07D23:33:..
trades| +`id`ts`tp`time!(`g#`long$();`long$();`float$();`timestamp$())
trade | (+(,`id)!,`u#`long$())!+`ts`tp`time!(`long$();`float$();`timestamp$..
quotes| +`id`bs`bp`ap`as`time!(`g#`long$();`long$();`float$();`float$();`lo..
..
```

## 5.3 Directories

The root namespace and all its children is designed for data. There is another type of namespace that is designed for functions and related configuration data. These special namespaces are called directories and begin with a single dot "`.`". Single letter directories are reserved for q. We can see all the directories that are loaded from `$QHOME/q.k` by starting a fresh instance of q.

```
$ q
q)key `
`q`Q`h`j`o
```

Just like other namespaces, we can use the \v command to list out the variables stored in the directory.

```
q)\v .q
,`csv
```

And we can inspect the directory directly.

```
q).q
            | ::
neg         | -:
not         | ~:
null        | ^:
string      | $:
reciprocal| %:
floor       | _:
..
```

The .q directory is where all the q functions which are implemented in k are stored. The other directories contain utility functions: .Q has functions for database maintenance, .h has functions for q's builtin web server, .j has q's JSON implementation and .o has functions for ODBC connectivity.

Defining a variable in a directory is the same as defining one in a namespace.

```
q).qtips.a:1
q).qtips.b:2
```

But directories offer another method of declaration. We can change the current directory with the \d system command and then declare the variable without fully specifying the path.

```
q)\d .qtips
q.qtips)buz:3
```

You can see how the prompt changes to include the directory name when we are not in the root directory. We can then return to the root directory and access the variable with the fully qualified name.

```
q.qtips)\d .
q).qtips.buz
3
```

Once we change the directory, all declared variables are scoped to the current directory. In addition, all variables accessed are assumed to exist in the current directory. You can open $QHOME/q.k to see how this is done to define the variables and functions in the .q, .Q, .h, .j, and .o directories. This same technique is used for all the qtips libraries.

## Accessing Global Variables

Changing directories to define functions provides one complication. All variables are assumed to be located in the current directory. To access data in other directories, their full name, including the directory, must be used. This does not work for variables in the root directory, however, because the root directory has no name. It is tempting to access the global variables with a double dot "..". This is close, but does not work.

```
q)a:1
q)\d .bar
q.bar)..a
'.
```

We must use the `value` or `get` operator on the fully scoped symbol representation of the variable.

```
q.bar)value `..a
1
```

An alternate method is to index into the root directory with the symbol representing the variable's name. This can be done with juxtaposition, bracket notation, or explicit use of the index operator "@".

```
q)a:1
q)\d .bar
q.bar)`. `a
1
q.bar)`.[`a]
1
q.bar)`.@`a
1
```

## 5.4 Namespaces vs. Directories

The terms *namespace* and *directory* are often used interchangeably. But while all directories are namespaces, not all namespaces are directories. I make this distinction to point out the subtle differences between the two.

Functions are designed to be used with data. We are using q primarily because we have data to store and analyze. Once we write our own functions and place them in a directory, it is then tempting to put our data in that directory as well. Unfortunately, q was not designed with this in mind. It would be nice to encapsulate all functions and associated data in a directory, but directories have limitations that discourage us from storing data in them.

• Directories can not contain views (discussed in the section called "Declaring a View" [242]).

- Automatic logging with the −l flag only records data updated in the root directory.

- Partitioned databases (discussed in Chapter 15 [201]) can not be loaded into directories.

---

**Q Tip 5.3** Scope function with directories, but datasets with namespaces

---

For these reasons, it becomes necessary to scope large datasets with namespaces, but not directories. In other words, although we should create functions within namespaces that begin with a ".", data should not. It may sometimes be useful to leave small configuration variables in the same directory as our functions, but datasets belong in namespaces located in the root directory.

Statistical functions, for example, can be placed in a .stat directory. But large datasets should be placed in namespaces representing their source. Dividend data from three different vendors can be differentiated: reuters.dividend, bloomberg.dividend and yahoo.dividend. In this way, all data from a single vendor can be safely imported into its own namespace. In addition, we can use the \a system command or tables operator to list all the tables from the vendor. Alternatively, we can create them as dividend.reuters, dividend.bloomberg and dividend.yahoo. Using the tables operator on the dividend namespace would then reveal the different dividend sources available.

Using namespaces also provides us the flexibility to add views to our datasets. Views allow access to derived data that gets (re)generated when, and only when, the underlying data changes and the view is accessed. If a view is never accessed, it is never executed. Views will be discussed in further detail in the section called "Declaring a View" [242].

## 5.5  Importing

Scoping libraries is a standard way to prevent different projects from accidentally declaring variables with the same name. There are times, however, when we would like to use a function or access data from another directory without having to specify the fully scoped name each time. In these cases we have explicitly decided that the variables imported from the other directory will not clash with our own.

**.util.use**

```
use:{system["d"] upsert $[99h=type v:get x;v;(-1#` vs x)!1#v]}
```

This use function accepts the name of a variable or a directory name and makes it available in the current directory. It first uses the get operator to find the actual data behind the symbol. The variable merged with the current directory if it is a dictionary itself. If it is a single element, however, the function must first wrap it in a single element dictionary. The upsert operator merges the two directories.

With the use function, we can import functions from the .stat directory into the root directory and access them without using their qualifying directory name. We can either import a single function,

```
q)use `.stat.skew
`.
q)skew
{avg[x*x2]%sqrt m2*m2*m2:avg x2:x*x-:avg x}
```

or the whole directory.

```
q)use `.stat
`.
```

The use function introduces the scalar conditional operator $[;;]. Depending on the type of the parameter passed to the function, different actions are taken. Each block between the semicolons is evaluated from left to right. If the first item evaluates to true, the second element is evaluated and returned. Otherwise, the third item is evaluated. If there are fourth and fifth blocks, then the third is treated as an *else if* statement and a true value will result in the fourth block being evaluated and returned. If all conditions evaluate to false, the last element is returned. This pattern can continue as long as you need. The benefit of using this scalar conditional operator construct is that each block is lazily evaluated. In contrast, each of the blocks in the vector conditional operator ?[;;] are evaluated before items are conditionally returned. Nothing is lazily evaluated, and only a single condition can be checked.

---

**Q Tip 5.4** Use scalar conditional $[;;] to implement lazily evaluated blocks

---

Conditional statements in q are rare because using null and positive/negative infinity transform typical conditionals into mathematical comparisons. This is demonstrated in Q Tip 17.5 [253]. There are some cases, however, where conditionals are necessary. Checking the type of a function parameter or the length of a list are the most common checks. Other languages may use a switch statement to implement conditional dispatch. Q, however, uses the scalar conditional operator $[;;] and its extended form $[;;...;]. Each block is lazily evaluated, thus allowing efficient condition checks.

The .util.tree [219] function introduced in the section called "Compressing a Directory Tree" [219] uses the extended conditional operator to efficiently dispatch between cases where the key operator returns a single file name, a list of files in a directory, or the empty list.

# Chapter 6

# A Random Walk

The concept of a random walk is simple but rich for its many applications, not only in finance but also in physics and the description of natural phenomena. It is arguably one of the most founding concepts in modern physics as well as in finance, as it underlies the theories of elementary particles, which are the building blocks of our universe, as well as those describing the complex organization of matter around us.

— Didier Sornette *Why Stock Markets Crash - Critical Events in Complex Systems (2003)*

A security's price history can be described as a random walk, with each movement up or down coming from our normally generated random numbers. To be precise, it is not the price that exhibits this behavior but the log price. If the price jumped up or down in this behavior, it would be possible for the price to become negative. A common model to describe a security's path is Geometric Brownian Motion.[1] With our ability to generate normally distributed random numbers, we are one function away from generating fictional security prices.

## 6.1 Geometric Brownian Motion

Our gbm function takes four parameters: the stock's volatility (also known as sigma), the stock's rate of drift, the interval time step, and the normal random realizations.

**.stat.gbm**

```
gbm:{[s;r;t;z]exp(t*r-.5*s*s)+z*s*sqrt t}
```

---

[1] Hull, John (2009). "12.3". *Options, Futures, and other Derivatives* (7 ed.).

The gbm function transforms a list of normal random variables into a list of returns scaled to the specified time interval, volatility and drift.

---

**Q Tip 6.1** Multiply instead of divide

---

Note how the gbm function multiplies by .5 instead of dividing by 2. CPUs can implement floating point multiplication faster than division. To take advantage of this, q has implemented vector division by an atom as multiplication by the atom's reciprocal. This can be seen clearly by the paradoxical difference between these two computations.

```
q) floor 3*7%3
7
q) floor 3*(1#7)%3
,6
```

The results should, in principle, be the same. But due to the inexact representation of some values in floating point notation, the results are different by a very small fraction. To see the difference, we can use the \P system command to display values with full precision. By default, q shows floating point numbers with up to 7 significant digits.

```
q) \P
7i
```

The same system command can be used to change this value. To display all digits, we can set the value to 0.

```
q) \P 0
```

We can then see that the results of the atomic operation are different from the vector operation.

```
q) 3*7%3
7f
q) 3*(1#7)%3
,6.999999999999991
```

Multiplying by the reciprocal results in the same value.

```
q) 3*(1%3)*7
6.999999999999991
```

---

**Q Tip 6.2** Compare with zero to compute exact equality

---

These small errors do not often cause problems when comparing floating point calculations because q implements equality with tolerance. Specifically, two floating point numbers are considered equal if the absolute difference between the numbers is less than $2^{-43}$ times the larger of the absolute values of the numbers. This also ensures that the only number equal to zero is 0. To test for equality without tolerance, always compare with 0. A more detailed discussion of q's comparison tolerance can be found on the Kx Wiki [tolerance] [265].

The benefits of multiplication over division extend to code readability. In order to divide by 2, an extra set of parentheses would be needed: `.5*s*s` vs `(s*s)%2`. This same technique is used in Chapter 17 [235] when we convert from nanoseconds to milliseconds. Instead of dividing by 1e6, the `.prof. stats` [240] function multiplies the time by 1e-6.

We can now generate a path with 252 (a commonly used number of business days in a year) daily steps for a stock with an annual volatility of 30%, growing at 5% a year.

```
q).stat.gbm[.30;.05;1%252] .stat.norminv 252?1f
1.001419 1.009522 0.9861329 1.009541 0.9986357 1.006547 1.035438 0.9861929 ..
```

These values represent the returns for each time interval. To find the cumulative effect of these changes we can multiply them together with the `prd` operator and multiply by the initial security value.

```
q)100*prd .stat.gbm[.30;.05;1%252] .stat.norminv 252?1f
159.2141
```

To see intermediate steps of the security price we can use the `prds` operator which produces a running product of all values.

```
q)100*prds .stat.gbm[.30;.05;1%252] .stat.norminv 252?1f
100.5395 99.76852 102.9526 100.6644 102.3929 102.9326 107.1463 108.5509 107..
```

The `prds` operator is an example of a uniform function.

## Uniform Functions

Like an atomic function, a uniform function returns an atom if called with an atom, and a list, of equal length, if called with a list. The returned values, however, are not the same as if the function were applied to each element separately. Each element of the list can affect the value returned for all other elements.

In addition to the `prds` operator, q includes a few more arithmetic uniform functions that also return the intermediate results of their computation. They all end with an `s`. Some, like `prds` have correspond aggregating functions that only return the last value.

**avgs**
> Each element is the average `avg` of all prior elements.

**deltas**
> Each element is the difference between itself and the prior value.

**fills**
> Each element is filled with the prior value.

**maxs**

Each element is the maximum `max` value of all prior elements.

**mins**

Each element is the minimum `min` value of all prior elements.

**prds**

Each element is the product `prd` of all prior elements.

**ratios**

Each element is the ratio of itself and the prior value.

**sums**

Each element is the summation `sum` of all prior elements.


## 6.2   Temporal Data

Every step in a security's price path corresponds to a date or time. The `gbm` function can actually compute path prices for uneven time steps. Let's take a quick diversion to discuss how q represents temporal (time based) data.

One reason q is a popular language for time-series analysis is because q makes manipulating dates and times easy. As mentioned in Section 3.3 [26], all temporal data is internally stored numerically. Q has overloaded the arithmetic operators to also manipulate temporal data. In our quest to generate simulated security prices, we will need to associate a security price with a date or time. After discussing temporal data types, we will create a function that generates realistic security prices for the time values we specify.


### Date

Dates in q are entered (and displayed) in YYYY.MM.DD format. They are internally represented as integers centered at 2000.01.01. We can recover the internal representation by casting the date to an integer.

```
q)"i"$2000.01.01
0i
```

Date manipulation is as easy as adding integers. To generate a list of dates we can start with an initial date and add a list of integers.

```
q)2000.01.01 + til 5
2000.01.01 2000.01.02 2000.01.03 2000.01.04 2000.01.05
```

Given that 2000.01.01 was a Saturday and this day has an internal representation of 0, all weekends are 7 days away from the numbers 0 and 1. If we take the modulus, base 7, of a date, weekends will have values 0 and 1.

```
q)(2000.01.01 + til 14) mod 7
0 1 2 3 4 5 6 0 1 2 3 4 5 6i
```

We can now create a function that filters a list of dates to only those that land on a weekday.

**.util.wday**

```
wday:{x where 1<x mod 7}
```

The `where` operator returns the indices for only those elements that return true. To only return the weekdays, the function uses the results of the `where` clause to index back into the original list.

```
q).util.wday 2000.01.01 + til 5
2000.01.03 2000.01.04 2000.01.05
```

The global variable `.z.D` returns the current date assuming the local timezone. To obtain the date with respect to GMT we can use the lowercase version of the same system variable `.z.d`.

## Time

Dates are good for inter-day data. But for intra-day data, we need to use a time data type. The proper type actually depends on how precise we need to be. We can save time values with minute, second, millisecond, or nanosecond precision. The first three are stored as 4-byte integers, while the nanosecond type is stored as an 8-byte integer.

Just as adding 1 to a date, has the logical result of adding 1 day, adding integers to the other time types, has the effect of adding a single unit of their precision.

```
q)00:00 + til 3
00:00 00:01 00:02
q)00:00:00 + til 3
00:00:00 00:00:01 00:00:02
q)00:00:00.000 + til 3
00:00:00.000 00:00:00.001 00:00:00.002
q)0D + til 3
0D00:00:00.000000000 0D00:00:00.000000001 0D00:00:00.000000002
```

The last example is in nanoseconds and is called a timespan in `kdb+`. Like the other time data types, it is a number that represents a window of time. When the value is less than one day (note the leading 0), it can also represent a specific time of day. The multitude of time types are convenient. It turns out, however, there is actually more flexibility if we limit ourselves to just using the timespan type. The timespan syntax allows us to represent any interval of time from days down to nanoseconds. For example, we can create lists of times with 30 minute intervals.

```
q)0D + 0D00:30*til 3
0D00:00:00.000000000 0D00:30:00.000000000 0D01:00:00.000000000
```

We can obtain the local time in milliseconds with the `.z.T` system variable (or `.z.t` for GMT) and the local time in nanoseconds with the `.z.N` system variable (or `.z.n` for GMT).

## Date and Time

It is also possible to have a single value that incorporates the date and time. `Kdb+` has two types of date/time values. The old type is called a datetime. It is saved in an 8-byte double. The integer component records the day of the year, while the fractional component represents the time (or fraction of a day). The local datetime can be obtained with the `.z.Z` system command (or `.z.z` for GMT).

In retrospect, storing time values in a double was not a good idea. Computers always record time at discrete intervals, so the floating point number was never needed. And in fact, the rounding error that sometimes occurs with floating point numbers has caused much confusion. When this value is displayed, q only prints three decimal points. The precision of the datetime, however, is much greater than milliseconds. If we generate a new datetime, and compare it with what is printed, we can see that they are not the same.

```
q) show z:.z.Z
2014.01.15T00:36:01.953
q) z~2014.01.15T00:36:01.953
0b
```

This is because the displayed value is just a rounded version of the true value. This also means datetimes should not be stored as keys in a dictionary. Integer values are the only safe way to store numeric data in a map/dictionary. As Arthur Whitney once told me, "Integers are God's gift to computing." To solve these problems, and increase precision to nanoseconds, `kdb+` introduced the timestamp in `kdb+` 2.6.

---

**Q Tip 6.3** Use `timestamps` instead of `datetimes`

---

Where the timespan indicates a duration, the timestamp indicates a specific time. Logically, subtracting two timestamps results in a timespan. And just like the timespan, the timestamp has nanosecond precision. The local timestamp can be obtained with the `.z.P` system command (or `.z.p` for GMT). Most computers only actually report the time down to microsecond precision. But if you use more advanced techniques to obtain nanosecond level timestamps, they will seamlessly fit into the new data type.

The `timestamp` is stored as the number of nanoseconds since the turn of the millennium 2000.01.01. More importantly, the value is stored in an 8-byte integer, thus making all comparisons between `timestamps` precise.

## 6.3   Path generation

One powerful feature of q is that mathematical operators are all atomic. That is, they work equally well on atoms and vectors (and dictionaries and tables). This means we can pass a vector of times to the gbm function to simulate paths with uneven time steps. In this example, we can create a more realistic price path by only computing the security price on weekdays.

```
q)s:.3;r:.05;dt:.util.wday 2001.01.01+til 365
q)tm:deltas[first dt;dt]%365.25
q)100*prds .stat.gbm[s;r;tm] .stat.norminv (count dt)?1f
100 100.1525 98.91791 97.59687 96.99619 94.84253 93.80587 92.75921 91.29922..
```

## Deltas

With weekends removed, the time between elements is no longer constant. We used the deltas operator to determine the number of days between each step.

```
q)deltas dt
366 1 1 1 1 3 1 1 1 1 1 3 1 1 1 1 1 3 1 1 1 1 1 3 1 1 1 1 1 3 1 1 1 1 1 3 1 1 1 1 3 1..
```

The first element of the list has no previous value to compare against. By default, deltas compares the first value with 0, which is not what we want. The deltas operator is quite special. It can be used in both monadic and dyadic form. If we pass two arguments to the function, q will use the first operand as the first element of comparison. To get the behavior we want, we can pass the list's first element as the first argument.

```
q)deltas[first dt; dt]
0 1 1 1 1 3 1 1 1 1 1 3 1 1 1 1 1 3 1 1 1 1 1 3 1 1 1 1 1 3 1 1 1 1 1 3 1 1 1 1 3 1 1..
```

---

**Q Tip 6.4** Use the dyadic form of deltas, ratios, differ and prev

---

Q has a total of four operators that share this ability: deltas, ratios, differ, and prev. The defaults for each operator are 0, 1, :: and 0N respectively. This is often exactly what we want. In our case, however, it would not be appropriate to compare the first date to 2000.01.01 (which is the date corresponding to the value of 0). To ensure that the first result of deltas is 0 we passed the first element of our list as the optional first operand. An alternate solution, which makes no assumptions about the data, is to pass a null value as the first operand.

We will be generating security paths with non-uniform time steps quite often. It is worth wrapping these steps in a function to be reused again. Just like the gbm function, the path function accepts the security sigma (or volatility), the rate of drift, and the time steps. The number of normal random realizations will be derived from the vector of time steps. Again, the simple multiplication by the initial security price has been left out.

**.sim.path**

```
path:{[s;r;t]
 z:.stat.norminv count[t]?1f;
```

```
p:prds .stat.gbm[s;r;deltas[first t;t]] z;
p}
```

Our `path` function can now generate daily security prices.

```
q)100*.sim.path[.3;.05](1%365.25)*.util.wday 2001.01.01+til 365
100 98.78096 97.76153 97.46765 96.09985 96.72204 97.5397 97.72342 96.95007 ..
```

The same function would also work if we removed public holidays. In fact, the `path` function will even work for intra-day prices.

```
q)100*.sim.path[.3;.05] (1%365D06)*0D09+0D00:01*til 1000
100 100.0417 100.0668 100.0189 100.0424 100.0574 100.0055 99.96756 99.94411..
```

---

**Q Tip 6.5** Factor algorithms into small reusable pieces

---

Factoring algorithms into a simple function allows us to change how we combine them without having to rewrite them. Making no assumptions about what types of time steps are passed to the `path` function allows us to use the same function for both inter- and intra-day periods. The same philosophy that guides the UNIX operating system works equally well with functional programming. Functions should be small and do one thing well.

## Ranges

Generating a list of numbers, whether they are days of the year, times of the day, or just plain integers is a common task. Factoring this into a range function will come in handy. The `rng` function accepts the stride width, starting value, and ending value.

**.util.rng**

```
rng:{[w;s;e]s+w*til ceiling(e-s)%w}
```

The function first determines the number of items between the starting and ending value. It uses the `til` operator to create an arithmetic sequence, multiplies it by the stride width, and offsets the list by the starting value. The `rng` function works with numeric and even temporal data. We can generate a list of dates for a single year,

```
q).util.rng[1;2000.01.01;2001.01.01]
2000.01.01 2000.01.02 2000.01.03 2000.01.04 2000.01.05 2000.01.06 2000.01.0..
```

or just two months by using q's internal `.Q.addmonths` function.

```
q).util.rng[1] . .Q.addmonths[2000.01.01;0 2]
2000.01.01 2000.01.02 2000.01.03 2000.01.04 2000.01.05 2000.01.06 2000.01.0..
```

## Projections

The first thing to notice in this example is that even though the `rng` function expects three arguments, we only called it with one. The result of calling a function with fewer arguments than expected is a new function that can be called with the remaining arguments. In this example, `.util.rng[1]` results in a function that expects the start and end values. The act of calling a function with fewer parameters than is needed to execute the function is called partial application or binding parameters. The result of binding parameters to a function is called a projection. Using semicolons, it is also possible to bind parameters other than the first. For example, we can bind the start and end values to create a projection that can be called with just the stride width.

```
q).util.rng[;10;20]  2
10 12 14 16 18
```

In these examples, the only reason to bind parameters and create projections is for syntactic elegance. It is, in fact, slightly slower. A more practical reason to use projections is to pass functions as parameters to other functions. This will be demonstrated in Section 17.3 [257].

## Dot Apply

The second thing to notice when we created a two month range of dates was that the last two arguments were passed to `rng` without actually using semicolons and brackets. After we bound the first argument of `rng` function, the resulting projection expected two arguments. The result of `.Q.addmonths` is a list of two dates that we want to use as parameters to the projection.

```
q).Q.addmonths[2000.01.01;0 2]
2000.01.01 2000.03.01
```

The dot operator `"."` accepts a multivalent function, projection or data structure (such as a keyed table introduced in Section 7.3 [85]), as its left operand and a list as its right operand. It then calls the right operand with each element of the list as if it had been called with bracket notation. In our example, the two dates are passed as the second and third arguments to `rng`.

We can now combine the `path` and `rng` functions to generate a price path for a single trading day.

```
q)100*.sim.path[.3;.05] .util.rng[0D00:01;0D09;0D15]%365D06
100 100.0437 99.99191 99.9817 99.92209 99.90936 99.87631 99.85888 99.86107 ..
```

## Rounding

To make our example a bit more realistic we also need to round the prices. In practice, we need to round prices to multiple precisions. Some prices are rounded to the nearest cent, while others are rounded to the nearest five cents. In some countries, prices are even rounded to the nearest dollar or even larger denominations. Our round function will need to be flexible enough to handle each of these cases. Writing a generic rounding function is actually quite simple.

**.util.rnd**

```
rnd:{x*"j"$y%x}
```

This function takes a rounding factor as its first argument x and an atom or list of numbers as the second argument y. It first scales the y argument by dividing by x. The function then rounds the number to the nearest integer by casting the value to an 8-byte integer with the "$" operator. And finally, it re-scales the value by multiplying by x. Using rnd to round our prices to the nearest cent looks like this.

```
q).util.rnd[.01] 100*.sim.path[.3;.05].util.rng[0D00:01;0D09;0D15]%365D06
100 100.09 100.12 100.16 100.15 100.16 100.19 100.17 100.25 100.19 100.12 1..
```

---

**Q Tip 6.6** Reserve the last function parameter for data

---

Notice how we chained three functions together without having to nest the opening and closing brackets. To achieve this flexibility, it is important to place the parameters that are used for configuration first, and those for data last. Ordering function parameters is sometimes more of an art than a science. For example, should the stride window for the rng parameter be first or last? Other languages place it last, as an optional parameter. Q, however, does not have the ability to declare optional parameters. Since we have already encountered an example where the start and end values are computed, experience tilts the argument in favor of passing them at the end - as data.

We can now generate a realistic price path for a single security. To expand our grasp of q we will need to generate and analyze intra-day datasets for multiple securities over multiple days. The data structures we have been using, namely atoms and lists, are not sufficient for the increased data complexity. The next chapter rounds out our knowledge of data structures by introducing dictionaries and tables.

Chapter 7

# Building a Table

I will, in fact, claim that the difference between a bad programmer and a good one is whether he considers his code or his data structures more important. Bad programmers worry about the code. Good programmers worry about data structures and their relationships.

— Linux Torvalds *Message to Git mailing list (2006-06-27)*

Like many programming languages, q has basic data types such as atoms, lists, and maps. In addition, q has a table type. Conceptually, a table is a matrix, or grid, of data with columns that can be indexed by name instead of number. Some tables have primary keys which then allow rows to be indexed by value. Kdb+ is considered a database because it has in-memory tables. Without tables, q would be just another scripting language. K became kdb+ when tables were embraced as a fundamental data type. To understand how tables have been integrated as a native data type we must first discuss dictionaries.

A single security path is easily stored in a list. When we expand our problem to multiple paths, we need the ability to store additional information with each path. At a bare minimum, we will need to associate a security ID with each path. To make the path useful, we will also need to associate a date/time with each element of the path. Our discussion begins with dictionaries.

## 7.1 Dictionaries

Dictionaries map keys to values. While other languages may use binary trees and/or hash tables as the internal data structure for their map implementation, kdb+ keeps it simple by using a pair of lists. Kdb+ operations are optimized for lists of values stored in contiguous memory. And while other languages must define a separate data type for ordered maps, the kdb+ dictionary is inherently ordered. Implementing a dictionary as a pair of lists allows q to take advantage of existing list algorithms. To map a list of dates to prices we first create two lists.

```
q)dt:.util.rng[1;2000.01.01;2001.01.01]
q)p:100*.sim.path[.3;.05] dt%365.25
```

We can then use the key operator "!" to bind the dates to the prices.

```
q)dt!p
2000.01.01| 100
2000.01.02| 98.66291
2000.01.03| 97.1703
2000.01.04| 99.40865
2000.01.05| 97.60011
2000.01.06| 96.97171
2000.01.07| 97.05328
..
```

Creating a dictionary is a constant time operation. The data in the dictionary has not been copied. It continues to refer to the dt and p lists until either one is modified. If we save the dictionary into a variable, we see the reference count of the prices is now 2.

```
q)d:dt!p
q)-16!p
2i
```

To retrieve the key and value list from the dictionary we can use the appropriately named key and value operators.

```
q)key d
2000.01.01 2000.01.02 2000.01.03 2000.01.04 2000.01.05 2000.01.06 2000.01.0..
q)value d
100 98.66291 97.1703 99.40865 97.60011 96.97171 97.05328 96.90366 96.25223 ..
```

Although the dictionary is stored as a pair of lists, we often think of dictionaries as lists of key-value pairs. In fact, we may find ourselves wanting to build a dictionary with a such a list. Although q does not have a specific syntax for building dictionaries with a list of pairs, it is not hard to do. Given a list of date/price pairs, we can create a dictionary by first flipping the list

```
q)pairs:((2000.01.01;100f);(2000.01.02;101f);(2000.01.03;99f))
```

Flipping a list of pairs creates the pair of lists that q requires when building a dictionary.

```
q)flip pairs
2000.01.01 2000.01.02 2000.01.03
100        101        99
```

We can now use the key operator "!" to bind the two lists. Instead of passing one list as the left operand and the other as the right operand, we can pass them both simultaneously by using the dot operator ".".

```
q)(!) . flip pairs
2000.01.01| 100
2000.01.02| 101
2000.01.03| 99
```

This is a special case when the q syntax parser needs help to fulfill our request. By default, a binary q operator, such as "!", is an *infix dyadic verb*. That is, it must be surrounded by left and right operands or called with bracket notation. To pass it as an argument to the dot apply operator ".", we must convert it into a *noun* by preventing its left or right arguments from being applied. This can be done by surrounding it with parentheses. To summarize the terminology, a verb must be passed a noun as an argument, while a noun can be passed as an argument to a verb.

## Manipulating

There are not many new operators to learn when manipulating dictionaries. This is because q's list manipulation operators are overloaded to work on dictionaries as well. We can, for example, reverse,

```
q)reverse d
2000.12.31| 104.3607
2000.12.30| 104.4279
2000.12.29| 103.6111
2000.12.28| 105.2337
2000.12.27| 104.634
2000.12.26| 107.516
2000.12.25| 108.0901
..
```

or take the first n elements of a dictionary.

```
q)2#d
2000.01.01| 100
2000.01.02| 98.66291
```

Other (value modifying) operators ignore the key and update the dictionary's values. We can reuse our .util.rnd [72] function without modification.

```
q).util.rnd[.01] d
2000.01.01| 100
2000.01.02| 98.66
2000.01.03| 97.17
2000.01.04| 99.41
2000.01.05| 97.6
2000.01.06| 96.97
2000.01.07| 97.05
..
```

Aggregate functions can also be applied to the dictionary's values but the result will no longer be a dictionary.

```
q) avg d
103.7808
```

## Indexing

Dictionaries are indexed by value, not position. To find the price on a specific date or dates, we index into our dictionary with the proper dates.

```
q) d:dt!p
q) d[2000.05.01]
97.73622
q) d 2000.03.30 2000.04.03
103.7118 101.2931
```

Notice how both bracket notation and juxtaposition work for dictionaries as well (though I would not encourage using brackets unless it is to enforce the ordering of execution within a long chain of operators). Critically, dictionary lookups are performed by iterating over each key element until an exact match is found. The corresponding value is then returned. For small dictionaries this can be faster than using more advanced techniques such as binary search or hashing. But for long dictionaries, this linear search will be very slow. In Chapter 8 [91], we will discuss how lists (and thus dictionaries) can be modified so q uses more efficient searching algorithms.

To create a dictionary with a subset of values, we can use the take operator "#".

```
q) 2000.05.01 2000.05.02#d
2000.05.01| 97.73622
2000.05.02| 98.49546
```

To take a single element from the dictionary we must create a single element list.

```
q) (1#2000.05.02)#d
2000.05.02| 98.49546
```

## Assignment

To update values, we can assign them directly,

```
q) d[2000.01.02]:99f
q) d
2000.01.01| 100
2000.01.02| 99
```

```
2000.01.03| 97.1703
2000.01.04| 99.40865
2000.01.05| 97.60011
2000.01.06| 96.97171
2000.01.07| 97.05328
..
```

or join with a new dictionary that has the list of new values we need to update.

```
q)show d,:2000.01.01 2000.01.02!101 102f
2000.01.01| 101
2000.01.02| 102
2000.01.03| 97.1703
2000.01.04| 99.40865
2000.01.05| 97.60011
2000.01.06| 96.97171
2000.01.07| 97.05328
..
```

Although we have modified the dictionary values, the underlying lists dt and p remain unchanged. We can refer back to the reference count to see that dt still has two references,

```
q)-16!dt
2i
```

but because the prices in the dictionary were modified, a copy of p was created, and its reference count has dropped back to one.

```
q)-16!p
1i
```

---

**Q Tip 7.1** Ensure dictionary keys are unique

---

When joining two dictionaries, q will merge common keys, and append new ones. But if we build a dictionary our self, it is possible to introduce duplicate keys.

```
q)show x:("aa"!1 2),"bb"!10 20
a| 1
a| 2
b| 10
b| 20
```

Q does not prevent us from doing this. But looking up a value in the dictionary will only find the first occurrence of each distinct key.

```
q)x"ab"
1 10
```

## Single Element Dictionaries

Creating dictionaries with a single element is a common task which unfortunately has a complicated solution. We can not just map one item to another.

```
q)2000.01.01!100
'type
```

The "!" operator is a heavily overloaded operator. Depending on the type of its operands it can perform different operations. To create a dictionary, both the left and right operands must be lists (even if they only contain a single value). The best way to create a single element list is to enlist the element.

```
q)enlist 2000.01.01
,2000.01.01
```

A slightly shorter notation for creating a list from an atom is to take a single element.

```
q)1#2000.01.01
,2000.01.01
```

And finally, a third way to create a single element list is to join an atom to the empty list, or the empty list to an atom.

```
q)(),2000.01.01
,2000.01.01
q)2000.01.01,()
,2000.01.01
```

---

**Q Tip 7.2** Use 0N! to debug data structures and functions

---

Each of these techniques converts an atom into a list. But when applied to a list, the outcomes are very different. We can use the 0N! operator to print the unformatted k data structure. The 0N! operator can be inserted anywhere within our code and other than printing its argument, has no side effects. This is very useful when debugging a function, as it adds logging without changing its behavior.

```
q)0N!enlist 2000.01.01 2000.01.02;
,2000.01.01 2000.01.02
q)0N!1#2000.01.01 2000.01.02;
,2000.01.01
q)0N!(),2000.01.01 2000.01.02;
2000.01.01 2000.01.02
```

The first example enlists a list. This creates a list of lists where the outer list only contains a single element (the inner list). The second example takes the first element from the list and discards all the rest. And the third example joins an empty list to a list which has no effect.

---

## Namespaces Revisited

Before we move on to tables, let's take another look at namespaces. We did not discuss it at the time, but a namespace (and therefore a directory) is actually a dictionary that stores variables and function definitions. If you recall, we inspected the `.q` directory by typing its name at the prompt. But now that we know namespaces are just dictionaries, we can perform many other operations on them as well. For example, we can request the list of variables in the `.q` directory.

```
q)key .q
``neg`not`null`string`reciprocal`floor`ceiling`signum`mod`xbar`xlog`and`or`..
```

Or we can reverse the directory to see the last few definitions.

```
q)reverse .q
eval | ![-6]
parse| k){$["\\"=*x;(system;1_x);-5!x]}
csv  | ","
show | k){1 .Q.s x;}
dsave| k){.[*x;1_x,y,`;:;@[;*!+a;`p#].Q.en[*x]a:. y];y}/:
rload| k){x:-1!x;.[*|`\:x;();:;.     x]}'
rsave| k){x:-1!x;.[`/:x,`;();:;.*|`\:x]}'
..
```

We can also index into the directory to find the definition of a specific function.

```
q).stat`pctile
{[p;x]x iasc[x]"j"$-.5+p*count x}
```

This is exactly what the dot operator "." in a function's name does - it descends into the dictionary and returns the appropriate value.

```
q).stat.pctile
{[p;x]x iasc[x] -1+ceiling p*count x}
```

Dot notation, however, is more strict than indexing a namespace. Instead of returning the generic null (`::`) for a missing definition, dot notation throws an error.

```
q).stat.missing
'.stat.missing
```

## 7.2   Tables

Dictionaries are good at mapping two sets of equally dimensioned data to each other. When the dimensions of our dataset begin to grow, dictionaries become cumbersome. One choice is to maintain multiple maps, each keyed by the same field but with different values. Another approach is to increase the complexity of the data stored in the map. Database tables are a popular data structure because they allow us to associate any number of attributes with each record. Our goal is to associate a date and a security ID with each price. In other languages, we would perhaps use nested maps. In q, however, there is a better way. To increase the number of fields in our dictionary let's first change the data structure.

## Dictionary of Lists

Instead of mapping each date to a price, we will convert our dictionary to be keyed on data field names. The values will now be the list of data elements - identifiers, dates and prices.

```
q) `id`date`price!(count[p]#0;dt;p)
id   | 0          0          0          0          0          0          0 ..
date | 2000.01.01 2000.01.02 2000.01.03 2000.01.04 2000.01.05 2000.01.06 20..
price| 100        98.66291   97.1703    99.40865   97.60011   96.97171   97..
```

We are no longer able to index into the dictionary by date to find a specific value, but we can extend the structure to include other fields. We could continue to expand our dataset to include the daily high, low and open prices, but for now let's focus on the fact that what we are building is a dictionary of lists. To access the data we need, we first index by field name (`id, `date or `price) and then by row number.

```
q)d:`id`date`price!(count[p]#0;dt;p)
q)d[`price;5]
100.8468
```

## Flipped Dictionary of Lists

This notation is not optimal. We are looking for a way to index the data by **row** first and then by **column**, just like databases access their data. In other words, we would like to transpose the data structure so we can access it by row-column instead of column-row order. The flip operator performs this exact operation. On a list of lists, the flip operator transposes the values.

```
q)(dt;p)
2000.01.01 2000.01.02 2000.01.03 2000.01.04 2000.01.05 2000.01.06 2000.01.0..
100        98.66291   97.1703    99.40865   97.60011   96.97171   97.05328 ..
q)flip (dt;p)
2000.01.01 100f
2000.01.02 98.66291
2000.01.03 97.1703
2000.01.04 99.40865
2000.01.05 97.60011
2000.01.06 96.97171
2000.01.07 97.05328
..
```

Similarly, we would expect that using `flip` on our dictionary of lists should create a list of dictionaries. Let's see what happens.

```
q)show t:flip `id`date`price!(count[p]#0;dt;p)
id date       price
-------------------------
0  2000.01.01 100
0  2000.01.02 98.66291
0  2000.01.03 97.1703
0  2000.01.04 99.40865
0  2000.01.05 97.60011
..
```

We can now index the data structure by row number to pull the dictionary we want.

```
q)t 4
id   | 0
date | 2000.01.05
price| 97.60011
```

And we can also access the data by row-column order.

```
q)t[4; `price]
97.60011
```

## Flip

This flipped dictionary of lists is, in fact, a table. Even though we can access each record individually, the data is still stored as a dictionary of lists.

Using the `flip` operator on a matrix of data, actually transposes the data. This operation is quite expensive. Using the `flip` operator on a dictionary of lists, however, does not transpose the data. It only records the fact that the data should be treated as a table. Keeping the data stored as lists minimizes memory usage, increases performance by allowing vectorized mathematical operations and creates a simple model for mapping the structures to disk for persistence. Looking at the internal representation shows us that it is still a flipped dictionary of lists.

```
q)0N!t;
+`id`date`price!(0 0 0 0 0 0 0 0 0 0 0 0 0 0 0 0 0 0 0 0 0 0 0 0 0 0 0 0 0 0 0 0 ..
```

The "+" character is actually the `flip` operator in the underlying k language. Note, however, that this does not work for all dictionaries of lists. To ensure that flipping a dictionary of lists is treated as a table, the keys of the dictionary must be symbols, and each of the lists must be of equal size (or be an atom which can be coerced into a list of matching length). We can actually define the `id` column without having to create a list of 0s. Kdb+ will take care of that for us.

```
q) flip `id`date`price!(0;dt;p)
id date       price
-------------------
0  2000.01.01 100
0  2000.01.02 98.66291
0  2000.01.03 97.1703
0  2000.01.04 99.40865
0  2000.01.05 97.60011
..
```

## Syntax

Flipping a dictionary of lists is but one way of creating a table. Another way is to create a list of dictionaries.

```
q) enlist `id`date`price!(0;2000.01.01;100)
id date       price
-------------------
0  2000.01.01 100
```

Kdb+ will always check a list of dictionaries to see if it can be converted to a table. If all dictionary keys are symbols, and are all matching in structure, kdb+ will compress all the matching dictionary fields into vectors of equal length, and convert the list of dictionaries into a dictionary of lists. This is a very useful feature but can be confusing the first time it is encountered.

The syntax for defining a table is similar to that of defining a non-uniform list. The data is surrounded with parentheses and the columns are separated by semicolons. In addition, however, we must specify each of the columns' names and identify the table's primary key (which we will discuss soon) with brackets. When there is no primary key, the brackets can be left empty.

```
q) ([]id:0;date:dt;price:p)
id date       price
-------------------
0  2000.01.01 100
0  2000.01.02 98.66291
0  2000.01.03 97.1703
0  2000.01.04 99.40865
0  2000.01.05 97.60011
..
```

Q also offers us the ability to drop the column name assignment if we are happy to have the variable names be the column names.

```
id:0
q) ([]id;dt;p)
```

```
id dt          p
---------------------
0   2000.01.01 100
0   2000.01.02 98.66291
0   2000.01.03 97.1703
0   2000.01.04 99.40865
0   2000.01.05 97.60011
..
```

## Table Manipulation

Like other lists, tables can be reversed, indexed and joined. Treating a table as a list of dictionaries is a natural extension to the q language. All list ordering operators treat the table as a list.

```
q) reverse t
id date       price
---------------------
0   2000.12.31 105.4232
0   2000.12.30 105.4052
0   2000.12.29 107.0373
0   2000.12.28 107.6605
0   2000.12.27 109.2849
..
```

And value modifying operators affect every row and column of the table.

```
q) string t
id    date         price
----------------------------
,"0" "2000.01.01" "100"
,"0" "2000.01.02" "98.66291"
,"0" "2000.01.03" "97.1703"
,"0" "2000.01.04" "99.40865"
,"0" "2000.01.05" "97.60011"
..
```

To retrieve the data from a table, we unflip it and request the value of the resulting dictionary.

```
q) value flip t
0          0          0          0          0          0          0         ..
2000.01.01 2000.01.02 2000.01.03 2000.01.04 2000.01.05 2000.01.06 2000.01 ..
100        98.66291   97.1703    99.40865   97.60011   96.97171   97.05328..
```

Accessing the list of table columns is just as easy.

```
q)key flip t
`id`date`price
```

But q provides a `cols` operator because not all tables are unkeyed and in-memory. The `cols` operator allows us to ignore the details of the table construction and simply access the list of fields that can be queried.

```
q)cols t
`id`date`price
```

Similar to taking a subset of fields from a dictionary, we can also take a subset of columns from a table.

```
q) `date`price#t
date       price
------------------
2000.01.01 100
2000.01.02 98.66291
2000.01.03 97.1703
2000.01.04 99.40865
2000.01.05 97.60011
..
```

And indexing by column name works as expected.

```
q)t `date`price
2000.01.01 2000.01.02 2000.01.03 2000.01.04 2000.01.05 2000.01.06 2000.01.0..
100        98.66291   97.1703    99.40865   97.60011   96.97171   97.05328 ..
```

But unlike a dictionary, taking the first (or last) few elements does not take the first, or last, few columns. Q has implemented the take operator "#" to return the first (or last) few records of the table.

```
q)2#t
id date       price
--------------------
0  2000.01.01 100
0  2000.01.02 98.66291
q)-2#t
id date       price
--------------------
0  2000.12.30 105.4052
0  2000.12.31 105.4232
```

To take the first (or last) few columns we can amend the "#" operator with the each-right adverb "/:".

```
q)2#/:t
id date
```

```
 ------------
 0   2000.01.01
 0   2000.01.02
 0   2000.01.03
 0   2000.01.04
 0   2000.01.05
 ..
```

In concept, "/:" has modified the "#" operator to take the first two fields from each of the table's rows (or dictionaries). In practice, a kdb+ table is not a list of dictionaries, but is a flipped dictionary of lists. And as such, the "#/:" operator merely performs the constant time operation of taking the first two columns. More will be discussed about the each-right adverb "/:" in the section called "Minimize Calls to each" [110].

Converting the dictionary to a table has allowed us to logically add new fields to the data structure. But it has also prevented us from indexing the table by date to obtain the price. We can recover this ability by converting the table to a keyed table.

## 7.3 Keyed Tables

An unkeyed table is conceptually a long list of records. Indexing into the table with a numeric index returns the specified row. Just as dictionaries allow us to access values by key instead of index, a keyed table allows us to access rows by key as well.

### Declaring a Key

The brackets in the table declaration are used to identify the table's primary key. If we declare a primary key by surrounding one or more columns by brackets, we can omit the first semicolon directly after the closing bracket.

```
q)show t:([id:0;date:dt]price:p)
id date      | price
-------------| --------
0  2000.01.01| 100
0  2000.01.02| 98.66291
0  2000.01.03| 97.1703
0  2000.01.04| 99.40865
0  2000.01.05| 97.60011
..
```

Another approach is to use the key operator "!" on an existing table to indicate the number of keyed columns.

```
q) show t:2!([]id:0;date:dt;price:p)
id date     | price
------------| --------
0  2000.01.01| 100
0  2000.01.02| 98.66291
0  2000.01.03| 97.1703
0  2000.01.04| 99.40865
0  2000.01.05| 97.60011
..
```

## Reordering Columns

There are times when the column we would like to use as a key is not the first column.

```
q) show t:([]price:p;id:0;date:dt)
price     id date
--------------------
100       0  2000.01.01
98.66291  0  2000.01.02
97.1703   0  2000.01.03
99.40865  0  2000.01.04
97.60011  0  2000.01.05
..
```

In this case we could reorder the columns of the table with the xcols operator and then apply the key.

```
q) 2!`id`date xcols t
id date     | price
------------| --------
0  2000.01.01| 100
0  2000.01.02| 98.66291
0  2000.01.03| 97.1703
0  2000.01.04| 99.40865
0  2000.01.05| 97.60011
..
```

## Simultaneous Keying and Reordering

Q provides the xkey operator to combine these operations.

```
q) `id`date xkey t
id date     | price
------------| --------
```

```
0  2000.01.01| 100
0  2000.01.02| 98.66291
0  2000.01.03| 97.1703
0  2000.01.04| 99.40865
0  2000.01.05| 97.60011
. .
```

These same operators can be used to unkey the table as well. Passing 0 to the key operator "!" or the empty list to the xkey operator will remove any key from the table.

```
q)t:([id:0;date:dt]price:p)
q)0!t
id date        price
--------------------
0  2000.01.01 100
0  2000.01.02 98.66291
0  2000.01.03 97.1703
0  2000.01.04 99.40865
0  2000.01.05 97.60011
. .
```

## Dictionary of Tables

We have recovered the ability to query prices by date (and now id). If we index into the table with an element from the key, we obtain the value.

```
q)t (0;2000.01.01)
price| 100
```

One way to query multiple records is to index with a list of lists.

```
q)t flip (0;2000.01.01 + til 5)
price
--------
100
98.66291
97.1703
99.40865
97.60011
```

But flipping a list of lists actually reorders the data in memory. A more efficient method of indexing a keyed table is to use a table instead.

```
q)t ([]id:0;date:2000.01.01 + til 5)
price
```

```
----------
100
98.66291
97.1703
99.40865
97.60011
```

In this case, there was no need to `flip` the data. True, a table is a flipped dictionary of lists. But as we mentioned in the section called "Flip" [81], this `flip` is just a layer of indirection, and not a reordering of memory.

Let's take a closer look at what happened when we indexed into our keyed table. The value returned was not the complete row of our desired records. Only the unkeyed portion of the data was returned.

When we index into a keyed table, `kdb+` searches the key for the rows that match our request and returns the non-key portion for those rows. If this sounds similar to how a dictionary works, it is no coincidence. A keyed table is, in fact, a dictionary whose key and value are tables. Remember that a dictionary maps a list of keys to a list of values. In the case of a keyed table, the list of keys is a list of dictionaries (a table), and the list of values is a list of dictionaries as well (another table). The solution is utterly brilliant. No new data types were needed to represent keyed tables. Syntax and operators that had already been available for dictionaries and tables were logically extended to keyed tables.

We can use the familiar dictionary operators to extract the key and value components of the dictionary.

```
q)key t
id date
------------
0   2000.01.01
0   2000.01.02
0   2000.01.03
0   2000.01.04
0   2000.01.05
..
q)value t
price
--------
100
98.66291
97.1703
99.40865
97.60011
..
```

With the knowledge that a keyed table is actually a dictionary of tables, we can create the keyed table by binding the key and value with the key operator "!".

```
q)([]id:0;date:dt)!([]price:p)
id date       | price
```

```
--------------|  --------
0  2000.01.01|  100
0  2000.01.02|  98.66291
0  2000.01.03|  97.1703
0  2000.01.04|  99.40865
0  2000.01.05|  97.60011
..
```

## Listing all Tables

To get a list of the tables in a given namespace, we can use the \a system command or the tables operator.

```
q)\a
`handle`price`prices`quote`quotes`ref`t`trade`trades
q)tables`
`handle`price`prices`quote`quotes`ref`t`trade`trades
```

In both cases, we can provide a namespace to query.

```
q)\a .o
,`TI
q)tables `.o
,`TI
```

The meta operator provides schematic information about the table. It returns a keyed table containing the **t**ype, **f**oreign-key and **a**ttribute of each **c**olumn.

```
q)meta t
c    | t f a
-----| -----
id   | j
date | d
price| f
```

We have not used foreign-keys or attributes yet so they are currently empty. We will discuss attributes in Section 8.2 [97].

We have covered a few ways of creating, accessing and manipulating keyed and unkeyed tables. We are now ready to add more security paths to our dataset. As the dataset grows, access time will begin to slow. Chapter 8 [91] introduces the important concept of attributes which are used to make data queries faster.

Chapter 8

# Large Tables

> In every major application area I can think of, it is possible to build a SQL DBMS engine with vertical market-specific internals that outperforms the "one size fits all" engines by a factor of 50 or so.
>
> — Mike Stonebraker *The Database Column*

Kdb+ excels at handling massive amounts of data (both in memory and on disk). It achieves extremely high performance by storing data in columns of contiguous memory. But efficient data storage is only half of the problem. To be a useful database, it must also be possible to efficiently retrieve data. Kdb+ does not use complex structures such as red-black or binary trees to store data. To gain query performance increases, kdb+ either saves extra information about the location of each element or uses knowledge of the data's layout to use faster search algorithms. To demonstrate these choices and their resulting performance gains we must first generate much larger tables.

We will start the chapter by generating a more realistic dataset which includes security paths for multiple ids and dates. Our focus will then move to discussing the different ways we can modify a table to increase query performance. Specifically, we will discuss concepts such as hashing, grouping and partitioning. Though these optimizations can only be applied to lists, tables also benefit because they are fundamentally a collection of lists.

## 8.1 Looping

In the last chapter we used the `.sim.path` [69] function to generate a price path for a single security. Passing in a list of volatilities or drift rate parameters will result in a `length error unless they are the same length as the time parameter. And even then, we will still only have a single security path which was created with time varying volatility and return parameters. To generate multiple paths we need to call the function multiple times.

## Each

To run a function multiple times in q requires the use of the each operator. Instead of writing an explicit loop to generate multiple paths, q requires us to provide a function and a list of function parameters. There is, of course, a loop in the underlying implementation, but we do not have to write the boiler-plate looping code ourselves. For example, we can use the same dates but generate different price paths for a variety of volatilities.

```
q)dt:.util.rng[1;2000.01.01;2001.01.01]
q)100*.sim.path[;.05;dt%365.25] each 10?1f
100 104.0532 101.8161 99.51862 100.2996 106.6656 105.1874 114.2953 120.1746..
100 100.0657 100.1356 100.1216 100.0929 100.1211 100.1334 100.1483 100.1658..
100 112.0581 118.1131 124.613  129.6531 128.6504 125.9266 122.0795 122.9674..
100 100.573  97.19478 101.7937 101.0252 96.68493 95.25461 96.4162  94.78584..
100 97.33557 96.99629 95.83718 95.89552 95.71721 95.47833 94.10744 87.28817..
100 101.0159 98.21908 97.87834 96.00932 101.6841 100.8119 99.44725 100.0587..
100 102.1442 102.0196 95.75811 98.37826 98.96145 95.99251 94.233   94.63246..
..
```

We provided the growth rate and the times, but left out the volatility. This created a function projection with a single missing parameter. We then used the each operator to apply the function to each of the volatilities.

## Each Left

Alternatively, we could have generated a single path, and multiplied it with a list of different starting prices. Only monadic functions can be used with the each adverb. To use the same right operand and vary the left operand, q provides the *each-left* "\ :" adverb.

```
q)(100?100)*\:.sim.path[.3;.05] dt%365.25
11 11.01933 10.93004 11.01261 11.02897 11.11024 10.89502 11.22275 11.39218 ..
42 42.07382 41.7329  42.04814 42.11061 42.4209  41.59917 42.85051 43.49743 ..
70 70.12304 69.55483 70.08024 70.18435 70.7015  69.33194 71.41752 72.49572 ..
13 13.02285 12.91733 13.0149  13.03424 13.13028 12.87593 13.26325 13.46349 ..
17 17.02988 16.89189 17.01949 17.04477 17.17036 16.83776 17.34425 17.60619 ..
68 68.11952 67.56755 68.07795 68.17908 68.68146 67.35103 69.37702 70.42441 ..
77 77.13534 76.51031 77.08826 77.20278 77.77165 76.26514 78.55927 79.74529 ..
..
```

In fact, we could have used the each operator by binding the starting price vector to the "*" operator which would have resulted in a monadic function.

```
q)*[1000?100]each .sim.path[.3;.05] dt%365.25
```

Using the *each-left* "\:" adverb, however, allows for much more elegant syntax.

## Each Right

Similarly, there is an *each-right* "/:" operator that applies the function and the left operand to each of the elements of the list passed as the right operand. We can reorder the multiplication and achieve the same result.

```
q).sim.path[.3;.05;dt%365.25]*/:100?100
```

## Each Both

Alternatively, we can also use the "'" operator to supply a list of volatilities **and** a list of growth rates.

```
q)100*.sim.path[;;dt%365.25]'[100?.1;100?.1]
```

In the case of two parameters, this is called *each-both*. But this operator is more general. It can (and will) *each* over as many arguments as are passed as its right operand.

Using each left, each right and each both provides a rare case where we can use infix notation with user defined functions just like builtin q operators. We are usually forced to use bracket notation to supply two parameters to a function. In these cases, however, we can pass the left and right operands on the left and right sides of the function, even if it is our own function.

```
q)100*(100?.1).sim.path[;;dt%365.25]'100?.1
```

We now have the tools to generate a table with multiple ids and price paths. In this example, we will generate price paths for ten ids.

```
q)n:10
q)p:(n?100)*(n?1f).sim.path[;;dt%365.25]' n?.1
q)show t:([]id:til n;date:n#enlist dt;price:p)
id date
---------------------------------------------------------------------..
0  2000.01.01 2000.01.02 2000.01.03 2000.01.04 2000.01.05 2000.01.06 2000.0..
1  2000.01.01 2000.01.02 2000.01.03 2000.01.04 2000.01.05 2000.01.06 2000.0..
2  2000.01.01 2000.01.02 2000.01.03 2000.01.04 2000.01.05 2000.01.06 2000.0..
3  2000.01.01 2000.01.02 2000.01.03 2000.01.04 2000.01.05 2000.01.06 2000.0..
4  2000.01.01 2000.01.02 2000.01.03 2000.01.04 2000.01.05 2000.01.06 2000.0..
..
```

The table now contains one row per ID. The time and price columns have vectors of values for each row.

## Ungroup

We can use the `ungroup` operator to unwind the nested data-structure. `Q` will repeat the `id` column enough times to ensure each row has a single ID/time/price combination.

```
q) ungroup t
id date       price
-------------------
0  2000.01.01 37
0  2000.01.02 37.47477
0  2000.01.03 37.28912
0  2000.01.04 37.55213
0  2000.01.05 37.85734
..
```

The syntax for generating a table with multiple ids and dates has become quite involved. We can write a function that encapsulates this routine, but we need to pay special attention to ensure we do not lose flexibility.

Once we write a function that generates a table of prices for a single ID, we can then call the function many times and merge the results. To ensure the function is generic, it must accept any type of time or date. In addition, the returned table should properly name the time or date column. The **generate price** function `genp` will of course need all the parameters to call `.sim.path` [69]. In addition, it will need the security `id` and initial Security price.

**.sim.genp**

```
genp:{[id;S;s;r;dtm]
 t:abs type dtm;
 tm:("np" t in 12 14 15h)$dtm;
 p:S*path[s;r;tm%365D06];
 c:`id,`time`date[t=14h],`price;
 p:flip c!(id;dtm;p);
 p}
```

The function starts by checking the type of the `dtm` parameter. To simplify the conversion of the date/time into fractions of a year, we cast the values to either `timestamp` or `timespan` types. We can then divide by `365D06`. If the date/time argument has a `date` component, we need to cast the value to a `timestamp`. Otherwise, casting to a `timespan` is sufficient. If the type is 12 (`timestamp`), 14 (`date`), or 15 (`datetime`), we use the character "p" to cast the values to a `timestamp`. Otherwise, we use the character "n" to cast the values to a `timespan`.

---

**Q Tip 8.1** Use array lookups to implement simple conditional statements

---

The third line of `genp` has an embedded conditional statement. `Q` automatically converts the boolean values `0b` and `1b` into the integers `0` and `1` when used to index a list or perform mathematical computations. In this example, we picked either an "n" or a "p" by indexing into the two element list "np" with the result of the conditional statement `t in 12 14 15h`. The same technique is used in the fifth line to pick one of two symbols - this time using bracket notation. When transforming the result of an if/else statement into one of two elements, it is often easier to perform an array lookup instead of using the scalar conditional operator `$[;;]`. A major benefit to this syntax is that array lookups are atomic, and therefore work for atoms, lists, dictionaries and tables.

```
q)"ny" 10101b
"ynyny"
```

An extension to indexing with a boolean is to index with the result of the `signum` operator. The `signum` operator returns -1, 0 or 1 depending if its operand is less than, equal or greater than zero. This operator is often used when determining the side of an order (buy or sell) or the side of a position (long or short) based on the sign of its quantity. Adding 1 to the results of `signum` allows us to index into a three element list.

```
q)"S B"1+signum 10 0 -10
"B S"
```

The `.sim.genp` [94] function then calls `.sim.path` [69] with the time converted to units of years. To build the price table, we must once again check the type of the date/time argument. By convention, we label the column `date` if the type is just the date. Any other type has a time component, so we label the column `time`. The sixth line of the function builds the price table as a flipped dictionary of lists.

We can now generate a table with prices across multiple dates,

```
q).sim.genp[0;100;.3;.03] .util.rng[1;2000.01.01;2001.01.01]
id date       price
-----------------------
0  2000.01.01 100
0  2000.01.02 101.2711
0  2000.01.03 100.4399
0  2000.01.04 98.23532
0  2000.01.05 100.3322
..
```

or times.

```
q).sim.genp[0;100;.3;.03] .util.rng[1;09:00;16:00]
id time  price
------------------
0  09:00 100
0  09:01 100.0323
0  09:02 99.98794
0  09:03 99.95417
0  09:04 99.99175
..
```

We can also call the function multiple times by **each**ing over the ids, initial security prices, volatilities and growth rates.

```
q)n:10
q)dts:.util.rng[1;2000.01.01;2001.01.01]
q).sim.genp[;;;;dts]'[til n;n?100;n?.3;n?.03]
+`id`date`price!(0 0 0 0 0 0 0 0 0 0 0 0 0 0 0 0 0 0 0 0 0 0 0 0 0 0 0 0 0 0 0 0 ..
+`id`date`price!(1 1 1 1 1 1 1 1 1 1 1 1 1 1 1 1 1 1 1 1 1 1 1 1 1 1 1 1 1 1 1 1 ..
+`id`date`price!(2 2 2 2 2 2 2 2 2 2 2 2 2 2 2 2 2 2 2 2 2 2 2 2 2 2 2 2 2 2 2 2 ..
+`id`date`price!(3 3 3 3 3 3 3 3 3 3 3 3 3 3 3 3 3 3 3 3 3 3 3 3 3 3 3 3 3 3 3 3 ..
+`id`date`price!(4 4 4 4 4 4 4 4 4 4 4 4 4 4 4 4 4 4 4 4 4 4 4 4 4 4 4 4 4 4 4 4 ..
+`id`date`price!(5 5 5 5 5 5 5 5 5 5 5 5 5 5 5 5 5 5 5 5 5 5 5 5 5 5 5 5 5 5 5 5 ..
+`id`date`price!(6 6 6 6 6 6 6 6 6 6 6 6 6 6 6 6 6 6 6 6 6 6 6 6 6 6 6 6 6 6 6 6 ..
..
```

## Raze

To join the resulting tables, we need to use the `raze` operator instead of `ungroup`. The `raze` operator creates a list by joining each of the elements of its argument. The operator starts with an empty list, and if the argument has any elements, appends the first element. It then joins that result with the next item in the list, and so on. In other words, it reduces one layer of nesting.

```
q)raze (1 2 3;4 5 6)
 1 2 3 4 5 6
```

When we call `raze` on our list of tables, it merges each of the tables into a single long table.

```
q)raze .sim.genp[;;;;dts]'[til n;n?100;n?.3;n?.03]
id date       price
--------------------
0  2000.01.01 18
0  2000.01.02 17.98979
0  2000.01.03 18.08106
0  2000.01.04 18.12056
0  2000.01.05 18.16953
..
```

---

**Q Tip 8.2** Return unkeyed tables by default

---

It is important that the tables being razed not be keyed. Keyed tables are dictionaries, and just as joining two dictionaries merges common keys, merging two keyed tables attempts to merge common rows. Our goal was to build a unique list of ID/time pairs. Attempting to find a common key would thus fail. As the table grows in length, the search for the common key will take progressively longer. The proper time to apply the primary key is after the table has been razed.

```
q)2!raze sim.genp[;;;;dts]'[til n;n?100;n?.3;n?.03]
id date     | price
------------| --------
0  2000.01.01| 89
0  2000.01.02| 88.66867
0  2000.01.03| 88.52082
0  2000.01.04| 87.29726
0  2000.01.05| 85.9732
..
```

## 8.2  Attributes

By default, q uses a linear search algorithm to find values within lists. This is efficient on small lists. Typical datasets, however, tend to be bigger than 10-20 items. Once our data begins to grow, we need to use better searching algorithms. We have two choices: use a binary search algorithm for sorted data, or a hashing algorithm for unique, grouped or partitioned data.

To take advantage of these faster algorithms we need to tag our data to indicate which method is most appropriate. Q has four different tags (or attributes): **s**orted, **u**nique, **p**arted and **g**rouped.

To apply each of the attributes to a list, we again use the take operator "#". But instead of a numerical left operand, we use a symbol corresponding to the attribute we would like to apply. For example, to enable the binary search algorithm, we apply the sort attribute.

```
q)x:`s#1 2 3
q)x
`s#1 2 3
```

### Querying Attributes

We can use the `attr` operator to obtain the attribute associated with any q value.

```
q)attr x
`s
```

If the data has no attributes, the null symbol is returned.

```
q)attr ()
`
```

We can use the null symbol to remove attributes from a list.

```
q)`#x
1 2 3
```

## Sort Attribute

Applying the sort attribute informs q to use a binary search algorithm to find the desired element(s). Applying the attribute to an unsorted list will fail.

```
q)`s#3 2 1
's-fail
```

Appending elements to a sorted list that invalidate the sorted criteria, will remove the attribute from the list. We can then use the `asc` operator to re-sort the list, and have the `s attribute automatically added back.

```
q)asc 3 2 1
`s#1 2 3
```

Similar to the `asc` operator, there is also a `desc` operator which, as the name implies, sorts the list in descending order. But unlike the `asc` operator, it does not apply an attribute.

```
q)desc 1 2 3
3 2 1
```

Using sorted data and the sort attribute `s adds no memory overhead to the processes. To see the benefit of applying the `s attribute to a list, we can use the `\t` system command to time how long it takes to find the last element of a long list using the default linear search algorithm. We can then apply the attribute to see how long it takes to use the binary search algorithm. In the section called "Generate" [26] we used the "?" operator with an atomic left operand to generate a list of random variables. When a list is passed as the left operand, "?" searches that list and returns the index where each of the right operands are found. If they are not found, the size of the list is returned (which obviously points to one passed the end of the list).

```
q)x:til 100000000
q)\t x ? last x
319
q)s:`s#x
q)\t s ? last s
0
```

The first timing indicates that it took 319 milliseconds to search through 100 million elements. The second timing reveals that it took less than 1 millisecond to perform the same lookup on a sorted list.

It is interesting to note that because no extra memory is needed to store the sort attribute `s, q applies the attribute to lists, even when no modification had been requested. In all other cases, q never modifies a variable unless you use in-place assignment or explicitly save the result back to the variable. The sort attribute `s is different. In this example, the application of the sort attribute `s has been applied to x even though we did not save the change.

```
q)`s#x:1 2 3
`s#1 2 3
q)x
`s#1 2 3
```

This trick is used to save memory by avoiding the need to copy the list.

## Binary Search

Even without the sort attribute `s, we can force a binary search on sorted data by using the binary search operator `bin`. This is useful when we know the data is sorted. The semantics of `bin` are slightly different however. The `bin` operator returns the first index that is not larger than the right operand. If the value exists, the proper index is returned. If it does not exist, `bin` returns an index of the closest (but not larger) value.

```
q)1 2 4 5 bin 3
1
```

In contrast, `binr` returns the index of the value that exists to the right of the non-existing element.

```
q)1 2 4 5 binr 3
2
```

Be careful not to use `bin` or `binr` with unsorted data, the results are undefined.

## Sorting Tables

Having covered the process of sorting data and using binary searches to improve access speed, we are now ready to apply the technique to large tables. After generating our keyed table, we need to sort the data by date and apply the sort attribute `s to the date column. Q provides the `xasc` operator to sort tables. It accepts a symbol (or list of symbols) representing the column name (or names) for its left operand and a table or table name for the right operand. Q's sort routine is stable: the ordering of equal items remains constant. Multi-column sorting is thus equivalent to successively sorting the table by each requested column starting with the last and ending with the first. For example, we can sort by ID first, and then by time within equivalent ids.

```
q)n:1000;dts:.util.rng[1;2000.01.01;2005.01.01]
q)t:2!raze .sim.genp[;;;;dts]'[til n;n?100;n?.3;n?.03]
q)`id`date xasc t
id date     | price
------------| --------
0  2000.01.01| 3
0  2000.01.02| 2.860272
```

```
0   2000.01.03| 2.760614
0   2000.01.04| 2.722993
0   2000.01.05| 2.754431
..
```

We can see the sort attribute has been added to the ID column.

```
q) ON! `id`date xasc t;
(+`id`date!(`s#0 0 0 0 0 0 0 0 0 0 0 0 0 0 0 0 0 0 0 0 0 0 0 0 0 0 0 0 0 0 0 0 ..
```

The same information is available by looking at the table's metadata.

```
q) meta `id`date xasc t
c    | t f a
-----| -----
id   | j   s
date | d
price| f
```

We can see how sorting the table (which applies the sort attribute `` `s ``) dramatically decreases lookup time by comparing the performance of row lookups with a table that has not been sorted.

---

**Q Tip 8.3** Use \t:n and \ts:n to time multiple runs of a single command

---

The query itself is already quite fast. To get a better feeling for how much performance gain we get by adding the sort attribute, we need to run the query multiple times. The \t and \ts system commands allow us to optionally supply a colon followed by a number of iterations.

```
q) \t:100 t`id`date!(999;2005.01.01)
782
```

After sorting the table, the query changes from a linear to binary search and the performance increases dramatically. By applying the xasc operator on the name of the table `` `t ``, the sort operation modifies the table directly.

```
q) `id`date xasc `t
q) \t:100 t`id`date!(999;2005.01.01)
1
```

This only works because t is a global variable. Sorting tables within functions requires us to sort the table and assign the result back to the original variable.

```
q) t: `id`date xasc t
```

Just as asc has a corresponding desc operator, there is also an xdesc operator that sorts a table in descending order.

The sort attribute is good for data that has a high number of distinct values - all listed in increasing order. If the data is not sorted, or there are many repeated values, as is the case for a table with both ids and dates, it is more appropriate to use one of the remaining attributes which rely on a hashing algorithm to quickly find the exact row or rows of the desired data. Each of these attributes (**u**nique, **g**rouped, and **p**artitioned) achieve a speed increases at the expense of using more memory. They use a hashing algorithm and either map the results to a single index (`` `u ``), an index and count (`` `p ``), or a list of indices (`` `g ``).

## Unique Attribute

The unique attribute `` `u `` is used when a list is guaranteed to have no duplicate entries. Placing the `` `u `` attribute on a list allows q to use a hashing algorithm to find the exact index for the desired element. No linear searches are performed. As the number of elements in the dataset grows, this is, by far, the fastest algorithm. Attempting to apply the `` `u `` attribute to a list with duplicate entries produces one of my favorite q error message.

```
q)`u#0 0
'u-fail
```

We can also apply the `` `u `` attribute to a table that has a single column primary key. Each element of the key is, by definition, unique.

For example, if we create a price history for only a single ID, we can reduce the number of columns in our primary key to 1 - the date. Instead of using the "!" operator to set the number of columns with primary keys, we can use the xkey operator to explicitly list the primary key of the table.

```
q)dts:.util.rng[1;2000.01.01;2005.01.01]
q)t:.sim.genp[0;100;.3;.03;dts]
q)show `date xkey t
date      | id price
----------| ----------
2000.01.01| 0  100
2000.01.02| 0  101.1747
2000.01.03| 0  101.8116
2000.01.04| 0  98.93706
2000.01.05| 0  99.53914
..
```

We must apply the attribute to the column before the key is added. A keyless table can be indexed by column name to extract a column.

```
q)t`date
2000.01.01 2000.01.02 2000.01.03 2000.01.04 2000.01.05 2000.01.06 2000.01.0..
```

We can then apply the attribute, and assign the column back into the table.

```
q)t[`date]:`u#t`date
```

We can see that the attribute was applied by displaying the table schema.

```
q)meta t
c    | t f a
-----| -----
id   | j
date | d   u
price| f
```

## Index Apply

This is standard syntax for modifying a member of any list.  It is such a common task that q has a shorthand for indexing into a list, applying an operation to the elements, and assigning the results back to the original list. Recall that we can use the index operator "@" to index into a list. This works equally well for a dictionary or table.

```
q)@[t;`date]
`u#2000.01.01 2000.01.02 2000.01.03 2000.01.04 2000.01.05 2000.01.06 2000.0..
```

The same operator has two more variants: one for applying a monadic functions and the other for a dyadic function. The first (3-argument) variant can be used to add attributes to table columns.

```
t:@[t;`date;`u#]
```

We can also pass a symbol as the first argument and q will apply the attribute directly to the table without creating a copy. In this example, we can remove the unique attribute `u by applying the null symbol.

```
q)@[`t;`date;`#]
`t
```

The second (4-argument) variant allows us to pass an extra argument to the operator to be used with a dyadic operator.

```
q)@[t;`price;%;100]
id date       price
-------------------
0  2000.01.01 1
0  2000.01.02 1.011747
0  2000.01.03 1.018116
0  2000.01.04 0.9893706
0  2000.01.05 0.9953914
..
```

---

**Q Tip 8.4** Use the `` `u `` attribute on dictionary keys to increase performance

---

In Section 7.1 [73] we discussed how dictionaries are stored as two separate lists: one for the keys and another for the values.

By default, looking up a value in a list (and therefore a dictionary) performs a linear search through each of the values until a match is found. By extension, this means that keys at the end of a dictionary will have slower retrieval time than keys at the beginning.

Adding the `` `u `` attribute to the key changes the lookup method from a linear search to a constant time hashing algorithm. For small dictionaries this will not offer any advantage, and may even make the lookup slower. But for dictionaries with more than around 80 elements, the `` `u `` attribute allows data retrieval to remain constant-time instead of growing linearly with the size of the dataset. It is easiest to place the attribute on the key when it is defined.

```
q)0N!d:(`u#0#`)!0#1
(`u#`symbol$())!`long$()
```

Appending new items leaves the key intact.

```
q)d[`qtips]:0
q)0N!d;
(`u#,`qtips)!,0
```

It is important to remember that applying attributes other than the sort attribute consumes memory. If the list is, either by itself or as a table column, saved to disk, the extra data structure needed to perform the hash lookup is saved as well.

## Partition Attribute

The unique attribute `` `u `` is perfect when we have a dictionary or a single column key, but is useless for a table with multiple keys. Multi-column keys permit duplicate values for any given column, but of course maintain uniqueness across the composite key. For a multi-column key we need to use the partition `` `p `` or group `` `g `` attribute.

Like the unique attribute `` `u ``, the partition attribute `` `p `` creates a map from each unique value to a row index. But in addition to the starting row index, it also stores the number of elements with the same value. This allows duplicate values, but also requires all instances of a specific value to be partitioned (or clustered) together. Sorting is a convenient way to partition a list. Even though sorting automatically applies the sort attribute `` `s ``, we can make searching even faster by applying the `` `p `` attribute instead.

We can once again generate a table with multiple ids and dates.

```
q)n:1000;dts:.util.rng[1;2000.01.01;2010.01.01]
q)t:raze .sim.genp[;;;;dts]'[til n;n?100;n?.3;n?.03]
```

The dates in this table cycle from 2000.01.01 to 2009.12.31 for each ID. We can partition the column by first sorting the table by date, and then applying the `p attribute. In addition, we can move the column to the front of the table by using the xcols function. Instead of repeatedly using the date column in each operation, we can create an anonymous function that applies all three steps.

```
q) show t:{x xcols @[;x;`p#] x xasc y}[`date] t
date       id price
-------------------
2000.01.01 0  78
2000.01.01 1  61
2000.01.01 2  6
2000.01.01 3  12
2000.01.01 4  21
..
```

We can see that the schema has also changed.

```
q) meta t
c    | t f a
-----| -----
date | d   p
id   | j
price| f
```

## Group Attribute

The group attribute `g works like the partition attribute `p but poses no restrictions on the data location. This flexibility comes at the price of extra memory. Applying the group attribute to a list causes q to create a mapping from the distinct hash values to a list of row indices. It is best used when the key values are scattered randomly over the list. It is used most in tables that are continuously being updated with new rows. To ensure fast query times, q updates its internal grouping map whenever new rows are added. This makes each update slower, but ensures fast query performance.

If we start again with the multiple date/id table, we can now apply the group attribute `g directly to the date column without sorting the data.

```
q)t:raze .sim.genp[;;;;dts]'[til n;n?100;n?.3;n?.03]
q) meta @[t; `date; `g#]
c    | t f a
-----| -----
id   | j
date | d   g
price| f
```

## Performance Considerations

To perform a table lookup, q first finds all rows in the table that match according to the first keyed column. Once all matches are found, it is able to narrow the search for any subsequent columns in the key. Adding an attribute on the first column of the key allows q to narrow the search extremely fast. Instead of performing a linear search on all rows, it can use a much more efficient algorithm depending on the attribute. But once the first column is used to narrow the search, attributes that may exists on the remaining column are ignored. A linear search is used for all remaining columns. It is therefore very important to make the first column as unique as possible.

Given the option of keying the table by date/id or id/date, the choice depends on the relative frequency of dates and ids. An extreme example should make this clear. If our table had 10,000 ids and 2 dates, keying first by ID and then by date allows the search to narrow the region down to 2 rows before beginning the linear search across dates. If, however, the table was keyed by date first and then by ID, the first column only narrows the secondary search down to 10,000 rows. Always use the most descriptive identifier as the first keyed column.

---

**Q Tip 8.5** Place the most descriptive column first

---

Table query performance critically depends on how fast q can narrow the search down to a few rows before it resorts to a linear comparison of any remaining keys. A single column primary key with the unique attribute `` `u `` is better than multiple columns. If you must have multiple columns in the key, ensure the most descriptive identifier is first and prefer the partition attribute `` `p `` over the group attribute `` `g ``.

Kdb+ imposes no limit to the number of attributes we apply. After the attribute on the first column is used, however, any further attributes are ignored. In our example, we can apply a `` `p `` attribute to the id and a `` `g `` attribute to the date column.

```
q)n:1000;dts:.util.rng[1;2000.01.01;2010.01.01]
q)t:raze .sim.genp[;;;;dts]'[til n;n?100;n?.3;n?.03]
q)meta @[t;`id`date;{y#x};`p`g]
c    | t f a
-----| -----
id   | j   p
date | d   g
price| f
```

Similar to other databases, kdb+ has an SQL-like syntax that allows users to limit the results of queries with a where clause. If a non-key column is often used to limit the rows within a where clause, applying an attribute to this column will also have obvious performance benefits. We will discuss q-SQL further in Chapter 14 [163].

It may seem that given enough memory, we should apply attributes to all columns of a table - just in case. Surely this would improve the performance of any potential query. This comes with an obvious cost of more memory, but it also slows down the addition of new rows. Each time a table is extended with new rows, each column attribute - other than the sort attribute - must be updated to include the new rows.

**Q Tip 8.6** Reapply attributes after filtering or deleting rows from a table

Kdb+ is optimized for tables that only grow (from the end) with time. Selecting a subset or deleting rows from tables is not only expensive, but also removes all attributes. Appending rows that invalidate attributes also removes them. It is important to reapply attributes to a table if the number of rows ever decreases. Because of these limitations, partitioned columns are typically only used with read-only tables.

It is useful to write a function that encapsulates each of these best practices. Setting attributes on in-memory tables is so critical for performance we should make it easy to do. The sattr function optimally sets attributes on tables with no key, a single key, and even multiple keys. A single column key will always have the primary identifier as the first column. Best practice, and performance, dictates that multi-keyed tables have the most descriptive column first. We can also require that unkeyed tables place the most distinguishing identifier first as well. With these restrictions in place, we can create a function to optimally key any table.

**.util.sattr**

```
sattr:{[t]
 c:first cols t;
 a:`g`u 1=n:count keys t;
 t:n!@[;c;a#]0!t;
 t}
```

The first line finds the name of the first column. This will be used when applying the attribute. The second line counts the number of keys in the table and picks the attribute. If the table has a single column key, we will apply the unique attribute `u. In all other cases we apply the group attribute `g. This includes cases where there is no key, and cases where the key has multiple columns. The fourth line of the function removes any primary key, applies the attribute, and then re-keys the table, if necessary.

We can see how the function applies the proper attributes to each type of table.

```
t:flip`a`b`c!"fff"$\:()
q)meta sattr t
c| t f a
-| -----
a| f   g
b| f
c| f
q)meta sattr 1!t
c| t f a
-| -----
a| f   u
b| f
c| f
q)meta sattr 2!t
```

```
c| t f a
-| -----
a| f   g
b| f
c| f
```

## Sorted Multi-Column Keys

Indexing into a multi-keyed table that has many unique values in each column of the key can become quite slow. Once the attribute in the first column is used, a linear search is performed for the remaining columns. To fix this behavior, we can sort the table and add a sort attribute `s to the whole key. This will inform kdb+ that it can use a binary search algorithm for the composite key. This significantly improves the performance of multi-keyed table queries. In addition, it allows us to do without memory intensive attributes such as `p and `g. But to sort a dictionary (and therefore a keyed table) by key, we have to write our own function because the asc operator sorts dictionaries by value, and not key.

**.util.kasc**

```
kasc:{$[`s=attr k:key x;x;(`s#k i)!value[x]i:iasc k]}
```

The kasc function accepts a dictionary as its only parameter. It begins by checking to see if its key is already sorted. If so, it can return the dictionary unchanged. Otherwise, the function uses the iasc operator to determine the proper transformation needed to sort the key. The iasc (and corresponding idesc ) operator performs the work behind both asc and xasc. Instead of actually rearranging the order of list elements, the iasc operator returns the index where each properly sorted element can be found in the original list. The asc operator uses these indices to index into the original list, thus returning a sorted copy. The benefit of separating out this functionality is that the results of iasc can be used to sort other lists without having to recompute the sort order.

The kasc operator uses the results of iasc to reorder both the key and value of the supplied dictionary. After the dictionary is reordered, the sort attribute `s is placed on the key. Since keyed tables are actually dictionaries, this same function can be used to make queries on multi-keyed tables faster too.

With our ability to generate large tables that are fast to query, we now turn our attention to generating a set of tables that will allow us to flex q's muscles.

Chapter **9**

# Trades and Quotes

> Nature isn't classical, dammit, and if you want to make a simulation of nature, you'd better make it quantum mechanical, and by golly it's a wonderful problem, because it doesn't look so easy.
>
> — Richard Feynman *Simulating Physics with Computers*

In Chapter 7 [73] we generated inter-day security paths. By changing the time units and column names, we can generate intra-day paths as well. Using this theoretical path as a foundation, we can generate a table representing the current bid and offer (or the price which someone is willing to buy or sell) in the market. We can then generate a table of trades based on the actual quotes we generated. It is, of course, not easy to simulate a real security's quotes and trades with perfection. But it sure is a wonderful problem. Generating these tables will serve two purposes: we will use them to experiment with q-SQL and the functions we write will be directly applicable when building our CEP engine.

## 9.1 Prices

Quote and trade prices do not typically occur at equally spaced intervals. To generate our dataset, we first need to generate unrounded prices at random times during the day. We will then round these values up and down to the nearest tick interval to generate bid and ask prices. And finally, we will take random samples of the quotes to generate trade prices and sizes.

### Ranges of Random Numbers

Let's first assume a seven hour trading day starting at 09:00 and ending at 16:00. We can simulate the random arrival of new quotes by using q's random number generator to create a list of timespans. It is convenient to write a utility function `randrng` that accepts the desired number of random values between a start and end value.

**.util.randrng**

```
q)randrng:{[n;s;e]s+n?e-s}
```

We can call `rndrng` and sort the results to generate a list of times appropriate for passing to `.sim.path` [69].

```
q)show asc .util.randrng[100000;0D09;0D16]
`s#0D09:00:00.330964475 0D09:00:00.358576141 0D09:00:00.571806728 0D09:00:0..
```

When we generated daily data, it was logical to use the same daily time steps for each security path. For inter-day data, however, each path will need its own time series. To do this we need to call `randrng` many times. Even though the arguments will be the same each time, we need to create a list with enough elements so we can use the `each` operator to loop through the list.

```
q)n:10
q).util.randrng[;0D09;0D16] each n#1000
0D09:48:37.616134230 0D09:50:08.642718382 0D13:12:18.183340150 0D13:29:30.3..
0D10:03:44.427754059 0D11:16:30.572151727 0D12:13:59.656830020 0D12:53:34.0..
0D14:51:11.628923714 0D12:21:09.472998473 0D12:34:29.292500987 0D13:29:30.9..
0D11:05:08.074615616 0D10:41:51.815845035 0D09:03:21.520249061 0D14:05:04.3..
0D13:39:55.835175924 0D13:47:07.251471485 0D14:01:19.034696705 0D10:29:37.3..
0D15:04:48.042074907 0D15:25:40.634973999 0D10:06:39.563455022 0D14:12:46.6..
0D09:59:56.081146784 0D14:23:01.336045078 0D12:39:22.523758504 0D13:33:30.9..
..
```

## Minimize Calls to each

But the results are not sorted. There are three ways we can sort each list. The first is to use the `each` operator again.

```
q)asc each .util.randrng[;0D09;0D16] each n#1000
0D09:00:06.434345338 0D09:00:17.704721912 0D09:00:25.153229758 0D09:01:10.9..
0D09:00:13.335137721 0D09:00:19.421626534 0D09:00:26.260013971 0D09:00:58.5..
0D09:00:36.423488985 0D09:01:22.767803594 0D09:02:20.268304757 0D09:02:58.7..
0D09:00:01.944398693 0D09:00:12.425742298 0D09:00:55.973527953 0D09:01:46.2..
0D09:00:05.528957303 0D09:00:20.622522756 0D09:00:55.145113449 0D09:01:03.6..
0D09:00:19.860274158 0D09:00:22.412710357 0D09:01:06.429284121 0D09:01:08.7..
0D09:00:10.265472717 0D09:00:14.560395106 0D09:01:27.335598003 0D09:01:49.5..
..
```

The second way is to use an anonymous function, or *lambda*, to sort the results of each call to `randrng`. This removes the second call to `each`.

```
q){asc .util.randrng[x;0D09;0D16]} each n#1000
```

---

**Q Tip 9.1** Use compositions to reduce calls to each

---

The final way to reduce the number of times we use the each operator is to use parentheses to force the creation of a function composition **before** it is applied to each argument.

```
q)(asc .util.randrng[;0D09;0D16]@) each n#1000
```

Since the "@" operator expects another argument, the contents of the parentheses can not be fully evaluated. The result is therefore a function composition expecting a single argument. A composition is the joining of two functions to create a third function. The right-most function can accept more than one argument, but the left function must be monadic. We can use this composition to loop over each of the parameters one at a time.

```
q)tms:(asc .util.randrng[;0D09;0D16]@) each n#1000
q)show p:raze .sim.genp'[til n;n?100;n?.3;n?.03;tms]
id time                 price
------------------------------------
0   0D09:00:55.048701446 25
0   0D09:01:11.404946129 24.9979
0   0D09:01:51.298170033 24.99438
0   0D09:02:38.248445112 24.98763
0   0D09:03:23.175540827 24.98553
..
```

## 9.2  Quotes

We do not actually see these prices in the market. We see bid and ask prices which are always at fixed increments. These increments, also called tick sizes, often depend on the price of the security. Low priced securities have small tick sizes, while high priced securities have large tick sizes. Rounding prices to the nearest tick requires the flexibility to change the rounding unit depending on the price of the security. Q provides a very flexible data structure to help us perform this rounding: the step function.

### Step Function

A step function is a discontinuous, monotonically increasing, piecewise constant line. Tick sizes, along with market maker maximum quote spreads, and minimum order sizes are typically defined as step functions. To represent a step function in q we create a dictionary with an extra sort attribute `s applied to the dictionary (not just its key).

For example, let's assume we need to round a security price to the nearest $0.01, $0.05, $0.10, $0.25, $.50 and $1.00 depending on its price. Let's also assume that the breakpoints for these rounding units are $5, $10, $25, $50 and $100. We can create a step function to represent this rule.

```
q)k:0n 5 10 25 50 100
q)v:.01 .05 .1 .25 .5 1
q)show sf:`s#k!v
    | 0.01
5   | 0.05
10  | 0.1
25  | 0.25
50  | 0.5
100| 1
```

The sort attribute `s distinguishes this step function from an ordinary dictionary. By using the 0N! operator, we can see that the sort attribute was added in two places: on the dictionary's key and on the dictionary itself.

```
q)0N!sf;
`s#`s#0n 5 10 25 50 100!0.01 0.05 0.1 0.25 0.5 1
```

It is the very first attribute that allows the dictionary to be treated as a step function. When we index into the step function, q will perform a binary search and return the value associated with the proper key location. We can now find the tick size for a list of prices.

```
q)sf 5 7 25 99 101f
0.05 0.05 0.25 0.5 1
```

To provide better intuition on how the step function works, it is useful to demonstrate its implementation. Let's first write a function that implements **d**ictionary **i**ndexing.

```
di:{value[x] key[x] ? y}
```

The function uses the "?" operator to find each element of y in the key of dictionary x. It then returns the values of the dictionary corresponding to those indices.

```
q)di[sf] 5 7 25 99 101f
0.05 0n 0.25 0n 0n
```

As we can see, it failed to find values for 7, 99 and 101 because they are not in the dictionary's key. We can implement a **s**tep **f**unction **i**ndexing function by changing the "?" operator to bin.

```
sfi:{value[x] key[x] bin y}
```

The query now returns the same values that indexing into the step function produced.

```
q)sfi[sf] 5 7 25 99 101f
0.05 0.05 0.25 0.5 1
```

Recall that keyed tables are actually dictionaries mapping one table to another. Just as we applied the sort attribute to our simple dictionary of lists, we can also apply it to a dictionary of tables. Looking up the same value returns the appropriate record in the table.

```
q)t:`s#([k]v)
q)t 99f
v| 0.5
```

Again, we can see the sort attribute has been applied to the keyed table as a whole, in addition to the dictionary's key (a table) and also the first column of the key.

```
q)0N!t;
`s#(`s#+(,`k)!,`s#0n 5 10 25 50 100)!+(,`v)!,0.01 0.05 0.1 0.25 0.5 1
```

## Rounding to the Nearest Tick

We can now write a function that uses a step function to round a price both up and down to the next tick.

**.sim.tickrnd**

```
tickrnd:{if[99h=type x;x@:y];(y;x+y:x*floor y%x)}
```

Like the .util.rnd [72] function, tickrnd can accept a single tick size as its first operand. If, however, a step function is passed in, tickrnd applies the step function to the price to obtain the tick size. The remainder of the function is quite similar to .util.rnd [72], except that instead of rounding to the nearest integer, tickrnd uses the floor operator to round down. It then returns that price and the price one tick above.

The function returns two lists. If we apply column names with the key operator "!" and flip the results, we obtain a new table which can be used to extend the original table. I have chosen bp and ap for names of the bid and ask price columns.

```
q)ts:`s#0n 5 50 100!.001 .005 .01 .02
q)flip `bp`ap!.sim.tickrnd[ts] p `price
bp    ap
-----------
92.99 93
92.99 93
92.98 92.99
92.97 92.98
92.97 92.98
..
```

## Extending a Table

Complex functions may return the results of multiple computations simultaneously. Instead of returning a simple vector, they might return a list of vectors. In these cases, it is easier to extend a table by concatenating a new table than by using the update statement to add each column individually. By building a table as a flipped dictionary of lists, we can efficiently add multiple columns to a table.

This often happens when attempting to compute multiple moving averages of a security price. Given an initial table,

```
q)tms:asc .util.randrng[n;0D09;0D16]
q)p:(n?100)*(n?1f).sim.path[;;tms%365D06]' n?.1
q)p:ungroup ([]id:til n;time:n#enlist tms;price:p)
```

we can add multiple moving average columns with a single line.

```
q)w:5 10 20
q)p,'flip (`$"w",/:string w)!w mavg\:p `price
id time                 price    w5       w10      w20
----------------------------------------------------------
0  0D11:44:08.408333212 77       77       77       77
0  0D13:24:52.436313349 77.11767 77.05884 77.05884 77.05884
0  0D13:29:48.897566590 77.04116 77.05294 77.05294 77.05294
0  0D14:05:49.055474437 76.82235 76.9953  76.9953  76.9953
0  0D14:16:40.286308117 77.03684 77.00361 77.00361 77.00361
..
```

Quotes also have sizes. For simplicity, we can just pick a few random values between 1 and a desired maximum quote size qs to represent the bid and ask sizes (bs and as respectively). Again, we will return a table to be concatenated to the original.

```
q)qs:100
q)flip `bs`as!1+count[p]?/:2#qs
bs as
-----
29 75
1  41
63 40
81 5
64 75
..
```

Putting the steps together, we now have a function that generates a quote table. It takes three arguments: the tick step ts (which can be a single value or a step function ), the maximum quote size qs and a table containing a price column.

**.sim.genq**

```
genq:{[ts;qs;p]
  q:p,'flip `bp`ap!tickrnd[ts] p `price;
  q:q,'flip `bs`as!1+count[p]?/:2#qs;
  q:`id`time`bs`bp`ap`as#q;
  q}
```

The fourth line picks only the columns we want, in the order we want them.

```
q)show q:.sim.genq[ts;qs] p
id time                 bs bp    ap    as
------------------------------------------
0  0D09:00:06.907428335 8  7.995 8      94
0  0D09:00:07.820572983 6  8     8.005 65
0  0D09:00:08.236355613 71 8     8.005 34
0  0D09:00:19.930412247 50 7.995 8      66
0  0D09:00:20.836932677 15 7.995 8      54
..
```

## 9.3  Trades

Given a quote table, a trade table can be generated by delaying its timestamps, taking a subset of rows and, for each row, either picking the bid or ask price and a fraction of its quantity.

### Delaying a Time Series

In practice, trades can occur in between quote updates, not just at the same time. This delay in timing makes it complicated to determine the prevailing quote at the time of each trade. The aj and wj q operators discussed in the section called "Asof Joins" [194] make this process easy. To ensure we model reality appropriately, we need to delay the trade time. We define a delay function that adds a random increment to each value that places it somewhere after the original value, and before the next. The function first generates a list of delays by computing the distance between each element with the deltas operator and multiplying it by a random fraction between 0 and 1. This fraction of the interval is then added back to the original value. Since each offset corresponds to the previous value, we must use the next operator to align the fraction and the original value.

**.sim.delay**

```
delay:{abs[type x]$x+next deltas[x]*count[x]?1f}
```

The next operator shifts all values back one element - creating a null entry in the last value.

```
q)next til 10
1 2 3 4 5 6 7 8 9 0N
```

Using the `next` operator with time series data should raise red flags. If at any point in time we look forward at the next value in our data, we have just created a look-ahead bias. Using these values in a backtest or profitability analysis would generate unachievable results. In this case, however, we are looking at the next **time** and not data point. This is, in effect, the same as looking back in time.

The `prev` operator is similar to the `next` operator. But instead of shifting the values backward, it shifts all values forward by one element.

```
q)prev til 10
0N 0 1 2 3 4 5 6 7 8
```

Using the `prev` function is so common with time series data, there also exists another function, `xprev` which allows us to shift the dataset forward by more than one entry.

```
q)5 xprev til 10
0N 0N 0N 0N 0N 0 1 2 3 4
```

---

**Q Tip 9.2** Use `xprev` with a negative left operand

---

Perhaps confusingly, there is no `xnext`. As mentioned, using the `next`, and obviously an `xnext`, operator should be avoided. But as this example shows, there may be cases where looking ahead is desired. Instead of writing our own `xnext` operator, we can actually call `xprev` with a negative left operand to obtain the same effect.

```
q)-5 xprev til 10
5 6 7 8 9 0N 0N 0N 0N 0N
```

## Casting Between Types

Multiplying values by a fraction will convert any integral type into a float. The intention of the function was to delay the values, not change their type. Before returning the delayed values, we need to convert them back to the original type. We can use the cast operator "$" with the type of the original list to recover the original type.

Casting between types can be done with a symbol, character, or numeric representation of the type. These three commands cast float to long values. Instead of truncating, casting rounds the value to the nearest whole number.

```
q)show x:5?100f
60.80809 53.62018 89.33856 35.64819 5.892398
q)`long$x
61 54 89 36 6
q)"j"$x
61 54 89 36 6
q)7h$x
61 54 89 36 6
```

The function can now be used to delay any list of values regardless of type. Using the index apply operator "@" we can delay the time column of the quote table.

```
q)@[q;`time;.sim.delay]
id time                bs bp    ap    as
----------------------------------------
0   0D09:00:07.346732638 8  7.995 8     94
0   0D09:00:07.921240577 6  8     8.005 65
0   0D09:00:18.533658118 71 8     8.005 34
0   0D09:00:20.242948201 50 7.995 8     66
0   0D09:00:22.118894773 15 7.995 8     54
..
```

Since trades occur less frequently than quote updates, we only need to pick a subset of the quotes to convert into trades. For this, we can define a `filter` function that accepts a fractional percentage and the list to be filtered.

### .sim.filter

```
filter:{y asc (neg"j"$x*n)?n:count y}
```

After counting the number of elements in the original list and multiplying by the desired percentage, the function uses the rand operator "?" operator with a negative left operand to generate non-repeating indices used to index into the original list. Before indexing, however, the indices are sorted to ensure the resulting list maintains its original order.

The last quote causes us some trouble. There is no *next* value to provide us with a delayed trade time. This is made clear by looking at the last value of a delayed list of numbers.

```
q).sim.delay 1 2 3 4f
1.444905 2.542917 3.00628 0n
```

For our purposes, we can assume there are no trades after the last quote. Before calling filter, we can throw the last quote away. We will also assume that only 30 percent of quotes become trades.

```
q).sim.filter[.3] -1_@[;`time;.sim.delay] q
id time                bs bp    ap    as
----------------------------------------
0   0D09:00:15.720338768 71 8     8.005 34
0   0D09:00:21.104934171 15 7.995 8     54
0   0D09:00:23.392346835 55 7.995 8     68
0   0D09:00:25.941771025 97 7.995 8     76
0   0D09:00:29.365944502 63 7.995 8     59
..
```

## Grouping

We have made one mistake, however. The quote table has intra-day data for many ids. We actually need
to delay (and drop the last row) for each ID. In the section called "By" [169], we demonstrate how q-SQL
can be used to apply functions to groups of data within tables. But this can also be done without resorting
to q-SQL. To do this, we need to split the table into chunks - grouped by ID. The `group` operator maps
each unique value in a list, to a list of indices where that value can be found.

```
q) group q`id
0|  0     1     2     3     4     5     6     7     8     9    10    11    12    13    14..
1|  1000  1001  1002  1003  1004  1005  1006  1007  1008  1009  1010  1011  1012  1013  10..
2|  2000  2001  2002  2003  2004  2005  2006  2007  2008  2009  2010  2011  2012  2013  20..
3|  3000  3001  3002  3003  3004  3005  3006  3007  3008  3009  3010  3011  3012  3013  30..
4|  4000  4001  4002  4003  4004  4005  4006  4007  4008  4009  4010  4011  4012  4013  40..
5|  5000  5001  5002  5003  5004  5005  5006  5007  5008  5009  5010  5011  5012  5013  50..
6|  6000  6001  6002  6003  6004  6005  6006  6007  6008  6009  6010  6011  6012  6013  60..
..
```

If we use the dictionary of indices to index back into the original table, we obtain a list of tables which
we can iteratively apply a function.

```
q) q group q`id
0| +`id`time`bs`bp`ap`as!(0 0 0 0 0 0 0 0 0 0 0 0 0 0 0 0 0 0 0 0 0 0 0 0 0 0..
1| +`id`time`bs`bp`ap`as!(1 1 1 1 1 1 1 1 1 1 1 1 1 1 1 1 1 1 1 1 1 1 1 1 1 1..
2| +`id`time`bs`bp`ap`as!(2 2 2 2 2 2 2 2 2 2 2 2 2 2 2 2 2 2 2 2 2 2 2 2 2 2..
3| +`id`time`bs`bp`ap`as!(3 3 3 3 3 3 3 3 3 3 3 3 3 3 3 3 3 3 3 3 3 3 3 3 3 3..
4| +`id`time`bs`bp`ap`as!(4 4 4 4 4 4 4 4 4 4 4 4 4 4 4 4 4 4 4 4 4 4 4 4 4 4..
5| +`id`time`bs`bp`ap`as!(5 5 5 5 5 5 5 5 5 5 5 5 5 5 5 5 5 5 5 5 5 5 5 5 5 5..
6| +`id`time`bs`bp`ap`as!(6 6 6 6 6 6 6 6 6 6 6 6 6 6 6 6 6 6 6 6 6 6 6 6 6 6..
..
```

In our case, we call `delay` and drop 1. After applying the composition to each table, we `raze` the
results to recover a single table.

```
q) raze (-1_@[; `time;.sim.delay]@) each q group q`id
id time                    bs bp     ap     as
-----------------------------------------------
0  0D09:00:06.993769423 8   7.995 8      94
0  0D09:00:08.084943027 6   8      8.005 65
0  0D09:00:10.468447612 71 8      8.005 34
0  0D09:00:20.576540831 50 7.995 8      66
0  0D09:00:22.217316109 15 7.995 8      54
..
```

Grouping a table and **each**ing over the groups is a very common operation. When the eached function
returns a result that is smaller than the originally grouped table, performance improvements can be made

by generating the grouped table within the function or composition, and not outside. This prevents a potentially large allocation of temporary memory. Since our returned table has one less row than the original, we can achieve a small performance gain by indexing into q within the composition. The benefits to this technique grow as the results shrink.

```
q)raze (-1_@[;`time;.sim.delay] q@) each group q`id
id time                   bs bp    ap    as
--------------------------------------------
0  0D09:00:06.993769423 8  7.995 8     94
0  0D09:00:08.084943027 6  8     8.005 65
0  0D09:00:10.468447612 71 8     8.005 34
0  0D09:00:20.576540831 50 7.995 8     66
0  0D09:00:22.217316109 15 7.995 8     54
..
```

The quote table times are now delayed mimicking the delay between quote updates and trade events. It has also been filtered to only those quotes that result in a trade. We now turn our attention to adding the trade size and price columns.

To know which price and size to use, we must first decide if the trade is a buy or sell. We can again use q's ability to pick random values - this time from the booleans 0b and 1b.

```
q)n?0b
100101010001111111111010001001001111110100110111100101001001100010001110001..
```

We must also determine what percent of the quoted size was traded. We will generate a random value between 0 and 1 to represent the percent traded.

```
q)n?1f
0.9266023 0.5977674 0.2253183 0.8698908 0.02786834 0.5412761 0.4120967 0.01..
```

We can now use these two values combined with the bid and ask sizes and prices to generate the trade size and price.

**.sim.trd**

```
trd:{[b;pct;bs;bp;ap;as](ceiling pct*?[b;bs;as];?[b;bp;ap])}
```

The trd function returns a list with two values: the trade size and the trade price. We use the ?[;;] operator two times to optionally select the bid or ask size and price. In addition, it multiplies the size by the pct traded and takes the ceiling of the final quantity to ensure the value is an integer and always greater than 0.

Applying this function to the data from the quote table results in a list of sizes and prices.

```
q).sim.trd[n?0b;n?1f] . q`bs`bp`ap`as
25     41    9    6    89    17    15    56 18   45    23    55    2..
19.005 19.02 19.03 19.02 19.04 19.025 19.005 19 19.02 19.01 19.035 19.035 1..
```

We use the indexing:[dot apply] operator "." to pass the bid and ask size and price to the `trd` function as a list of lists. After adding a key for the column names, we flip the result and concatenate the tables.

```
q)t:q,' flip `ts`tp!.sim.trd[n?0b;(n:count q)?1f] . q`bs`bp`ap`as;
q)t
id time                  bs bp    ap    as ts tp
----------------------------------------------------------
0  0D09:00:06.907428335 8  7.995 8        94 3  8
0  0D09:00:07.820572983 6  8     8.005 65 37 8.005
0  0D09:00:08.236355613 71 8     8.005 34 4  8.005
0  0D09:00:19.930412247 50 7.995 8        66 13 7.995
0  0D09:00:20.836932677 15 7.995 8        54 10 7.995
..
```

The `gent` function combines the filtering and trade generation code.

**.sim.gent**

```
gent:{[q]
 q:filter[pct] raze (-1_@[;`time;delay] q@) each group q`id;
 t:q,' flip `ts`tp!trd[n?0b;(n:count q)?1f] . q`bs`bp`ap`as;
 t:`id`ts`tp`time#t;
 t}
```

The fourth line of the function will again pick the exact columns we want, in the order we want them.

```
q)show t:.sim.gent[.3] q
id time                  ts tp
--------------------------------
0  0D09:00:07.069086418 4  7.995
0  0D09:00:11.173569078 1  8.005
0  0D09:00:23.366481880 37 7.995
0  0D09:00:24.985832966 37 8
0  0D09:00:35.687299321 42 8
..
```

This completes the business logic of our CEP engine. We now have functions that can simulate the evolution of a hypothetical stock price, generate quotes, and finally produce trades. Before we can transform these functions into a real-time CEP engine, we need a few tools that are typically included in the core libraries of many programming languages. The next chapter implements libraries for parsing command line options, logging messages, and creating repeating timer events.

# Chapter 10

# CEP Engine Components

> You don't have to be a genius or a visionary or even a college graduate to be successful. You just need a framework and a dream.

> — Michael Dell

We can now generate quote and trade tables with data for multiple ids. The techniques and functions we used will be useful in the section called "Market Data Functions" [140] when we complete the CEP engine. In this case, the functions will be used to generate quote and trade records (not tables) in real-time. Out of the box, kdb+ does not provide any libraries for application development. To begin writing real applications, we need, at a minimum, a logging library and an options parsing library. To write a CEP engine, we will also need a flexible timer library. This chapter covers the implementation of a timer library that allows multiple events, a logging library that permits customizable levels of verboseness, and a command line option library that automatically generates usage messages.

## 10.1  Timer Events

The combination of q's efficient table manipulation and kdb+'s event callbacks creates a powerful platform for performing real-time computations. A kdb+ CEP engine is nothing more than a long-running q process that responds to events. These events can be generated both internally by timers or externally from client messages. By default, kdb+ offers a single timer that can be triggered at a fixed frequency. To make a more complex engine, we need the ability to run multiple events, on multiple time schedules, for arbitrary periods of time. To achieve this, we need to write our own timer utility.

## Starting the Timer

Kdb+ has an internal timer that calls a custom function at a specified interval. The interval is defined in milliseconds. If a finer grained timer is needed, you should consider redesigning the algorithm to be event based, instead of timer based. The timer can be started in one of two ways. The timer interval can be passed to the q process on startup with the −t command line argument or changed with the \ t system command. Once the timer is running, it will call the function stored in the **timestamp** .z.ts system variable. By default, this value is undefined and thus has no effect. The global timer will call the function stored in .z.ts with a single argument: the current time. As a simple demonstration of the timer's operation, we can print the time.

```
q)\t 1000
q).z.ts:{show x}
q)2015.03.06D10:00:06.770709000
2015.03.06D10:00:07.770709000
2015.03.06D10:00:08.770709000
2015.03.06D10:00:09.770709000
\t 0
```

Setting the timer interval to 0 turns it off.

The single timer is useful for simple applications. More complicated applications need multiple timers. Some applications require events to run at specific times in the future. Other applications require events to run at fixed intervals for a specific number of times. And yet other applications require the flexibility to keep running an event until a custom condition is met. If we design the framework correctly, we can allow for all three scenarios with a single interface.

## Table Prototypes

The first step in creating the timer utility is to create an empty table to hold the list of timer events. The table must have all the necessary columns, and the columns need to be of the correct type. Once the engine is started, new rows will be added and removed from the table. But since we do not know what data should be in the table, we will declare an empty table.

The timer.job table needs three fields: a name for the event, the function to run, and the time it needs to run. The most verbose syntax to generate a timer.job table would be to cast empty lists to the proper data type using the type's symbolic representation.

```
q)([]name:`symbol$();func:();time:`timestamp$())
name func time
--------------
```

We see that the name column will hold symbols, the function column is an untyped list, and we will be saving timestamps in the time column. The func column is declared as an untyped list so we can save symbols, symbol lists, and even anonymous functions in the column.

This syntax is quite clear. The syntax becomes unwieldy, however, when we declare a table with many columns. Using the character representation of each data type makes the table definition more compact.

```
q)([]name:`$();func:();time:"p"$())
name func time
--------------
```

The repetition of casting is still glaring. Remembering that a table is really a flipped dictionary of lists opens up a more concise format for table definitions.

```
q)show timer.job:flip `name`func`time!"s*p"$\:()
name func time
--------------
```

The definition first generates an empty list for each data type. We need to use the "s" character for symbols and the "*" character for an untyped list. The declaration then uses the key operator "!" to add a key to the list and then flips the result. Declaring empty tables is very common when kdb+ is used as a CEP engine. We will use this syntax many times.

## Untyped Columns

There is one problem with empty tables that have untyped columns. Once a single row is added, kdb+ will convert untyped lists into typed lists of the appropriate type. We can see this by adding a single row to the table.

```
q)meta timer.job upsert (`;`;.z.P)
c    | t f a
-----| -----
name | s
func | s
time | p
```

---

**Q Tip 10.1** Insert an empty row to prevent untyped columns from collapsing

---

Once the list is converted to a typed list, we will not be able to insert values of other types. This would prevent us from inserting anonymous functions into the table. To prevent this from happening, we need to insert a single row into the table where the func column is an untyped list.

```
q)meta timer.job upsert (`;();.z.P)
c    | t f a
-----| -----
name | s
func |
time | p
```

An easier way to achieve this is by taking a single row from the anonymous table at the time of definition.

```
q)show 1#flip`name`func`time!"s*p"$\:()
name func time
--------------
```

But the `timer.job` table is special. In order to run the events in the correct order, the elements of the timer will be sorted in descending chronological order. To ensure this place-holder record stays at the top, and never gets run, we will add the record with an infinite `time` field. Using the name of the table as the left operand for `upsert` appends the data in-place and returns the table name. We can then use the `get` operator to retrieve the table stored in the variable `timer.job`.

```
q)get `timer.job upsert (`;();0Wp)
name func time
--------------
           0W
```

## Nulls and Infinities

One very special feature of kdb+ is that all (but two) numerical and temporal data types have defined values for null and positive and negative infinity. Null and infinite float values are represented by the numbers 0n, 0w and -0w respectively. They correspond to the IEEE representation of NaN, +inf and -inf. Integral values, however, do not have internationally recognized values for these concepts. To handle these values, we must designate three existing values as magic. Kdb+ has made our life easier by implementing this for us. Using two's complement representation for signed numbers, the range of negative values is always one more than the range of positive values. Kdb+ uses the smallest value for null which makes the range of positive and negative values equal. The next smallest integer value is used for negative infinity, while positive infinity is stored as the largest integer value. These three values have similar syntax as their float counterparts but use capital letters instead.

```
q)0N -0W 0W
0N -0W 0W
```

We can see their underlying representation by computing a few offsets from positive infinity.

```
q)0W + 3 2 1 0 -1
-9223372036854775806 -0W 0N 0W 9223372036854775806
```

To represent null or infinity for other types, we must add the qualifying type character after the 0W. For example, we can find the largest and smallest 4-byte integer as well.

```
q)0Wi + 3 2 1 0 -1i
-2147483646 -0W 0N 0W 2147483646i
```

The `boolean` and `byte` types are the only types that do not have a null value. The `boolean` type, by definition, only has two values: `0b` and `1b`. Neither of these are classified as null. We can confirm this by using the `null` operator to test for nullness.

```
q)null 01b
00b
```

There is just no room in the data type to represent a missing value. The `byte` type has the same problem. By definition, a byte can be one of 256 values. Kdb+ does not treat any of these values as null.

There are many benefits to using nulls and infinities. Nulls provide a way to acknowledge that you do not know a value. Atomic operations propagate null values.

```
q)1+1 2 0N
2 3 0N
q)
```

Aggregate functions tend to ignore them. For example, computing the average of a vector ignores all nulls.

```
q)avg 1 2 0N
1.5
```

But when computing an average of a list of vectors (a matrix), it is not possible to ignore just a few null elements. In this case, the nulls propagate.

```
q)avg (1 2 0N;3 0N 5)
2 0n 0n
```

Q provides two operators to handle missing values: the dyadic fill operator "^" and the monadic `fills` operator. The fill operator "^" is atomic and can thus be used with both atoms and lists. Every null element of the right operand is filled with the corresponding element from the left operand.

```
q)0 1 ^ (1 2 0N;3 0N 5)
1 2 0
3 1 5
```

It is common practice in financial computations to fill quantities with 0, bid prices with 0 or -0w, and ask prices with 0w. Missing trade prices pose an interesting problem, neither 0, -0w, nor 0w make sense. Without any other information, perhaps the most appropriate trade price would be the last known trade price. This is where the `fills` operator is useful. The `fills` operator fills forward the last non-null value. A daily price series with missing points on holidays can be cleaned by using the `fills` operator.

```
q)fills 1.23 1.25 1.22 0n 1.24
1.23 1.25 1.22 1.22 1.24
```

Positive and negative infinity are values that can, if used properly, simplify code. In our case we have used a positive time infinity to ensure that the first row of our table is never inspected and thus never removed.

With the appropriate data structure in place, we can move on to writing the interface for the timer utility.

## Implementing a Timer Utility

The basic functionality of the timer utility can be implemented in four functions. A merge function to insert new timer events, an add function that converts timestamps to GMT before calling merge, a run function that executes an event from the timer.job table, and finally a loop function that is called from the kdb+ timer and checks the timer queue for runnable events.

The kdb+ timer will be called every few milliseconds. It is important to make its operation as efficient as possible. Kdb+ is optimized for appending data to the end of lists. To prevent a large relocation of memory when removing elements from a list, it is important to remove them from the end as well. To ensure we are always modifying the end of the timer.job table, we will sort the data in descending time order after appending any new elements. The merge function is a composition of the xdesc and upsert operators. The arguments are therefore the same as upsert's: a table as the first argument and a record as the second.

**.timer.merge**

```
merge:`time xdesc upsert
```

The add function accepts the table name, the event name, the function to run, and the time to run it.

**.timer.add**

```
add:{[t;n;f;tm]
 r:(n;f;gtime tm);
 t:merge[t;$[0h>type tm;r;reverse flip r]];
 t}
```

## Time Zones

The first line creates a record to be merged into the table. Kdb+ calls the .z.ts callback with the current time in GMT. But to make the timer library easy to use, we will allow it to accept times in the local time zone. Instead of converting the time from GMT to local time every time the timer wakes up, we convert the event time from local time to GMT before inserting the row into the timer.job table. The gtime operator converts timestamps and datetimes from local time to GMT. When it is time to call the function, we can convert the timestamp back to local time with the ltime operator.

We can make the add function flexible by allowing a single event to be passed with a list of times. Instead of merging the row into the table directly, we first check to see if the type of the tm variable is greater than 0. Negative types are atoms, while lists are equal or greater than 0. If we detect a list, we can then `flip` the record and q will properly expand the single record into multiple records - one for each time.

```
q)flip (1; til 5)
1 0
1 1
1 2
1 3
1 4
```

## Flexible Return Values

When writing functions to operate on global variables, it is tempting to embed the table name directly in the function. This, however, limits the function to be used on only that table. A better approach is to pass the table as an argument and return the modified table as a result. This allows the function to be used to modify global tables (when the table name is passed as an argument) and local tables (when the actual table is passed). Passing the table name also has the advantage of being more efficient, as operations performed on global symbols do not need to make a copy of data structures. They update values in-place.

**Q Tip 10.2** Allow functions to operate on both tables and table names

Both the `merge` and `add` function return copies of the table passed in as the first argument. This allows us to use the functions to generate modified copies of the `timer.job` table or, alternatively, to modify the table in place. Like many q operators, these functions can accept both a table and a table name as their first argument. If a table is passed to the functions, a copy is returned. If the table name is passed, the global variable will be modified.

We can modify the table in-place and see that the value changes.

```
q).timer.add[`timer.job; `a; `.q.show;.z.P]
`timer.job
q)timer.job
name func    time
-----------------------------------------------
     ()       0W
a    `.q.show 2015.03.06D15:20:59.669131000
```

or use the actual table, and obtain a new table as the result.

```
q).timer.add[timer.job; `a; `.q.show;.z.P]
name func    time
-----------------------------------------------
     ()       0W
```

```
a       `.q.show 2015.03.06D15:21:06.108952000
a       `.q.show 2015.03.06D15:20:59.669131000
```

As designed, the add function can also generate multiple events.

```
q).timer.add[`timer.job; `a; `show;.z.P+0D00:00:05* til 10]
`timer.job
q)show timer.job
name func  time
----------------------------------------
      ()    0W
a     `show 2015.03.06D15:27:43.056751000
a     `show 2015.03.06D15:27:38.056751000
a     `show 2015.03.06D15:27:33.056751000
a     `show 2015.03.06D15:27:28.056751000
..
```

Let's move on to the main routine that periodically checks the timer.job table for runnable events. In order to be used as the .z.ts callback, the last argument of the function must be the current time. We also pass the table as the first argument.

**.timer.loop**

```
loop:{[t;tm]while[tm>=last tms:t`time;t:run[t;-1+count tms;tm]];t}
```

## While

The loop function uses the while operator to check the last job in the table. If it was scheduled to run before the current time, the run command is called with the event's row number and the result is written back to the variable t. Using the while operator is typically shunned in the q community. Using uniform functions or the each family of adverbs is the preferred method of running a function over each element of a list. In this case, however, the while operator is exactly what we need. During the execution of an event, it is possible that events were added to (or deleted from) the timer.job table. It is therefore important to inspect the potentially modified table after each iteration. The while operator allows us to do this.

The final piece of the puzzle is running the event. We know the function parameters: the table, the event's row index, and the current time in GMT.

**.timer.run**

```
run:{[t;i;tm]
 j:t i;
 t:.[t;();_;i];
 r:value (f:j`func),ltime tm;
 if[not null r;merge[t;(j`name;f;tm+r)]];
 t}
```

## Drop

The second line of the function indexes into the table to find the job `j`. This syntax works even if the name of the table was passed to the function. The second line deletes the row from the table. If we had limited the function to only work on tables, and not table names, we could have used the drop operator `"_"`.

```
t:t _ i;
```

But this syntax does not work with table names. In order to allow our code to work with both tables and table names, we use the dot apply operator `"."` just like q's `upsert`.

```
q) upsert
.[;();,;]
```

Given its utility and relation to `upsert` it is tempting to write a new `drop` operator. A neat little trick, which should only be tried at home, is to define a dyadic function in the `.q` namespace and call it using infix notation.

```
q).q.drop:.[;();_;]
q)timer.job drop 1
name func time
--------------
          0W
```

The third line of the `run` function pulls the scheduled function from the `e` dictionary, saves it into the variable `f` and appends the current (local) time. This list is then passed to the `value` operator for evaluation and the results are saved in `r`. The last line of the function reschedules the event to run again if the result is not null. This allows us to add a single event, and have it run for an unspecified number of times until the function does not return a time to be rescheduled.

Allowing the function to determine when it should be rescheduled allows us to customize the timer's behavior without having to complicate its interface. For example, we can write a utility function to run jobs until a specified time. The `until` function accepts the **d**elay, the **e**nd time, the **f**unction, and the current **t**ime.

### .timer.until

```
until:{[d;et;f;tm]if[tm<et;@[value;f,tm;0N!];:d]}
```

## Trap

If the current time is before the end time, the function is called using the *trap* version of apply. When called with three arguments, the apply operators (both `"@"` and `"."`) can be passed a function, an argument list, and finally a function to process any errors and optionally return an alternate result. This stops the function from aborting and allows us to reschedule the function even if it encountered an error. In this case, we just print the error with `ON!`. In other cases, you may decide to print a special log message, or return a default value.

We can define an event `e` as a list, starting with the function `until` followed by all the arguments except the timestamp, which will be added when the function is called. When we start the `kdb+` timer, and add this event to the `timer.job` table, the event will print the current time every second for the next 30 seconds.

```
q)\t 100
q)e:(`.timer.until;0D00:00:01;.z.P+0D00:00:30;`.q.show)
q).timer.add[`timer.job;`a;e;.z.P]
`timer.job
q)2015.03.06D23:32:11.369173000
2015.03.06D23:32:12.369173000
2015.03.06D23:32:13.369173000
2015.03.06D23:32:14.369173000
2015.03.06D23:32:15.369173000
```

We now have a robust timer interface which will allow us to add multiple events that can run once, repeatedly, or until a desired time. The timer utility allows us to start a `kdb+` server that simulates real-time market data for both trade and quote messages. Before writing the functions to generate the events, we will introduce a logging utility to help document and debug a real-time system.

## 10.2  Logging

Performance and memory usage are two critical components of any CEP engine. To track down bottle-necks, we need to see how long functions take, and how much memory they allocate. Having a robust logging library at our disposal allows us to pepper the code with statements that record the current time and memory consumption of the `kdb+` process. We can then pinpoint where time and memory are being spent. Used appropriately, calls to the logging routines also help document the code.

The current date and time are easy to obtain with the `.z.D` and `.z.T` system variables. Logging the current memory utilization is a bit harder. Before diving into the implementation of the logging library, we must understand how `kdb+` manages and reports its memory utilization.

### Memory

Kdb+ keeps track of every allocated byte and provides functions to access this information. The `\w` system command returns a list of numbers which represent the number of bytes used in different parts of the application.

```
q)\w
113760 67108864 67108864 0 0 2147483648
```

If given a parameter, the command returns the number of symbols and associated memory usage.

```
q)\w 0
762 27614
```

This data is conveniently returned in a dictionary with descriptive keys by the internal `.Q.w` function.

```
q).Q.w[]
used| 119616
heap| 67108864
peak| 67108864
wmax| 0
mmap| 0
mphy| 2147483648
syms| 571
symw| 18607
```

The first element indicates how much memory is currently being used by kdb+. The second field shows how much memory has been allocated on the heap (or reserved from the operating system). Kdb+ uses a memory pool to allow memory to be quickly reserved and freed. When more memory is needed than exists in the pool, kdb+ will allocate additional multiples of 64MB blocks. The increased heap (pool) size can be seen in the second field of the `\w` command.

The third field indicates the high water mark for the heap memory. When the process memory limit has been reached, q will coalesce blocks of unused memory that are at least 64MB, and return them back to the operating system. If kdb+ is still unable to allocate a requested block of memory, a `wsfull error is thrown and the process will die. Otherwise, the heap allocation will decrease but the high water mark will not.

**Q Tip 10.3** Use continuous garbage collection with limited memory

It is possible to request memory to be coalesced by using the garbage collection operator `.Q.gc`. In addition, q can be configured to automatically release blocks of memory that are at least 64MB by setting the command line option −g to 1. This is useful when running q on a machine with a limited amount of memory or running the 32-bit version of q which is limited to 4GB. This adds a small constant overhead, but also prevents the process from suddenly stalling or aborting after hitting the memory limit.

The fourth field is the hard limit placed on the kdb+ process by the user. When no limit is specified, the field displays a 0 and the actual limit will be two times the system's physical memory (located in field six). More will be discussed on this memory limit in Q Tip 11.10 [152].

If we scale the output of `\w`, we can see that out of the 2GB of memory on my machine, q allocates 64MB on startup.

```
q)system["w"]%4 xexp 10
.0.1087 64 64 0 0 2048
```

The fifth field does not relate to RAM allocation. It represents the amount of memory mapped from disk. We will cover this field in Chapter 15 [201]. The first three fields are most relevant for our use: the current memory usage, the current memory reserved, and the maximum memory used.

## Logging Library

The logging library starts by declaring four variables.

```
h:-2
lvl:2
unit:"BKMGTP"
mult:5 (1024*)\ 1
```

The first two variables configure where and when logs are printed. The first is the handle used to log messages. It defaults to STDERR (-2). As suggested in Q Tip 2.2 [12], we have declared it negative so q automatically adds newlines. To change the destination of the messages to STDOUT, we can set the value to -1. We could, in fact, redirect the messages to a file or network socket if we set .log.h to the handle returned from the hopen operator.

The definition of mult demonstrates how to use the scan operator to call a monadic function iteratively for a fixed number of times. In this case, the monadic function (1024*) multiplies its argument by 1024. We start the iteration with the value 1, and iteratively call the function 5 more times.

```
q)5 (1024*)\ 1
1 1024 1048576 1073741824 1099511627776 1125899906842624
```

The log level lvl is the second configurable variable. It is used to filter the messages by severity. Setting the value to -1 will turn logging off altogether. 0 will only show errors, 1 is for warnings, while info, debug, and trace messages are successively higher values. By default, it is set to 2 which will display error, warning, and info messages.

The last two variables are used to convert the memory usage reported in bytes by kdb+ to human readable values. To make the values easier to read, the library scales these values into units of the maximum allocated memory.

The next three lines of the logging library are the functions that format the log message.

### .log.hdr

```
mem:{@[string"i"$(3#x)%mult m;2;;;unit m:mult bin x 2]}
hdr:{string[(.z.D;.z.T)],mem system "w"}
msg:{if[x<=lvl;h " " sv hdr[],(y;$[10h=type z;z;-3!z])]}
```

The mem function reformats the system generated memory. We can see how the function reports the currently used memory, the total allocated memory and the maximum memory used by this process.

```
q).log.mem system "w"
,"0"
"64"
"64M"
```

The `hdr` function combines the current time and memory usage into a list of character vectors. The `msg` function accepts the log level, a character vector representation of that level, and the value to log. If the log is suitable for printing, based on the global `lvl` variable, the header is generated and printed with the message. Instead of constantly joining character vectors with spaces, each of the functions generates a list of character vectors. These lists are joined with spaces a single time with the `sv` operator as the last step before printing.

The `-3!` operator used in the `msg` function is a q primitive that generates a character vector representation of any q data type. It is useful for cases when we need to represent a complex data type on a single line. Small lists, dictionaries and tables can be printed without newlines. The final display of the text will still be truncated by the display width mentioned in Q Tip 5.2 [56].

```
q)-3!`a`b!1 2
"`a`b!1 2"
```

The last 5 lines of the library define functions designed to be used by the library user. They declare the `err` (error), `wrn` (warning), `inf` (info), `dbg` (debug), and `trc` (trace) projections of the `msg` function.

```
err:msg[0;"[E]"]
wrn:msg[1;"[W]"]
inf:msg[2;"[I]"]
dbg:msg[3;"[D]"]
trc:msg[4;"[T]"]
```

We can see how the messages change as memory is allocated,

```
q).log.inf "on start"
2015.03.06 09:34:34.300 0 64 64M [I] on start
q)x:til 10000000
q).log.inf "after allocation"
2015.03.06 09:34:41.861 128 192 192M [I] after allocation
```

and then recovered.[1]

```
q)delete x from `.
`.
q).log.inf "after recovery"
2015.03.06 09:35:11.573 0 192 192M [I] after recovery
```

---

[1] Deleting variables from memory is covered in the section called "Using q-SQL on Dictionaries" [188].

From the last line we can see how the current memory usage is 0MB, but that the maximum size allocated was 192M. The middle number, indicates that this memory has not been freed to the operating system. We can force the memory to be recovered by calling the kdb+ garbage collector.

```
q).Q.gc[]
134217728
q).log.inf "after gc"
2015.03.06 09:39:09.207 0 64 192M [I] after gc
```

The .Q.gc operator returns the number of bytes freed. Though the memory currently used is still 0MB, and the maximum value ever reached remains the same, the amount used by the process has dropped by 134217728 bytes (or 128MB) back to the initial value of 64MB.

## 10.3  Command Line Options

To write a useful CEP engine, we will need to configure the process at startup. We have already seen how −g and −w control memory management and how −t can set how frequently the timer is run. The complete list of single letter system command line options can be found on the Kx Wiki [cmdline] [266].

Q provides access to the list of command line options (excluding the single letter system options) in the .z.x system variable.

```
$ q cep.q −eod 22:00 −db qdb
KDB+ 3.2 2015.03.04 Copyright (C) 1993−2015 Kx Systems
m32/ 4()core 2048MB nick nicks−macbook.local 192.168.1.103 NONEXPIRE
q).z.x
"−eod"
"22:00"
"−db"
"qdb"
```

### Configuration

We can write our own library to access these options in a useful format and automatically generate usage statements. The library begins by declaring a table to hold each of the options, their default value, and documentation used when displaying a usage banner.

```
config:1#flip `opt`def`doc!"s**"$\:()
```

The options are saved as symbols "s", and the default values and documentation are saved as untyped lists "*". Using an untyped list is needed to allow the default values to vary in type. And since the documentation will be saved as a character vector, it too must be saved in an untyped column. Following

Q Tip 10.1 [123], we prevent the untyped list from automatically collapsing to a typed list by ensuring that the list has at least one entry with an empty list.

Our CEP server will require five parameters: a file path to load reference data, a time to run the end of day processing, a directory to save the market data, a debug flag, and a log level to control how much logging is displayed. We can insert each of these options into a copy of the `config` table.

```
c:.opt.config
c,:(`ref;`:ref.csv;"file with reference data")
c,:(`eod;0D23:59;"time for end of day event")
c,:(`db;`:db;"directory to save tables at eod")
c,:(`debug;0b;"don't start engine")
c,:(`log;2;"log level")
```

The table now has one empty row, and five options.

```
q)c
opt   def                   doc
------------------------------------------------------
      ()                    ()
ref   `:ref.csv             "file with reference data"
eod   0D23:59:00.000000000  "time for end of day event"
db    `:db                  "end of day dump location"
debug 0b                    "don't start engine"
log   2                     "log level"
```

## Parsing User Command Line Arguments

We can build a `getopt` function to combine our configuration table `c` and the command line arguments `x` to define a parameter list for our application.

**.opt.getopt**

```
getopt:{[c;h;x]
 p:(!). c`opt`def;
 p:.Q.def[p] .Q.opt x;
 p:@[p;h;hsym];
 p}
```

The second line of the function extracts the `opt` and `def` columns. It then uses the key operator "!" to create a dictionary mapping the options to their default values. Just as we did in Chapter 7 [73], we need to surround the key operator "!" with parentheses. We can then use the dot apply operator "." to generate the parameter dictionary.

```
q)show p:(!). c`opt`def
 | ()
```

```
ref   | `:ref.csv
eod   | 0D23:59:00.000000000
db    | `:db
debug| 0b
log   | 2
```

The first step in processing the command line arguments is calling the internal `.Q.opt` operator to convert the list of command line arguments into a dictionary.

```
q).Q.opt .z.x
eod| "22:00"
db | "qdb"
```

---

**Q Tip 10.4** Write utility functions that only operate on their parameters

---

To keep our `getopt` function generic, we will expect the user to pass the contents of `.z.x` to the function. This gives the user of the library the opportunity to manipulate the command line character vector before calling `getopt`.

The real magic occurs in the next operator: `.Q.def`. The first parameter of `.Q.def` is our dictionary of default values. Besides providing values for missing command line arguments, the dictionary provides a template for determining the types of each command line parameter. When merging the default values with the command line parameters, each parameter will get cast to the proper type.

```
show p:.Q.def[p] .Q.opt .z.x
ref   | `:ref.csv
eod   | 0D22:00:00.000000000
db    | `qdb
debug| 0b
log   | 2
```

The variable p now contains the `eod` and `db` parameters that were passed on the command line, as well as the default values for `ref` and `log`. But we are stuck with one problem. Notice that the db value was converted to a symbol but not a handle. Q does not differentiate between symbols and handles (starting with a `":"`). Any command line arguments we specify as a handle will be cast to a symbol. It is up to us to cast them back. The second argument of the `getopt` function is a list of symbols that need casting to handles. The last line of the `getopt` function converts the symbols to handles by using the `hsym` operator. In reality, it has not changed the type of the symbol, it has just prepended a `":"` character.

```
q)@[p;`ref`db;hsym]
ref   | `:ref.csv
eod   | 0D22:00:00.000000000
db    | `:qdb
debug| 0b
log   | 2
```

## Generating Usage Text

The descriptive text we provided during the configuration initialization not only documents the code, but enables us to generate a usage banner that can be displayed when users start the kdb+ process with a -help option.

**.opt.usage**

```
usage:{[c;f]
 u:enlist "usage: q ",(string f)," [option]...";
 a:wrap[(7#" "),"-";" "] string c`opt;
 a:a,'wrap["<";"> "] c`doc;
 a:a,'wrap["(";")"] -3!'c`def;
 u,:a;
 u}
```

The usage function takes two arguments, the .opt.getopt [135] configuration and the name of the file passed to the q process on startup. This file is stored in the .z.f system variable and is returned as a symbol.

```
q).z.f
`cep.q
```

The first line of the function concatenates the q script with a simple message indicating how to run the script. The remaining lines of the function build the usage text for the options, one column at a time: first the command line argument, then the text describing the desired parameter, and finally the default value.

To make this easier, a wrap utility function is used to add characters to the left and right of the desired text. It also ensures all rows have the same width. The wrap function accepts a left hand character vector, right hand character vector, and a list of strings to wrap.

```
wrap:{[l;r;s](max count each s)$s:l,/:s,\:r}
```

## Justifying Text

The right hand text is appended to each character vector in s and then the left hand text is prepended and saved back into the same variable s. To justify the text, we used the cast operator "$" with an integer argument. The resulting text will be padded with spaces until the desired text length is achieved. If a positive value is used, the text is left justified.

```
q)8$"qtips"
"qtips   "
```

Negative values right justify.

```
q)-8$"qtips"
"    qtips"
```

The `wrap` function counts the length of each character vector and left justifies them to be the same length as the longest character vector.

If we call the `usage` function with all elements of `c` except the first empty row, and pass the results to the STDERR file handle `-2`, we can see how the usage statement prints each of the configuration items in justified columns.

```
q)-2 .opt.usage[1_c] .z.f;
usage: q cep.q [option]...
       -ref   <file with reference data>   (`:ref.csv)
       -eod   <time for end of day event>  (0D23:59:00.000000000)
       -db    <end of day dump location>   (`:db)
       -debug <don't start engine>         (0b)
       -log   <log level>                  (2)
```

The timer, logging and command line parsing libraries are three vital components of a CEP Engine framework. Using internal q functions and leveraging the table data structure, we have been able to create flexible libraries with minimal coding and effort. We now move on to actually starting the engine.

Chapter 11

# Running a CEP Engine

Inside every large program is a small program struggling to get out.

— Charles Antony Richard Hoare *Efficient Production of Large Programs (1970)*

We have spent the last few chapters writing small reusable functions. They were written and tested at the `q)` prompt. But everything that can be done from the interactive q session can also be performed in a non-interactive kdb+ server (or daemon process). It is time to compose a larger program by combining each of the developed libraries.

The job of a kdb+ server is to load and configure libraries, open a port for communication and start the timer. Server processes run unattended, so any configuration must be performed on the command line or through configuration files. This chapter begins by creating a few tables to store our CEP generated data. It also implements timer callbacks and adds the events to the `timer.job` table. We will then learn how to import configuration files as kdb+ tables and finally start the CEP engine.

## 11.1 Generating Market Data

This is, hopefully, the most exciting chapter of the whole book. Until now, we have been introducing all the fundamentals of q, and designing a set of tools to help support our CEP engine. When kdb+ is launched, the code loaded, and the timer started, our engine will begin generating data. Starting with fictional price paths that follow a random walk, the CEP engine will generate quotes by rounding the prices up and down to the nearest tick. From there, it will generate trades that occur randomly at either the bid or offer price. The data generated during this process will be saved to in-memory tables. And at the end of day, the data will be saved to disk.

## Market Data Tables

We begin with empty price, trade, and quote tables. In our simulation we will keep one set of tables for storing each of the price, quote and trade updates. But we will also keep another set of tables to maintain the most recent update for each `id`. This second set of tables will have the `id` column set as the primary key, and all data inserted into the table will be updated in-place instead of appended to the end. We will use the `.util.sattr` [106] function to apply the proper attributes for each table.

```
ref:.util.sattr 1!flip `id`px`ts`qs`vol`rfr!"jffjff"$\:()
prices:.util.sattr flip `id`px`time!"jfp"$\:()
price:.util.sattr 1!prices
trades:.util.sattr flip `id`ts`tp`time!"jjfp"$\:()
trade:.util.sattr 1!trades
quotes:.util.sattr flip `id`bs`bp`ap`as`time!"jjffjp"$\:()
quote:.util.sattr 1!quotes
```

The first table `ref` is needed to store static reference information for each ID in our simulation. In addition to the security ID, it contains the initial price for the simulation `px`, tick spread `ts`, maximum quote size `qs`, volatility `vol`, and risk free rate `rfr`. The remaining tables are populated by the CEP engine.

## Market Data Functions

We next write three functions to perform the cascading operations of generating security prices, quotes, and finally trades. Each function accepts the `id` that should be operated on, and the current time which will be provided by the timer. The functions compute new values and `upsert` the results into both the keyed and unkeyed `price(s)`, `trade(s)` and `quote(s)` tables.

The **upd**ate **p**rice function `updp`, obtains the most recent price record from the `price` table and uses the `.stat.gbm` [63] function to propagate the price forwarded based on the volatility and growth rate found in the `ref` table. After creating a dictionary `p` with the new price and current time cast to a `timespan`, the function inserts the record into both the real-time and historical price tables.

### .md.updp

```
updp:{[id;tm]
 .log.dbg "updating price for ", string id;
 p:`price id;
 r:`ref id;
 z:.stat.norminv rand 1f;
 f:.stat.gbm[r`vol;r`rfr;(tm-p`time)%365D06;z];
 p:`id`px`time!(id;f*p`px;tm);
 `price`prices upsert\: p;
 }
```

The last line of the `updp` function only contains a closing brace. Because the previous line ends in a semi-colon the return value of the function is the generic null `::`.

## Generic Null

This generic null value `::` has no display text and is considered null. To prevent the colons from being interpreted as a double assignment operator, we need to wrap them with parentheses when performing operations. It is not a numeric type, but does obey tests for nullness.

```
q)null (::)
1b
```

When functions have no explicit return value, they actually return the generic null `::`. We can see this by calling a function that returns nothing.

```
q)(::)~{}[]
1b
```

We can also see that this is the first value populated in all namespaces to prevent them from becoming typed lists.

```
q).q
          | ::
neg       | -:
not       | ~:
null      | ^:
string    | $:
reciprocal| %:
floor     | _:
..
```

---

**Q Tip 11.1** Return null from update-only functions

---

Returning a null value prevents q from having to reference count the returned value. In addition, when such a function is executed with a call to `each`, returning a null value prevents q from allocating memory to save the result vector. This small change can make a noticeable difference for short functions that are called very often, potentially using a call to `each`. The return value for an event callback function such as `updp` is never used so we do not return anything.

Similarly, the **upd**ate **q**uote `updq` function obtains the most recent price and generates bid and ask prices with the `.sim.tickrnd [113]` function based on the reference data found in the `ref` table. The function then merges the bid and ask prices with the dictionary `q`. Two random quote sizes are also generated and merged using the same technique. Finally, the function inserts the new values into the real-time and historical quote tables. Note that since these functions were defined within the `.md` directory, all global variables referenced by the function are also assumed to be in the `.md` directory. To access the `price(s)`, `quote(s)` and `trade(s)` tables in the root directory, we must indirectly access them through their symbolic names: `` `price `` and `` `quote `` for example.

**.md.updq**

---

```
updq:{[id;tm]
 .log.dbg "updating quote for ", string id;
 px:`price[id; `px];
 r:`ref id;
 q:`id`time!(id;tm);
 q,:`bp`ap!.sim.tickrnd[r `ts] px;
 q,:`bs`as!1+2?r `qs;
 `quote`quotes upsert\: q;
 }
```

The last function, **upd**ate **t**rade updt, uses the .sim.trd [119] function to generate a trade size and price based on the prevailing market bid-offer. After merging the fields with the trade dictionary t, it is inserted into the real-time and historical trade tables.

**.md.updt**

```
updt:{[id;tm]
 if[not id in key `quote;:(::)];
 .log.dbg "updating trade for ", string id;
 q:`quote id;
 t:`id`time!(id;tm);
 t,:`ts`tp!.sim.trd[rand 0b;rand 1f] . q `bs`bp`ap`as;
 `trade`trades upsert\: t;
 }
```

**Q Tip 11.2** Use if statements to exit functions early

The first line of the updt function follows Q Tip 4.5 [43] and limits the if statement to a single line. It returns early if no valid quote is available. Exiting a function early if no further processing can be done is one of the most common uses for the if operator in CEP engines. Remember to maintain a consistent return value when exit a function early. In this case we return the generic null.

## Saving Market Data

To complete the market data library, we need a function that writes the data to disk. If we save the data in a specific format, kdb+ will allow us to re-load the data, along with data from many other days, as an historical database. Kdb+ can save a complete table into a single file, or spread the table's columns across different files. The latter approach allows us to query a subset of columns without having to load the entire table. Saving a table across multiple files is called splaying a table. It is not possible to splay a keyed table, so the dump function must first unkey the price, quote and trade tables before calling the .Q.dpft operator. Once done, the tables are re-keyed.

**.md.dump**

```
dump:{[db;tm]
 dt:"d"$tm;
 .log.inf "dumping tables in ", 1_ string ` sv db,`$string dt;
 0!/:`price`quote`trade;
 .Q.dpft[db;dt;`id] each `price`quote`trade`prices`quotes`trades;
 1!/:`price`quote`trade;
 }
```

The internal `.Q.dpft` operator takes care of generating the proper directory structures and files. As the name of the function indicates, it accepts a **d**irectory, **p**artition, sort **f**ield and **t**able name. Our dump function computes today's date from the current time and calls `.Q.dpft` once for each unkeyed table. The function plays an integral part in the kdb+ tickerplant product. And even though the functions in the `.Q` namespace are not intended for daily use, many of them have become standard operators. More documentation on other useful functions located inside the `.Q` directory can be found in the .Q "unreference" [qunref] [265].

The `.Q.dpft` operator imposes a few restrictions, however. The operator requires us to reference the table by name, so it can save the table to disk with the same name. This prevents us from renaming tables when writing to disk. It also uses the `.Q.en` operator to enumerate any symbol columns. As we will see in Section 15.2 [211], the `.Q.en` operator gives us no choice but to save the enumerations in a file called sym. And finally, each time we use `.Q.dpft` it writes over the old table. When manipulating very large datasets, it is desirable to store more data on disk than fits into memory. To store the data, we must record it in chunks. `.Q.dpft` does not allow this. Working around this limitation requires us to either perform each of `.Q.dpft`'s steps by hand or write a new function that appends to, instead of writing over, the existing data.

## 11.2  Server Sockets

A kdb+ server needs to start and stay running while it listens for events. When started from an interactive terminal, a kdb+ session will continue running while waiting for updates from STDIN. When used as a server, however, STDIN is closed, and the kdb+ process will exit immediately after the last command is executed. To prevent the server from exiting, we must open a server socket.

### Opening a Port

To create a server socket we can either use the −p command line option or open it at run-time using the \p system command. A positive port number starts the process in single threaded mode. Each client connection is serviced sequentially, and modifications to internal data structures are allowed.

**Q Tip 11.3** Use a negative port to make kdb+ read-only

A negative port number, however, puts the server into multi-threaded input queue mode and queries can be handled simultaneously. To ensure high performance, kdb+ does not lock data structures. Allowing multiple simultaneous client queries must therefore require each client to have a read-only view of the data. This can be used to our advantage if we want to prevent clients from modifying our data. One drawback of multi-threaded mode, however, is that views (which will be mentioned in the section called "Declaring a View" [242]) can not recompute within a client query. Doing so would modify the internal state of the server.

To allow the operating system to dynamically allocate the next available port, positive and negative infinity 0W may also be used. We can then use the \p system command to retrieve the allocated port.

```
$ q -p 0W
KDB+ 3.2 2015.03.04 Copyright (C) 1993-2015 Kx Systems
m32/ 4()core 2048MB nick nicks-macbook.local 192.168.1.103 NONEXPIRE
q)system"p"
63366i
```

Once the server socket is open, q will remain running until an explicit call to exit is called, or an external process kills it.

Before starting the main processing of the CEP engine, we need to configure our libraries. We first load the command line options and save the **p**arameter dictionary for future use.

```
p:.opt.getopt[c;`ref`db] .z.x
```

If the -help argument is passed to the process, we can display the usage banner and exit.

```
if[`help in key p;-1 .opt.usage[c;.z.f];exit 1]
```

The exit code of a successful application is 0. To indicate an error, we can call the exit operator with a custom value. In our case, we exit with a return code of 1.

After customizing the log level we check the debug flag and start the application.

```
.log.lvl:p `log
if[not p`debug;main[p;.z.P]]
```

## 11.3   Text Files

Passing arguments on the command line is perfect for controlling the general running behavior of a process. But other parts of the server may require finer grained configuration. In our case, we need to configure each security with different prices, tick spreads, quote sizes, volatilities and risk free rates. Command line arguments are not flexible enough for this. We can configure each security by creating a CSV file and loading it as a kdb+ table.

Q provides a very concise and flexible syntax for loading delimited files.

## Loading Delimited Files as Tables

The 0: operator is used to convert lines of text into a table, and back again. To load a delimited text file as a table we provide a list of conversion types and the delimiter as the left operand, and the file to process as the right.

```
q) ("JSFFJFF*";1#",") 0: `:ref.csv
id sym price tick size quote size volatility rate description
------------------------------------------------------------
0  abc 110   0.05      30         0.35       0.01 "security 0"
1  def 80    0.05      50         0.25       0.01 "security 1"
2  ghi 10    0.01      100        0.12       0.01 "security 2"
3  jkl 5     0.01      300        0.09       0.01 "security 3"
4  mno 2     0.005     1000       0.5        0.01 "security 4"
```

Choosing the types for each column is a fine art. When should you use and 4-byte integer versus an 8-byte long? When is a 4-byte time better than an 8-byte timespan? Should you save prices as 4-byte single precision floats instead of 8-byte double precision floats? Should you save an order ID as character vector or a 16-byte GUID. Each decision has a tradeoff between space and precision.

One of the most subtle decisions that needs to be made is whether to load text as a character vector or symbol. For short identifiers like security tickers that will be repeated multiple times within the system, converting the character vector into a symbol enables text equality tests to be performed with a single pointer comparison. Each instance of the symbol actually references the same location in memory. If, on the other hand, the character vector will be used once, with repetition unlikely and perhaps discarded, converting the character vector to a symbol will actually waste memory. Symbols are stored in a global map and never deleted. Once all references to a character vector are lost, however, the memory is recovered.

---

**Q Tip 11.4** Load descriptive text as character vectors, identifiers as symbols

---

A security's description is a good example where character vectors should be used (and thus the use of the "*" character to load the field). In our case, we have no need for symbols, or the description. We can change the list of types to skip the field by using a space " ", and stop loading columns before reading the description column by leaving off the last type.

```
q) ("J FFJFF";1#",") 0: `:ref.csv
id price tick size quote size volatility rate
---------------------------------------------
```

```
0   110    0.05     30      0.35     0.01
1   80     0.05     50      0.25     0.01
2   10     0.01     100     0.12     0.01
3   5      0.01     300     0.09     0.01
4   2      0.005    1000    0.5      0.01
```

**Q Tip 11.5** Only load desired columns from text files

Each column loaded from a text file must be cast to a specific data type. For large files, this can add a large amount of memory and processing time. If there are columns that will ultimately be thrown away, it is better to prevent them from being parsed to begin with. Using a space character " " informs q to skip the column altogether. Any columns that occur after the defined set will also be ignored.

**Q Tip 11.6** Use boolean and character types for increased efficiency

It is easy to use 8-byte integers, 8-byte floats, symbols, dates, and timespans for loading all types of data. We can not go wrong by using too much memory. But using the correct type will save disk space and make computations faster. The boolean type "B" can be used to import a column of 0s and 1s (and even y/Ys and n/Ns). And if a column of data will only be a single character long, importing the values as the characters type "c" will allow us to perform fast equality comparisons.

## Column Names

Often, we do not control how columns are named within text files. While there is no technical restriction on how columns can be named, they must obey variable naming conventions if we want to access them with q-SQL. Column names with spaces, leading numbers or non alphanumeric characters will not be accessible with q-SQL. Columns with names that match q operators will cause trouble as well. This is a common problem with columns called `group`, `type`, `div` and those named after statistical computations such as `min`, `max`, `med`, `avg`, `sdev`, `svar`. One option is to specifically rename each column.

**Q Tip 11.7** Use `.Q.id` to ensure column names are q-SQL compliant

Conflicting column names is such a common problem that kdb+ has created an internal function `.Q.id` to make column names q-SQL compliant. Not only does it remove characters that trip up the q-SQL parser, it also appends a 1 after any column name that happen to match any q operator name.

Neither of the following columns can be queried with q-SQL.

```
q) enlist (`$"pct%"; `div)!"ff"$\:()
pct% div
-------- 
```

Using `.Q.id` fixes this.

```
q).Q.id  enlist  (`$"pct%";`div)!"ff"$\:()
pct div1
--------
```

In our case, some column names have spaces and must be renamed. We can do this ourselves with the `xcol` operator.

```
q)show t:`id`px`ts`qs`vol`rfr xcol("J FFJFF";1#",") 0: `:ref.csv
id px  ts    qs   vol  rfr
--------------------------------
0  110 0.05  30   0.35 0.01
1  80  0.05  50   0.25 0.01
2  10  0.01  100  0.12 0.01
3  5   0.01  300  0.09 0.01
4  2   0.005 1000 0.5  0.01
```

We do not have to rename all the columns. But those we do rename must be at the front of the table. There is no operator to rename columns in the middle of the table, but we can implement this ourselves.

### .util.mapcol

```
mapcol:{[d;t](c^d c:cols t) xcol t}
```

The `mapcol` function accepts a dictionary as its first argument and a table as its second. The dictionary maps a set of existing column names to new column names. The function starts by obtaining the existing column names with the `cols` operator and saves them into a variable `c`. It then indexes into the dictionary to find the new column names. Any column that does not exist in the dictionary will now be null. To fix this, we use the old column names stored in `c` to fill the list before renaming the table's columns with the `xcol` operator.

```
q)t:("J FFJFF";1#",") 0: `:ref.csv
q).util.mapcol[(`$("tick size";"quote size"))!`ts`qs] t
id price ts    qs   volatility rate
------------------------------------------
0  110   0.05  30   0.35       0.01
1  80    0.05  50   0.25       0.01
2  10    0.01  100  0.12       0.01
3  5     0.01  300  0.09       0.01
4  2     0.005 1000 0.5        0.01
```

## Saving Tables as Delimited Files

The `0:` operator can also convert tables to text. Passing the delimiter (which can be any character we want including a tab `"\t"`) as the left operand and the table as the right, creates a list of character vectors ready to be written to disk.

```
q)"\t" 0: t
"id\tpx\tts\tqs\tvol\trfr"
"0\t110\t0.05\t30\t0.35\t0.01"
"1\t80\t0.05\t50\t0.25\t0.01"
"2\t10\t0.01\t100\t0.12\t0.01"
"3\t5\t0.01\t300\t0.09\t0.01"
"4\t2\t0.005\t1000\t0.5\t0.01"
```

To save the file to disk, we use the 0: operator, yet again.

```
`:ref.txt 0: "\t" 0: t
```

## Loading Data Without Column Names

It is also common to find text files without column headers. We can create a tab delimited text file without row headers by dropping the first row of the list of character vectors before saving the data to disk.

```
q)`:ref.txt 0: 1_"\t" 0: t
```

The read0 operator allows us to load a file as a list of character vectors, having been split on new lines.

```
q)read0 `:ref.txt
"0\t110\t0.05\t30\t0.35\t0.01"
"1\t80\t0.05\t50\t0.25\t0.01"
"2\t10\t0.01\t100\t0.12\t0.01"
"3\t5\t0.01\t300\t0.09\t0.01"
"4\t2\t0.005\t1000\t0.5\t0.01"
```

Even though the file has no column headers, it is still possible to load the data into a table. We can use the 0: operator again, but must change the syntax slightly. Instead of using a character vector with a single element, we need to pass a single character as the second element of the right operand. Q will parse the file and return a list of properly parsed lists, but without column headers.

```
q)("JFFJFF";"\t") 0: `:ref.txt
0    1    2    3    4
110  80   10   5    2
0.05 0.05 0.01 0.01 0.005
30   50   100  300  1000
0.35 0.25 0.12 0.09 0.5
0.01 0.01 0.01 0.01 0.01
```

To convert the lists into a table, we can create a dictionary of lists and flip the result.

```
q)flip `id`px`ts`qs`vol`rfr!("JFFJFF";"\t") 0: `:ref.txt
id px ts    qs    vol  rfr
--------------------------------
0  110 0.05  30    0.35 0.01
1  80  0.05  50    0.25 0.01
2  10  0.01  100   0.12 0.01
3  5   0.01  300   0.09 0.01
4  2   0.005 1000  0.5  0.01
```

## 11.4 Pulling it All Together

We have covered all the material needed to run the CEP engine. Our final task is to connect all the pieces. The last line of cep.q calls the main function. Its job is to load reference data and add the timers for updating the price, quote, and trade tables, as well as dumping the data at the end of day.

**main**

```
main:{[p;tm]
 r:("J FFJFF";1#",") 0: p`ref;
 `ref upsert `id`px`ts`qs`vol`rfr xcol r;
 `price upsert flip ((0!ref)`id`px),tm;
 tms:(n:count ids:key[ref]`id)#tm;
 u:genu[p`eod;ids];
 .timer.add[`timer.job; `updp;u[d:n?0D00:00:01; `.md.updp];tms];
 .timer.add[`timer.job; `updq;u[d+:n?0D00:00:01; `.md.updq];tms];
 .timer.add[`timer.job; `updt;u[d+:n?0D00:00:01; `.md.updt];tms];
 .timer.add[`timer.job; `dump;(`.md.dump;p`db);p[`eod]+"d"$tm];
 }
```

---

**Q Tip 11.8** Initialize programs and libraries with a function call

---

Q does not force us to put all of a program's runnable code inside a single function called main. But doing so makes for easy debugging. Passing a "-debug 1" command line argument to our CEP engine will load all the server's code without starting the engine. We can then inspect the server and/or execute our own code. Similarly, .q libraries files should not initialize data structures by default. Initialization should be encapsulated within a function. This allows the library user to initialize, or even re-initialize, the library when wanted or needed.

### Initializing Values

The main function starts by loading the reference data from a configuration file.

```
q) ("J FFJFF";1#",") 0: p `ref
id price tick size quote size volatility rate
----------------------------------------------
0  110   0.05      30         0.35        0.01
1  80    0.05      50         0.25        0.01
2  10    0.01      100        0.12        0.01
3  5     0.01      300        0.09        0.01
4  2     0.005     1000       0.5         0.01
```

It then loads the ID, price and current time into the `price` table. These will be used as initial values for the market data server price path.

```
q) `price upsert flip ((0!ref)`id`px),tm;
q)price
id| px  time
--| ------------------------------------
0 | 110 2015.03.06D12:48:52.761120000
1 | 80  2015.03.06D12:48:52.761120000
2 | 10  2015.03.06D12:48:52.761120000
3 | 5   2015.03.06D12:48:52.761120000
4 | 2   2015.03.06D12:48:52.761120000
```

The remaining lines of the `main` [149] function add the `.md.updp` [140], `.md.updq` [141], and `.md.updt` [142] events to the timer. We need to call `.timer.add` [126] with a list of times in order to add multiple items to the timer simultaneously. The fourth line of `main` saves the list of ids into `id`, the number of ids into `n` and a list of times into `tms`. Each of these variables are needed for the calls to `.timer.add` [126].

The utility function `genu` builds the multi-dimensional list needed to call `.timer.until` [129].

**genu**

```
genu:{[et;ids;d;f]flip(`.timer.until;d;et;flip(f;ids))}
```

We can see how it generates a list of parameters.

```
q)genu[0D23:59;0 1;1 2+00:01;`.md.updp]
`.timer.until 00:02 0D23:59:00.000000000 (`.md.updp;0)
`.timer.until 00:03 0D23:59:00.000000000 (`.md.updp;1)
```

The end time and the list of ids never changes, so we can create a projection u that can be reused for each call to `.timer.add` [126].

```
 u:genu[p`eod;ids];
```

## Adding Timer Events

We can then add timer events for each stage of the transformation from price to trade. We generate a random delay between calculations for each `id`. And the delay in each stage of the calculation (price, quote and trade), gets progressively longer.

```
.timer.add[`timer.job; `updp;u[d:n?0D00:00:01; `.md.updp];tms];
.timer.add[`timer.job; `updq;u[d+:n?0D00:00:01; `.md.updq];tms];
.timer.add[`timer.job; `updt;u[d+:n?0D00:00:01; `.md.updt];tms];
```

The last line of the function creates a single timer event to save all data to disk.

```
.timer.add[`timer.job; `dump;(`.md.dump;p`db);p[`eod]+"d"$tm];
```

To create the `datetime` needed for the end of day timer, we add the end of day `timespan` supplied on the command line,

```
q)p`eod
0D23:59:00.000000000
```

to the `date` obtained by casting the current time.

```
"d"$tm
```

We could have used the `.z.D` system variable to obtain the current day, but it is better to use the passed-in parameter to permit flexibility.

---

**Q Tip 11.9** Pass event dates and times as parameters

---

One of the main goals of recording market data is to reuse it later for analysis or backtesting. Time is often an input to calculations. But to be useful in simulation it is important that the functions obtain the time as a parameter instead of using system variables. Declaring the time parameter as the last parameter to a function allows a projection of the function to be used with the timer utility as well. When used in a CEP engine, the function will obtain the time from the timer. And when used in simulation, the time can be generated from market data.

## Stopping the Engine

We have finished all the coding necessary to start the market data CEP engine. But before we turn it on, it is important to know how to stop it. Once we start the engine, it will continuously generate prices, quotes and trades. Each update is being saved into an unkeyed table, slowly increasing the memory consumption of the `kdb+` process. Left unchecked, this will grow and has the potential of consuming more memory than exists on your computer. At some point, this will render your computer inaccessible. We have two choices to prevent this. The first is to turn the timer off.

```
q)\t 0
```

**Q Tip 11.10** Always start q with a memory limit

The second option is to place a limit on the memory available to the q process. Once this limit is reached, the process will die with a `wsfull error indicating that the **w**orkspace is **full**. This allows us to keep collecting data, while still protecting the machine from accidentally allocating too much memory. The − w command line option allows us to specify the maximum memory in megabytes. For example, we can limit the process memory to 200MB.

```
$ q -w 200
```

We will end the chapter by starting the CEP engine with a timer that runs every 100 ms on port 5001. It has a custom end of day dump time and directory to save the data.

```
$ q cep.q -w 200 -t 100 -p 5001 -eod 16:00 -db qdb
```

A lot of work goes in to creating a stable CEP engine. But the features that make the language so easy to develop in, also make it insecure. Once the CEP engine has been started with a server socket, any client connecting to the engine has full read and write access. Our attention must turn to securing the server against unauthorized access. The next chapter discusses the callbacks that kdb+ provides for us to customize the default security model and client connection handling.

# Chapter 12

# Security

> Don't call us, we'll call you.
>
> — The Hollywood Principle

Kdb+ achieves its simplicity and efficiency by relying on the file system for many of its features. Similarly, a large amount of security can be achieved by using the operating system's user/group permissions to enable and disable data access. This security model is valid for disk-based data access. But anyone connecting to a running kdb+ process has full read and write access to its data. This includes any data on the file system accessible by the server. Now that we have started our CEP engine, we need to worry about who connects to the process, and what they can see and/or modify. Continuing along its focus on simplicity, kdb+ provides facilities for authentication, but leaves authorization to us.

In addition to providing facilities to authenticate by username and password, kdb+ allows us to customize its behavior at each stage of the connection life cycle. From initial login and port opening, through each client query, and finally to connection shutdown, kdb+ allows us to change its behavior by executing our callbacks. Callback (or event) based programming reverses the standard program flow. Instead of continuously checking the state of each client connection, kdb+ acts like a Hollywood producer and calls us when the state has changed.

## 12.1   Username and Password

All communication with a kdb+ server begins with authentication. A username and password are sent (in clear text) during the initial handshake with clients. It is, of course, valid to pass an empty character vector for both of these parameters. It is up to the server to decide if the values are acceptable to allow further communication. The values are ignored by default, but can be checked by starting the q session with a −u flag followed by the name of a file that contains a list of colon delimited usernames and passwords. The password can either be in clear text or encoded with the md5 hashing function. We can use q to append an entry into the password file for user "nick" and password "qtips".

```
q)h:hopen`:../psswd.txt
q)neg[h] 0N!"nick:",raze string md5 "qtips"
"nick:72fcf42466c7b4e7ae7ad6e25bbf3ae9"
-4i
q)hclose h
```

The first line uses the hopen operator to open the file ../psswd.txt for writing and saves the file handle in the variable h. It then converts the password "qtips" into a hashed byte vector with the md5 operator. After converting it into a character vector and joining it with the username "nick" it appends the text to the file by indexing into the file handle h. In this case, we used a negative file handle so q adds the trailing newline. For completeness, we then close the file handle. We can now restart the kdb+ process and limit client connections to only those users who connect with a known username and password.

```
$ q -u ../psswd.txt -p 5001
```

The hopen operator can accept either an integer port for connections on the localhost, or a handle matching the following pattern.

```
`:[server]:[port][:user[:password]]
```

All parameters are optional but there must be a minimum of two colons. Leaving all parameters blank will cause the kdb+ process to open a connection to port 0. If the q process has not opened a server socket with the −p command line argument or the \p system command, the resulting network handle will be 0, and can be used as if it was a connection to a separate process. The only difference is that asynchronous communication is not possible.

```
q)hopen `::
0i
```

If both client and server are running on the same host, we can leave the server blank, but must include the port.

```
q)hopen `::5001
'access
```

We were unable to connect in both of these cases because we did not specify the username and password. To properly gain access to the server, we must provide the correct username and password.

```
q)hopen `::5001:nick:qtips
4i
```

It is also possible to supply a connection timeout by passing a two element list: with the connection symbol as the first element and the timeout in milliseconds as the second.

```
q) hopen (`::5001:nick:qtips;100)
4i
```

If the password file could be modified from within q, the security of the process would be compromised. To prevent this, the -u command line argument also limits file modification to only those files below the starting directory. It is thus a good policy to place the password file above the working directory of the kdb+ server. Q allows you to throw caution to the wind and disable this restriction by using the -U command line argument instead.

After q performs the optional file based authentication, it triggers two events which allow further authentication customization. First, the **authentication cookie** .z.ac event allows us to use corporate *single sign-on* infrastructure to permission a client based on an HTTP cookie. This callback is only called when HTTP requests are made. If this event is not customized, or if a longer lasting TCP socket connection is established, the **password** .z.pw event is called with two arguments: the username (passed as a symbol) and the password (passed as a character vector). We can customize this method to return the boolean value 1b if the user is allowed access. We can, for example, redefine the event to reject all access to "nick" regardless of the contents of psswd.txt.

```
q) .z.pw:{[u;p] not `nick=u}
```

Providing these callbacks allows us to implement any form of authentication we desire. It is also possible to embed all communication within an SSH tunnel. This is important because the username and password are sent in plain text.

## 12.2 Connection Attributes

Once the client has been authenticated, the connection is considered open, and the **port open event** .z.po is called with the new network handle. This event is useful for querying and storing client attributes. Many global variables which are normally set to local values, are redefined to provide relevant information about the client. For example, instead of providing information about my machine, the following variables would allow inspection of the client's connection.

```
q) .z.u
`nick
q) .z.a
-1062731412i
q) .z.w
0i
```

The **username** .z.u is only as valid as the security used to validate it. The **address** .z.a is obtained from the network connection, and **who** operator .z.w provides the network handle used to communicate with the client. This is also passed as an argument to the .z.po event.

The address in its raw form may be unfamiliar to most. It is actually just the integer representation of the four byte TCP/IP address. To obtain the commonly used decimal representation of the IP address we must split the integer into four bytes, and then cast them into short integers.

```
q)"h"$0x0 vs .z.a
192 168 1 5h
```

Alternatively, we can use the `.Q.host` operator to convert the address from an integer to the host name.

```
q).Q.host .z.a
`nicks-macbook.local
```

It is useful to store these client attributes when the client initially connects. We can create a table and modify the `.z.po` callback to populate it.

```
handle:.util.sattr 1!flip `h`active`user`host`address`time!"ibss*p"$\:()
.z.po:{[h]`handle upsert (h;1b;.z.u;.Q.host .z.a;"i"$0x0 vs .z.a;.z.P);}
```

The `.z.po` callback is never called for the handle `0i`. To record the hostname and IP address of the current process, we can need to call it ourselves.

```
q).z.po 0i
q)handle
h| active user host                address     time
-| -----------------------------------------------------------------------
0| 1         nick nicks-macbook.local 192 168 1 5 2015.03.06D10:51:29.578256000
```

---

**Q Tip 12.1** Use boolean flags instead of deleting rows

---

We include a `time` column to record when the connection was established. In addition, we keep an `active` column to indicate if the connection has been subsequently closed. The active flag allows us to record that the connection no longer exists without having to delete rows. Kdb+ is optimized for data insertion, and not deletion. Since columns are stored in contiguous memory, values deleted from any place other than the end must result in data being copied to a new memory location. In addition, deleting rows from a table clears all attributes from the columns. Including a boolean `active` column allows us to invalidate specific rows without having to move memory or invalidate attributes.

We can update the value of the `active` flag by redefining the **p**ort **c**lose `.z.pc` event. To update only the `active` and `time` columns the `.z.pc` event must upsert a dictionary instead of a list of values. This allows us to specify which columns need to be updated.

```
.z.pc:{[h]`handle upsert `handle`active`time!(h;0b;.z.P);}
```

To test the event handling, we can open and close a connection from a separate q session.

```
q)hclose hopen `::5001
```

The `handle` table now has an inactive connection.

```
q)handle
handle| active user host          address   time
------|  ------------------------------------------------------------
4     | 0          nick nicks-macbook 127 0 0 1 2015.03.06D13:45:26.561484000
```

When building a server that accepts client connections, it is useful to log all client activity. The logging library was designed to allow its header to be customized. We can modify the `.log.hdr` [132] function to include more descriptive client information. Instead of just including the date and time, we can change the header to include the user, handle, and host as well.

```
\d .log
hdr:{string[(.z.D;.z.T;.z.u;.z.w;.Q.host .z.a)],mem get"\\w"}
```

When logging the active q session, the results are not surprising.

```
q).log.inf "test"
2015.03.06 20:31:38.604 nick 0 nicks-macbook 0 64 192M [I] test
```

But when a client connects and executes a query, the logs will indicate the client information.

## 12.3  Finer Grained Event Handling

Between the time the client connection is established and closed, queries can arrive in different formats. Some are synchronous and expect immediate responses: native kdb+ **port get** `.z.pg`, HTTP **port post** `.z.pp`, and **port http get** `.z.ph`. Others are asynchronous and discard all return values: native **port set** `.z.ps` and **web socket set** `.z.ws`. It is possible to intercept each of these events and customize their access. To start with, you might want to log each access request to see who is accessing your server.

Asynchronous communication is used when responses are not needed immediately and the full context in which the initial request was made is encoded in the response. If the response to an asynchronous message is not initiated immediately from within the callback, it is mandatory to record the client's network handle found in `.z.w` in a variable that can be referred to later when the response is ready to be delivered.

Messages that are sent over network handles are serialized for network transportation. Upon receipt, the messages are then deserialized. This happens on all network handles, except the internal handle 0.

It is possible to see how these messages are actually serialized with the $-8!$ operator.

```
q)-8!`qtips
0x010000000f000000f5717469707300
```

The $-9!$ operator performs the deserialization.

```
q)-9!0x010000000f000000f5717469707300
'qtips
```

If an error is encountered during deserialization, a `` `badmsg `` error is thrown.

```
q)-9!0x010000000f000000f5717469707301
'badmsg
```

To help debug ill-formed network messages, `kdb+` allows us to customize the **bad message** `.z.bm` callback. Prior to printing the `` `badmsg `` error, `.z.bm` is called with the bad byte vector. You can print the vector or save it for future inspection.

During the processing of client queries, whether from STDIN, or from a client handle, there is a possibility that a global variable is modified. When such an event occurs, the **value set** `.z.vs` event is triggered. The event is passed two parameters: the name of the modified variable as well as a list of indices that were modified. In the case of a full assignment, as opposed to a partial amend, the second parameter is passed the empty list `()`. The `.z.vs` event can be used for debugging and logging variable modifications.

Before a `kdb+` process **exit**s, the `.z.exit` event is triggered. This provides one last chance for a process to cleanup. The `kdb+` process may exit due to any number of reasons. If the process ran out of memory, it will not be possible to allocate any more memory in the `.z.exit` event either. For this reason, the complexity of this event should be kept to a minimum. In fact, it is always possible to externally kill the `kdb+` process without giving q the ability to call this event. You should therefore not rely on this event to be called before every exit.

No matter how hard we have worked to write robust code, the moment we move code from our home directory into a testing or production environment, there will invariably be scenarios we have not predicted. Q will throw an exception, or the published data will be invalid, and we will then need to debug the problem. This is especially true when a CEP engine handles free-form client requests. The next chapter explains the debugging environment and demonstrates ways we can use it to step through functions.

# Chapter 13

# Debugging

Everyone knows that debugging is twice as hard as writing a program in the first place. So if you're as clever as you can be when you write it, how will you ever debug it?

— Brian Kernighan *The Elements of Programming Style (2nd Edition)*

Q developers continuously optimize their code. After a few rounds of optimization, even the smartest developer may have trouble debugging their own code. Adding extra print statements is not the only way to debug q. The chapter begins by demonstrating the q debugging interface. It then shows how to debug errors resulting from client queries. And finally, the chapter concludes by giving an example of conditional "breakpoints" can be used to inspect the local state of a function.

## 13.1 The Debugging Interface

Once we have started the CEP engine, and clients begin querying the server, we will invariably encounter errors. When errors are generated from the q command line, a debugging session is started. The debugging session allows us to inspect the local variables, stop execution, and continue execution with a specific return value.

For instance, if we attempt to find how many times 0 can be divided by `` `a ``, q throws an exception and enters a debugging session.

```
q)0 mod `a
k){x-y*x div y}
'type
*
`a
```

```
0
q.q))
```

The first line of the error displays the function receiving the error. The next line displays the error itself. This is followed by the function that caused the error and all of its arguments.

The prompt has changed to have the namespace the function was defined in (in the case .q) and another closing parentheses. If we cause yet another error, we would enter a second level of debugging, and another closing parentheses would appear.

While in the debugging session, we can inspect all the local variables to see what may have caused the problem. If the offending function has multiple execution blocks, we can rerun them, one by one, to see which block threw the error.

---

**Q Tip 13.1** Function variables default to the empty list in the debugger

---

All local variables are initialized to the empty list (). We can determine how far a function progressed before throwing the exception by checking which variables still have the default value and which have been successfully re-assigned.

If the function that threw the error was a few calls deep in the stack, we may want to debug the function one level above. To rise one level in the stack, we can use the "′" command. If however, we prefer to let the code continue by providing a valid return value, we can exit the function by entering a colon ":" optionally followed by the desired return value.

```
q.q)):0
0
```

Typically, though, there is something wrong with our code, and it needs to be fixed. Continuing execution with a correct value, does not fix that problem. Once we have determined the problem, the best thing to do would be to exit the debugging session. As mentioned in the section called "Single Backslash" [12], a single backslash will exit one level of debugging.

```
q.q))\
q)
```

## 13.2  Trapping Errors

There are cases where the process causing the error is another q instance or even a compiled library interfacing with the running q process. In either of these two cases, the error message is printed, but the debugging session is not initiated. To trap these errors for debugging, we must turn on the error trapping flag with the \e system command.

To demonstrate its use, we can set q's internal timer to wake up every 5 seconds and define the timer callback to be an invalid function.

```
q)\t 5000
q).z.ts:{0 mod `a}
q)'type
div
0
`a
```

In this case, the error is printed, but the debugging session is not started. After we enter \e 1, the next occurrence of the error immediately enters the debugging session.

```
q)\e 1
q)k){x-y*x div y}
'type
div
0
`a
q.q))
```

Once we have determined the error, it is important to reset the system variable so the debugging session is not initiated with every error. This can be done with \e 0.

## 13.3  Breakpoints

There are times when bugs in the code do not signal an exception, but in fact return null values or empty lists. The q debugging environment does not allow us to step through each line of the code checking the local variables along the way.

**Q Tip 13.2** Use breakpoints to debug functions

But we can use q's ability to dynamically redefine functions to our advantage. If we define a function and purposefully insert an unknown variable name, the debugging session will automatically start the next time the undefined variable is accessed.

```
q)f:{break;x+y}
```

With this breakpoint in place, we can then inspect each of the local variables.

```
q)f[1;2]
{break;x+y}
'break
q))x
1
q))y
2
```

Sometimes invalid values only occur under special conditions. For these cases, we can create condition breakpoints. By placing the undefined variable inside an appropriately constructed `if` block, we can force q to only enter the debugging session when our special condition is met. In this example, we only trigger the breakpoint when x is null.

```
q)f:{if[null x;break];x+y}
```

The function works as expected when called with proper parameters.

```
q)f[1;2]
3
```

But a null value will trigger the debugging session so we can inspect the other parameters.

```
q)f[0N;2]
{if[null x;break];x+y}
'break
q))y
2
```

We have now developed a fully functioning CEP server, and discussed how to secure and debug it. In the process, we have not used a single line of q-SQL. But q-SQL is arguably one of q's most popular features. Functionally, there is nothing that q-SQL provides that can not be done with q. But q-SQL offers a familiar syntax and optimizations for querying large datasets. We now transition from the CEP engine which manipulates small datasets, to q-SQL which is best for very large datasets.

# Chapter 14

# Q-SQL

> Relational processing entails treating whole relationships as operands. Its primary purpose is loop-avoidance, an absolute requirement for end users to be productive at all, and a clear productivity booster for application programmers.
>
> — E. F. Cod *Relational Database: A Practical Foundation for Productivity (1982)*

SQL is popular because it provides a standard syntax for filtering, sorting, grouping, and joining data. While q-SQL does not conform to common SQL standards, it is similar enough to be easily learned. Many operations available in q-SQL can also be done with q operators. But it is much easier to type, read, and maintain code that is written in q-SQL. In addition, since q-SQL syntax is quite strict, q can use a combination of lookaheads and parallelism to optimize queries on large datasets.

## 14.1   Syntax

Q-SQL syntax differs slightly from standard SQL, but has all the standard features. We can sort, select, update and delete rows. We can filter, aggregate and group queries. We can create indexes that are sorted, unique or partitioned. And we can even create views and add, drop, and join tables.

But the real benefit of using q-SQL relies on the fact that we are not limited to standard SQL functions. We can use any q or user defined function to manipulate datasets. And because q has been optimized for array processing, performing database queries is very fast. But to use q-SQL efficiently, it is important to understand the underlying vector nature of kdb+. Understanding how a complete CEP engine can be written without any q-SQL should arm you with the necessary knowledge to integrate efficient user defined functions with concise q-SQL.

## Select

Whether you generate data yourself, load it from disk with the `\l` system command, or connect to a running `kdb+` server, the first thing you will need to do is narrow the set of columns in the dataset to only those you need.  Carrying around extra columns is a common cause of poor query performance. Let's create a dataset to begin our example.

```
q)dts:.util.rng[1;2000.01.01;2005.01.01]
q)show t:raze .sim.genp[;100;.3;.03;dts] each til 10
id date       price
--------------------
0  2000.01.01 100
0  2000.01.02 100.0632
0  2000.01.03 100.122
0  2000.01.04 99.74749
0  2000.01.05 98.30914
..
```

Using the `select` statement, we can create a new table with only the columns we request. The simplest query is to select all the columns. If we do not specify which columns to select, `q` will return them all.

```
q)select from t
id date       price
--------------------
0  2000.01.01 100
0  2000.01.02 100.0632
0  2000.01.03 100.122
0  2000.01.04 99.74749
0  2000.01.05 98.30914
..
```

To select a subset of columns, we can provide a comma separated list of column names after the `select` statement.

```
q)select id,date,price from t
id date       price
--------------------
0  2000.01.01 100
0  2000.01.02 100.0632
0  2000.01.03 100.122
0  2000.01.04 99.74749
0  2000.01.05 98.30914
..
```

We can even rename columns in our selection.

```
q)select id,date,px:price from t
```

```
id date       px
--------------------
0  2000.01.01 100
0  2000.01.02 100.0632
0  2000.01.03 100.122
0  2000.01.04 99.74749
0  2000.01.05 98.30914
..
```

To create the new columns we used a colon ":" just as we would have done when assigning a new variable in q. It is important to realize that even though we created a new table by selecting data from t, we did not actually make a full copy of the data. Kdb+ is a *column* oriented database, and as such, columns are contiguous blocks of memory that can be passed as references.

**Q Tip 14.1** Conservatively query table columns

A reference to a column is kept until the data is modified. When this occurs, q creates a full copy of the data. It is therefore important to limit the number of columns queried from a table to only those that we need.

In addition to selecting existing columns, we can generate new columns that are derived from data already existing in the current table. For example, we can round the price column to the nearest cent.

```
select id,date,.util.rnd[.01] price from t
id date       price
--------------------
0  2000.01.01 100
0  2000.01.02 100.06
0  2000.01.03 100.12
0  2000.01.04 99.75
0  2000.01.05 98.31
..
```

Notice how I did not provide a column name to the rounded price. Kdb+ infers the column name based on the order of the arguments. This is an important technique in making q-SQL more succinct and therefore readable. This is discussed in more detail in Q Tip 17.1 [241].

## Where

In addition to limiting the columns in our table, we can also limit the rows. The where operator achieves this by evaluating a conditional statement and only returning the rows where the condition evaluates to true. For example, we can select only those rows for the month of February 2000.

```
q)select from t where date.month = 2000.02m
id date       price
```

```
--------------------------
0   2000.02.01 100.2401
0   2000.02.02 102.6694
0   2000.02.03 101.7217
0   2000.02.04 100.5921
0   2000.02.05 98.9701
..
```

We can include multiple `where` clauses by separating them with a comma ",".

```
q)select from t where id = 1,date.month = 2000.02m
id date        price
--------------------------
1   2000.02.01 103.147
1   2000.02.02 103.1715
1   2000.02.03 104.0317
1   2000.02.04 105.79
1   2000.02.05 107.4212
..
```

---

**Q Tip 14.2** Apply the fastest and most restrictive `where` clauses first

---

It is important to note that even though each `where` clause is evaluated from right to left, the clauses themselves, separated by commas, are each applied from left to right. In addition, only the rows that are selected by the first clause are passed for evaluation to the second clause and so on. Subsequent conditions are only applied to rows that pass all prior conditions. It is therefore important to order your `where` clauses properly. Placing the most restrictive clause first ensures that the remaining clauses have fewer rows to operate on. It is also better to place simple and efficient conditions first, and leave computationally intensive conditions for the end. This limits the number rows that the inefficient condition must be applied to.

Using the comma separator "," is similar to using the `and` operator. The `and` operator, however, must evaluate both sets of conditions to find the rows where both sets evaluate to true. Using the `and` operator loses the short-circuit features of ",". The following query returns the same results but is less efficient. Notice also that we must use parentheses to force the order of operations we desire.

```
q)select from t where (id = 1) and date.month = 2000.02m
id date        price
--------------------------
1   2000.02.01 103.147
1   2000.02.02 103.1715
1   2000.02.03 104.0317
1   2000.02.04 105.79
1   2000.02.05 107.4212
..
```

In contrast, there is no short-circuit syntax for queries looking for rows that match either one condition `or` another. In this case, both conditions must be evaluated in-full. Again, we must use parentheses to prevent q's right to left parsing from misinterpreting our request. To find rows that are for either ID = 1 or for days in February 2000, we can perform the following query.

```
q)select from t where (id = 1) or date.month = 2000.02m
id date       price
--------------------
0  2000.02.01 100.2401
0  2000.02.02 102.6694
0  2000.02.03 101.7217
0  2000.02.04 100.5921
0  2000.02.05 98.9701
..
```

**Q Tip 14.3** Use De Morgan's Laws to optimize `where` clauses

This is where some knowledge of boolean algebra can help. If we rearrange De Morgan's Laws[1], which state that `not(A or B)` is the same as `not(A) and not(B)`, we find that `A or B` is the same as `not(not(A) and not(B))`. Instead of selecting rows that match a series of `or` conditions, we can delete rows that do not match a series of `where` clauses.

## Delete

An inefficient `or` statement can be easily converted to use a comma by negating each of the conditions and replacing the `select` statement with `delete`. To obtain rows that are for either ID = 1 or for days in February, we can delete rows that are not for ID = 1 and not in February.

```
q)delete from t where not id = 1, not date.month = 2000.02m
id date       price
--------------------
0  2000.02.01 100.2401
0  2000.02.02 102.6694
0  2000.02.03 101.7217
0  2000.02.04 100.5921
0  2000.02.05 98.9701
..
```

There are cases, however, when blindly applying De Morgan's Laws produces different results. Since `kdb+` filters the results following each comma delimited condition, it is possible to construct `where` clauses that violate the conditions under which De Morgan's Laws apply. If a condition relies on the results of a uniform or aggregate function, it must be placed as the first `where` clause. All remaining

---

[1] http://en.wikipedia.org/wiki/De_Morgan's_laws

clauses should only use atomic functions. If a second condition uses uniform or aggregate functions, the resulting table will not match the original query.

It is therefore important to ensure the results of these different approaches are exactly the same. A naive solution would be to test for equality.

```
q)a:select from t where (id = 1) or date.month = 2000.02m
q)b:delete from t where not id = 1, not date.month = 2000.02m
q)a=b
id date price
-------------
1  1    1
1  1    1
1  1    1
1  1    1
1  1    1
..
```

But this provides a cell by cell comparison. To determine if the whole table is exactly equal, we can use the match operator "~".

```
q)a~b
1b
```

The `delete` statement can also be used to remove columns from a table.

```
q)delete id from t
date       price
-----------------
2000.01.01 100
2000.01.02 100.0632
2000.01.03 100.122
2000.01.04 99.74749
2000.01.05 98.30914
..
```

But unlike the `select` statements, we can not issue a `delete` statement with both columns and rows specified.

```
q)delete id from t where date.month=2000.02m
'nyi
```

This is the first time we have seen the `nyi error. No doubt you will see it many more times. It stands for **n**ot **y**et **i**mplemented and indicates that the implementation is in some way controversial. Until a dominant use case has been determined, it will not be implemented. In this case, it is not clear what should be done when attempting to delete a few cells from a table. Specifying both columns and row conditions in a `select` statement always returns a table as its result. But what would deleting data from specific rows and columns return? Would it return a list of dictionaries where some dictionaries had fields removed? Or would it return a table with those specific fields nulled out? The answer is not clear. Returning a list of dictionaries would explode the amount of memory taken by the data structure, and its usefulness questionable. On the other hand, if we wanted the fields to be null, we could achieve the same result with the `update` statement. Both proposals fail to provide a convincing reason for implementation.

## Update

While the `select` and `delete` statements are typically used for reducing the number of columns in a table, the `update` statement can be used to modify values or add new columns. Instead of selecting the ID, date and rounded price columns, we could have just rounded the prices.

```
q) update .util.rnd[.01] price from t
id date        price
--------------------
0  2000.01.01 100
0  2000.01.02 100.06
0  2000.01.03 100.12
0  2000.01.04 99.75
0  2000.01.05 98.31
..
```

The tables we have generated have all been stored in memory. Later we will discuss ways to persist them to disk. This will provide more flexibility when querying large datasets. But it will also limit our ability to modify the data. Querying data from disk can only be done with the `select` statement. Both `delete` and `update` will not work. To actually change data on disk, we will need to `select` the data into memory, modify the data, then save it to disk again. We will discuss different ways of saving data to disk in Chapter 15 [201].

## By

The real power of q-SQL comes when we combine `select`, `delete` and `update` statements with the `by` clause. By themselves, `select`, `delete`, `update` and `where` are simple transformations that do not actually simplify standard q syntax very much. We can, for example, select columns,

```
q) `id`date#t
id date
-------------
0  2000.01.01
0  2000.01.02
0  2000.01.03
0  2000.01.04
0  2000.01.05
..
```

filter the rows,

```
q)t where 2000.02m="m"$t `date
id date       price
--------------------
0  2000.02.01 100.2401
0  2000.02.02 102.6694
0  2000.02.03 101.7217
0  2000.02.04 100.5921
0  2000.02.05 98.9701
..
```

and modify values.

```
q)@[t; `price;.util.rnd[.01]]
id date       price
--------------------
0  2000.01.01 100
0  2000.01.02 100.06
0  2000.01.03 100.12
0  2000.01.04 99.75
0  2000.01.05 98.31
..
```

But implementing the by clause is a bit more involved. An example implementation is given in Section 14.2 [179] when writing the .util.pivotq [183] function. Using the by clause with q-SQL, however, simplifies things considerably. For example, we can find the average price for each ID.

```
q)select avg price by id from t
id| price
--| --------
0 | 179.7995
1 | 186.054
2 | 101.1568
3 | 112.2339
4 | 107.68
..
```

or add a new column with price returns for each security.

```
q)update ret:deltas[0n;log price] by id from t
id date       price ret
-------------------------------
0  2000.01.01 100
0  2000.01.02 100.06 0.0001371565
0  2000.01.03 100.12 0.0001276343
0  2000.01.04 99.75  −0.0008135982
0  2000.01.05 98.31  −0.00315577
```

The by clause performs three actions. It first groups the query using the columns in the by clause. It then iterates over each group and applies our query. The final step depends on whether we used a select or update statement. The select statement sorts the results while the update statement aligns the results to match the location of the original query.

We can see how the results of the select query have the sort attribute automatically applied to the first column. This makes subsequent queries faster.

```
q)meta select avg price by id from t
c    | t f a
-----| -----
id   | j   s
price| f
```

The key itself has the sort attribute as well.

```
q)0N!select avg price by id from t;
(`s#+(,`id)!,`s#0 1 2 3 4 5 6 7 8 9)!+(,`price)!,123.4993 124.3238 112.2379..
```

By adding extra column names after the by clause we can even group by more than one column. For example, we can compute the average price for each ID and week combination.

```
q)select avg price by id,date.week from t
id week       | price
--------------| --------
0  1999.12.27| 100.0316
0  2000.01.03| 98.9953
0  2000.01.10| 97.69468
0  2000.01.17| 97.02881
0  2000.01.24| 101.4942
..
```

The key still has the sort attribute applied. But with repeated values in the id column, a partition attribute `p is applied instead of the sort attribute `s.

```
q)meta select avg price by id,date.week from t
c    | t f a
-----| -----
id   | j   p
week | d
price| f
```

## Dot Notation

As you can see, we are not limited to grouping by fields in the table, we can even group by derived data. In this case we used q's *dot* notation to access different forms of the temporal data. Instead of grouping by the date, we grouped by the week (which is still an actual date but represents the first day of the week). There are many other ways of using *dot* notation to cast between temporal data types. But while it is easy to use, *dot* notation does not add extra functionality over direct casting. For example, we could have written the same query by casting each date to a week explicitly.

```
q) select avg price by id, `week$date from t
id date       | price
--------------| --------
0  1999.12.27| 100.0316
0  2000.01.03| 98.9953
0  2000.01.10| 97.69468
0  2000.01.17| 97.02881
0  2000.01.24| 101.4942
..
```

You will notice however that q changes the column name when you use dot notation, but not when casting. Of course in either case you can choose the column name yourself by assigning a name directly.

Using dot notation is not limited to dates. The constituent parts of all temporal types (months, date-times, minutes, seconds, timestamps, and timespans) can be extracted as well. And the constituent parts themselves are not limited to the seven temporal types. We can also extract the year, month of year, day of month, hour of day, minute of hour and second of minute (all integer values) of the date or time values.

```
q) `year`mm`dd`hh`uu`ss$\:2001.09.11D08:46
2001 9 11 8 46 0i
```

In addition to using dot notation in q-SQL, q allows us to use it on global variables as well. Here is an example of extracting the minute component from a timespan representing midnight.

```
q) tm:0D
q) tm.minute
00:00
```

---

**Q Tip 14.4** Explicitly cast between types

---

Unfortunately the use of dot notation does not work on function parameters or variables.

```
q) {x.minute}0D
{x.minute}
'x.minute
```

Given that explicit casting works for both global and local variables, it is safer to always use explicit casting instead of using dot notation.

```
q) `minute$0D
00:00
q) { `minute$x}0D
00:00
```

## By Gotchas

The select ...   by query is very powerful, but easy to use incorrectly. When a simple select query with a by clause is executed, all values for each group are returned.

```
q) select price by id,date.week from t
id week       | price
--------------| ------------------------------------------------------------------
0  1999.12.27| 100 97.58377
0  2000.01.03| 99.08814 96.36225 94.31315 93.19448 93.58785 92.4247 92.48023
0  2000.01.10| 90.47419 90.6332 93.07564 93.92358 94.58776 92.93978 92.17413
0  2000.01.17| 93.94096 94.24428 91.36118 92.51848 95.23733 93.43914 95.92783
0  2000.01.24| 93.93053 92.05195 92.2714 90.57179 91.64911 93.45228 92.62375
..
```

There are times where this comes in handy. But accidentally doing this can cause `type errors that are hard to track down. We may want, for example, a single price by ID and date. And instead of using the xkey operator to define a two column primary key, we use a select ...   by query to perform what we think is the same operation.

```
q) select price by id,date from t
id date       | price
--------------| --------
0  2000.01.01| 100
0  2000.01.02| 100.0632
0  2000.01.03| 100.122
0  2000.01.04| 99.74749
0  2000.01.05| 98.30914
..
```

But we get a `type error when attempting to create a CSV file.

```
q)"," 0: select price by id,date from t
k){$[t&77>t:@y;$y;x;-14!'y;y]}
'type
```

---

**Q Tip 14.5** Check the `meta` of tables that cause `` `type `` errors

---

The problem occurs because the `price` column is not a list of numbers. It is a list of lists of numbers. The best way to diagnose the problem is by using the `meta` operator to check the type of each column.

```
q)meta select price by id,date from t
c     | t f a
------| -----
id    | j   p
date  | d
price | F
```

The `price` column has a capital "F" indicating that instead of being a vector of floats, the column is represented as a mixed list where each element is a list of floats. The proper way to fix the problem is to use an aggregating function such as the `sum`, `avg`, `med`, `first` or `last` operators.

```
q)"," 0: select last price by id,date from t
"id,date,price"
"0,2000-01-01,100"
"0,2000-01-02,100.0632"
"0,2000-01-03,100.122"
"0,2000-01-04,99.74749"
"0,2000-01-05,98.30914"
"0,2000-01-06,97.507"
..
```

In time series tables, a common operation is to find the most recent record of each column. Instead of using the `last` operator on each column, q allows us to simplify the query, and increase the performance, by not specifying any columns.

```
q)select by id from t
id| date       price
--| -------------------
0 | 2004.12.31 236.6237
1 | 2004.12.31 238.8049
2 | 2004.12.31 83.98941
3 | 2004.12.31 237.1457
4 | 2004.12.31 156.202
..
```

## Exec

It is often assumed that `exec` is a special case of `select`. But in fact, the reverse is true. The `select` statement always returns a table, while the `exec` statement can return anything: an atom, list, dictionary, or table. If a dictionary is returned, it can take on one of five different forms. The most familiar would be a keyed table. But other return types are also possible. We begin our demonstration with an atom.

```
q)exec first price from t
100
```

Querying for more than a single value returns a list.

```
q)exec price from t
100 97.58377 99.08814 96.36225 94.31315 93.19448 93.58785 92.4247 92.48023 ..
```

This same operation can of course be performed with simple indexing. The power of exec becomes more apparent when we use it to access dictionaries. If we query multiple columns, exec returns the data as a dictionary.

```
q)exec id,date,price from t
id   | 0          0          0          0          0          0          0 ..
date | 2000.01.01 2000.01.02 2000.01.03 2000.01.04 2000.01.05 2000.01.06 20..
price| 100        97.58377   99.08814   96.36225   94.31315   93.19448   93..
```

It will also return a dictionary if we query for a single field, but provide it with a label.

```
q)exec px:price from t
px| 100 97.58377 99.08814 96.36225 94.31315 93.58785 92.4247 92.48..
```

The select statement is a layer around exec that, in addition to providing optimizations for querying large historical databases, flips the result of exec.

```
q)flip exec id,date,price from t
id date       price
--------------------
0  2000.01.01 100
0  2000.01.02 100.0632
0  2000.01.03 100.122
0  2000.01.04 99.74749
0  2000.01.05 98.30914
..
```

But exec can return four more types of dictionaries, depending on the types of the key and value. Selecting a single column in both the key and value generates a simple dictionary.

```
q)exec last price by date from t where id = 0
2000.01.01| 100
2000.01.02| 100.0632
2000.01.03| 100.122
2000.01.04| 99.74749
2000.01.05| 98.30914
```

```
2000.01.06| 97.507
2000.01.07| 98.71857
..
```

Selecting multiple values in either the key or value, or explicitly providing a name generates a table. When both key and value are tables, the result is the same as that produced by the `select` statement: a keyed table.

```
q)exec px:last price by id,date from t where id = 0
id date      | px
-------------| --------
0  2000.01.01| 100
0  2000.01.02| 100.0632
0  2000.01.03| 100.122
0  2000.01.04| 99.74749
0  2000.01.05| 98.30914
..
```

But there are two other dictionaries that can be created (though their usefulness can be questioned). We can create a dictionary where the key is a table and the value is a list.

```
q)exec price by date:date from t where id = 0
date      |
----------| --------
2000.01.01| 100
2000.01.02| 100.0632
2000.01.03| 100.122
2000.01.04| 99.74749
2000.01.05| 98.30914
..
```

Or even a dictionary where the key is a list and the value is a table.

```
q)exec price:price by date from t where id = 0
          | price
----------| --------
2000.01.01| 100
2000.01.02| 100.0632
2000.01.03| 100.122
2000.01.04| 99.74749
2000.01.05| 98.30914
..
```

## Exec by

We have seen how q returns the last row of every column when a `select by` query does not specify any columns. By performing an `exec by` query we can apply any operation across multiple columns.

For example, instead of selecting the first date and price for every ID,

```
q)select first date, first price by id from t
id| date        price
--| ----------------
0 | 2000.01.01 100
1 | 2000.01.01 100
2 | 2000.01.01 100
3 | 2000.01.01 100
4 | 2000.01.01 100
..
```

We can exec a table and use the `first` operator a single time.

```
q)exec first ([]date;price) by id:id from t
id| date        price
--| ----------------
0 | 2000.01.01 100
1 | 2000.01.01 100
2 | 2000.01.01 100
3 | 2000.01.01 100
4 | 2000.01.01 100
..
```

This works because calling `first` on the table creates a dictionary. The `by` clause causes one dictionary to be created for each `id`, and the resulting list of dictionaries is then promoted to a table.

---

**Q Tip 14.6** Simplify queries by using `exec by`

---

When a single operation is performed over many columns, or multiple operations are performed on the same set of data, using an `exec by` statement can considerably simplify your code. When the result of each statement within an `exec by` query is a dictionary with conforming keys that are symbols, q will promote the list of dictionaries to a table. To generate a dictionary we can either perform a single operation on a table, or assign a key to a function that returns multiple values.

Time series data is often summarized with candle stick charts. Each candle stick is plotted with the open, high, low, and close values of each time window. This can computed by using a `select by` clause.

```
q)s:select id,date.week,p:price from t
q)select o:first p,h:max p,l:min p,c:last p by id,week from s
id week       | o        h        l        c
--------------|---------------------------------------
0  1999.12.27| 100      100.0632 100      100.0632
0  2000.01.03| 100.122  100.122  97.507   99.71328
0  2000.01.10| 99.36008 99.63464 95.70985 96.14122
0  2000.01.17| 96.24896 99.87957 95.87985 99.87957
0  2000.01.24| 98.72707 103.3749 98.72707 102.9145
```

```
..
```

This was a lot of typing. It even took me a few tries to fit the query within the boundaries of the page. Long and complicated q-SQL queries can often be simplified by moving the algorithm to a function. In this case, we are performing a list of functions on the same dataset. This can be factored out.

**.stat.ohlc**

```
ohlc:{`o`h`l`c!(first;max;min;last)@\:x}
```

Using this function with the `exec` statement allows us to simplify everything.

```
q)exec .stat.ohlc price by id,date.week from t
id week       | o        h        l        c
--------------|  -------------------------------------------
0  1999.12.27| 100      100.0632 100      100.0632
0  2000.01.03| 100.122  100.122  97.507   99.71328
0  2000.01.10| 99.36008 99.63464 95.70985 96.14122
0  2000.01.17| 96.24896 99.87957 95.87985 99.87957
0  2000.01.24| 98.72707 103.3749 98.72707 102.9145
..
```

---

**Q Tip 14.7** Factor complex q-SQL statements into functions

---

Complex computations often require multiple q-SQL statements to implement. After the final column is created, the intermediary columns are no longer needed. These same computations can be written more efficiently and take less memory by moving them into a function and assigning the results back into the desired table. The factored computation can also be unit tested outside of q-SQL.

Similarly, we can write a function to compute summary statistics, and use it in a q-SQL statement. The five basic summary statistics used to describe a dataset are the count, min, max, average (or median), and the standard deviation. You can of course add skew and kurtosis.

**.stat.summary**

```
summary:{`n`mn`mx`md`dv!(count;min;max;med;sdev)@\:x}
```

Using the labels `count`, `min`, `max`, `med`, or `sdev` as column names is completely valid. But if we did that, it would be impossible to use q-SQL to query the columns. The q parser would interpret them as builtin operators. For this example, we shorten the labels to one or two letters.

```
q)exec .stat.summary price by id,date.week from t
id week       | n mn       mx       md       dv
--------------|  -------------------------------------------
0  1999.12.27| 2 100      100.0632 100.0316 0.04467704
0  2000.01.03| 7 97.507   100.122  98.8496  0.9250627
```

```
0   2000.01.10| 7 95.70985 99.63464 97.49647 1.725384
0   2000.01.17| 7 95.87985 99.87957 96.63348 1.321148
0   2000.01.24| 7 98.72707 103.3749 101.3572 1.500534
..
```

## 14.2    Pivot Tables

Although much more flexible than `select`, `exec` is used far less frequently. The `select` statement is both more intuitive and well known due to its existence in standard SQL. Pivot tables are one case where `exec` permits unrivaled functionality, and thus provides incentive for us to understand its usage and syntax.

### Long and Skinny

The best designed kdb+ tables are *long and skinny*. Our price path table is an example of such a table. Humans, however, like to view tables that are *short and fat*. Using the `pivot` function introduced in this section, we can transform a long and skinny table to short and fat.

```
q)dts:.util.rng[1;2000.01.01;2005.01.01]
q)show t:raze .sim.genp[;100;.3;.03;dts] each til 10
q)"i"$.util.pivot 2!select id,date,price from t
date      | 0   1   2   3   4   5   6   7   8   9
----------| -------------------------------------
2000.01.01| 100 100 100 100 100 100 100 100 100 100
2000.01.02| 100 100 102 100 99  101 98  104 99  100
2000.01.03| 100 98  104 98  98  100 100 104 102 101
2000.01.04| 100 100 105 97  97  99  101 103 103 99
2000.01.05| 98  103 104 97  99  100 100 106 103 100
..
```

---

**Q Tip 14.8** Only transform tables into pivot tables for presentation

---

Pivot tables are the perfect format for presenting data and submitting to charting packages. But once a pivot table has been created, we are left with a single set of data. Any calculations that require other fields from the original table are impossible to perform. For this reason, generation of a pivot table should be one of the last steps in any analysis. Adding an extra summary column and row at the end and bottom of the table is probably the only other adjustment we are likely to make to our pivot table.

When deciding which field to place in the column headers, remember that data takes up more room horizontally than vertically. We should place the field with the fewest distinct items in the column headers. Vertical scrolling is also more natural. Had we reversed the column and row headers in the previous example the table would be quite short but the data would run off the screen. A robust `pivot` function should be able to easily swap the column and row labels.

The `pivot` function introduced in this section takes a single argument: a keyed table. It derives all configuration parameters from the incoming table. As we will see, we can swap keys, column headers and pivoted data by simply rearranging the columns of the keyed table.

### Building a Pivot Table

To build a pivot table we must first understand precisely what we want to build. Looking at the table above, we see that we need to summarize the data by date. This gives us a clue that we will be using a `by` clause. It is also important to remember that although a table is stored as a dictionary of lists, q will promote a list of conforming dictionaries to a table. Combining these two constructs, we can get a good start at building our pivot table. We first create a dictionary mapping each ID to its price and group by year. The trick, however, is to use an `exec by` statement.

```
q)exec id!price by date from t
2000.01.01| 0 1 2 3 4 5 6 7 8 9!100 100 100 100 100 100 100 100 100 100f
2000.01.02| 0 1 2 3 4 5 6 7 8 9!97.58377 99.73487 100.782 100.5971 99.445 9..
2000.01.03| 0 1 2 3 4 5 6 7 8 9!99.08814 95.66496 99.18316 100.4701 99.0398..
2000.01.04| 0 1 2 3 4 5 6 7 8 9!96.36225 93.06001 99.74824 100.3953 101.163..
2000.01.05| 0 1 2 3 4 5 6 7 8 9!94.31315 90.28146 100.6231 100.9441 102.603..
2000.01.06| 0 1 2 3 4 5 6 7 8 9!93.19448 92.99005 100.3045 103.5482 100.396..
2000.01.07| 0 1 2 3 4 5 6 7 8 9!93.58785 94.42756 101.9615 104.1397 98.7785..
..
```

Each date now has a dictionary of prices. To turn the key into a table, we need to assign the list of dates a label.

```
q)exec id!price by date:date from t
date      |
----------| -----------------------------------------------------------------..
2000.01.01| 0 1 2 3 4 5 6 7 8 9!100 100 100 100 100 100 100 100 100 100f
2000.01.02| 0 1 2 3 4 5 6 7 8 9!97.58377 99.73487 100.782 100.5971 99.445 9..
2000.01.03| 0 1 2 3 4 5 6 7 8 9!99.08814 95.66496 99.18316 100.4701 99.0398..
2000.01.04| 0 1 2 3 4 5 6 7 8 9!96.36225 93.06001 99.74824 100.3953 101.163..
2000.01.05| 0 1 2 3 4 5 6 7 8 9!94.31315 90.28146 100.6231 100.9441 102.603..
2000.01.06| 0 1 2 3 4 5 6 7 8 9!93.19448 92.99005 100.3045 103.5482 100.396..
2000.01.07| 0 1 2 3 4 5 6 7 8 9!93.58785 94.42756 101.9615 104.1397 98.7785..
```

And to promote the list of dictionaries to a table, we need to convert the keys to symbols. We will also cast the prices to integers to fit on the screen.

```
q)exec (`$string id)!"j"$price by date:date from t
date      | 0    1    2    3    4    5    6    7    8    9
----------| -------------------------------------------------
```

```
2000.01.01|  100 100 100 100 100 100 100 100 100 100
2000.01.02|  101 99   102 101 101 99   101 99  100 100
2000.01.03|  101 100 106 99   100 97   101 98  100 102
2000.01.04|  100 101 108 98   100 97   102 102 104 101
2000.01.05|  98   101 106 98   99   94   98  103 106 102
..
```

We now have a simple command to create pivot tables. Unfortunately, the ease with which we created the pivot table masks a problem typically found in daily use. Our dataset has a price for every symbol on every day. Q promoted these dictionaries to a table because each dictionary had the same number of fields. But if our dataset is not complete, we will be left with a list of dictionaries.

```
q)exec (`$string id)!"j"$price by date:date from 1_t
date      | _____
----------|
2000.01.01|  `1`2`3`4`5`6`7`8`9!100 100 100 100 100 100 100 100 100
2000.01.02|  `0`1`2`3`4`5`6`7`8`9!98 100 101 101 99 99 101 103 99 99
2000.01.03|  `0`1`2`3`4`5`6`7`8`9!99 96 99 100 99 97 100 104 99 100
2000.01.04|  `0`1`2`3`4`5`6`7`8`9!96 93 100 100 101 93 101 103 102 101
2000.01.05|  `0`1`2`3`4`5`6`7`8`9!94 90 101 101 103 92 103 99 101 101
2000.01.06|  `0`1`2`3`4`5`6`7`8`9!93 93 100 104 100 90 104 100 103 104
2000.01.07|  `0`1`2`3`4`5`6`7`8`9!94 94 102 104 99 91 105 102 101 109
..
```

The key of the dictionary remained a table, but the value reverted to a list of dictionaries. To recover the table, we must ensure each dictionary has the same number, and ordering, of elements. We can do this by first constructing a unique list of ids. Using this list we can reshape each dictionary to ensure they conform.

```
q)u:`$string distinct t`id
q)exec u#(`$string id)!"j"$price by date:date from 1_t
date      | 0  1   2   3   4   5   6   7   8   9
----------| ------------------------------------
2000.01.01|     100 100 100 100 100 100 100 100 100
2000.01.02| 98 100 101 101 99  99  101 103 99  99
2000.01.03| 99 96  99  100 99  97  100 104 99  100
2000.01.04| 96 93  100 100 101 93  101 103 102 101
2000.01.05| 94 90  101 101 103 92  103 99  101 101
..
```

Even though we are missing the first value, we ensured that each dictionary had the same dimensions, and q promoted the list of dictionaries to a table - inserting a null value for each missing field.

## Writing a Pivot Function

This is a very useful routine, but the syntax has become a little too complicated to type each time we want a pivot table. The first step of generalizing the pivot code is moving the code to a function.

```
pivot:{[t]
 c:`$exec string asc distinct id from t;
 p:exec c#(`$string id)!price by date:date from t;
 p}
```

The problem with this function is that it assumes knowledge of three things. It assumes we want to display the price as the data element, group the data by date and pivot the table by id. We could change the function to pass these three values as parameters. But how can we modify the q-SQL to have dynamic fields?

One way is to build a character vector, convert it into executable form with the parse operator, and evaluate the result with the eval operator.

**.util.pivots**

```
pivots:{[c;g;d;t]
 s:"exec (`$exec string asc distinct ",string[c]," from t)";
 s,:"#(`$string ",string[c],")!",string d;
 s,:" by ", ","  sv ":" sv'string flip 2#enlist g,();
 s,:" from t";
 p:eval @[parse s;1;:;t];
 p}
```

We can now pass in the desired columns and obtain a pivot table.

```
q)"i"$ .util.pivots[`id;`date;`price] t
date       | 0   1   2   3   4   5   6   7   8   9
-----------| ---------------------------------------------
2000.01.01| 100 100 100 100 100 100 100 100 100 100
2000.01.02| 100 100 102 100 99  101 98  104 99  100
2000.01.03| 100 98  104 98  98  100 100 104 102 101
2000.01.04| 100 100 105 97  97  99  101 103 103 99
2000.01.05| 98  103 104 97  99  100 100 106 103 100
..
```

The result of the parse command is called a *parse tree*. It is a list of elements starting with a function followed by its parameters - which may themselves be parse trees. This syntax is called parse tree notation.

```
q)0N!parse "select from t";
(?;`t;();0b;())
```

When used in a global context, this translation from a character vector to parse tree notation works well. But when used from within a function, it can not access local variables. From the previous example, we can see how `parse` converted the table `t` to the table's *name* `t`. The last line of the `.util.pivots` function uses the index apply operator `"@"` to replace the second element of the parse tree to the actual local table `t`;

Instead of generating the parse tree notation each time the function is called, we can write the functional form ourselves. To understand what the syntax must look like, we can use the `parse` operator on our q-SQL to generate the necessary parse tree command. We can then customized the result.

```
q) 0N!parse "exec c#('$string id)!price by date:date from t";
(?;`t;();(,`date)!,`date;,(#;`c;(!;($;,`;($:;`id));`price)))
```

We can make the function customizable by removing the hard-coded columns, introducing variables, and using the functional select operator `?[;;;]`.

### .util.pivotp

```
pivotp:{[c;g;d;t]
 u:`$string asc distinct t c;
 pf:{x#('$string y)!z};
 p:?[t;();g!g,:();(pf;`u;c;d)];
 p}
```

In addition to the four-argument functional select, there is also a five- and six-argument functional select that permits us to specify what sublist of elements we would like returned as well as the sorting function to use. These will be demonstrated in Q Tip 14.10 [187]. Replacing the `"?"` with a `"!"` transforms the functional select into a functional update (or even a functional delete if `0b` is passed for the `by` clause in the third parameter). Once again, we can determine the correct syntax to use by passing a sample q-SQL statement through the `parse` operator.

In fact, we can pivot without using q-SQL. We will, of course, have to implement the grouping and sorting that the `by` clause performs for us.

### .util.pivotq

```
pivotq:{[c;g;d;t]
 u:`$string asc distinct t c;
 p:asc[key p]#p:group (g,())#t;
 p:u#/:('$string t c)[p]!'t[d] p;
 p}
```

The first line of the function creates the list of column headers by obtaining the unique list of items in column `c`, sorting them and then casting them to symbols. The second line groups the table by column `g` and sorts it as well (mirroring the behavior of the q-SQL by clause). The final line of the function groups the data in column `d`, applies the key from column `c` and reshapes each of the dictionaries with the unique list of keys.

**Q Tip 14.9** Use functional `select`/`update` to parameterize by clauses

That was a lot of work to replicate the functionality of a q-SQL by clause. As mentioned in the section called "By" [169], we can implement the functionality of each of the q-SQL statements `select`, `delete`, `update` and `where` in standard q. But just as q-SQL shines when used with the by clause, functional select and functional update are a perfect choice when the by clause of a query must be dynamically generated. In most other cases, using the functional form of `select` and `update` can be overkill.

Using functional select, we can make our pivot function even easier to use. We know that the three column parameters must already exist in the table. If we mandate that the table also be keyed, we can have a contract between the function and the caller. We will use the last column of the table as the data, the last column of the key will be the pivot column, and the remaining columns of the key will be used for grouping. If this is not the ordering of the table, then the caller can easily create the proper table by selecting the columns into a new table and re-applying the key.

**.util.pivot**

```
pivot:{[t]
 u:`$string asc distinct last f:flip key t;
 pf:{x#(`$string y)!z};
 p:?[t;();g!g:-1_ k;(pf;`u;last k:key f;last key flip value t)];
 p}
```

With a flexible pivot function, we can summarize the results of any query.

```
q)"i"$.util.pivot select by id,date.year from t
id| 2000 2001 2002 2003 2004
--| -------------------------
0 | 95    130  233  224  237
1 | 138   165  229  205  239
2 | 121   121  88   105  84
3 | 97    62   117  146  237
4 | 67    84   93   147  156
..
```

To swap the key and column fields, we just reorder the by clause.

```
q)"i"$.util.pivot select by date.year,id from t
year| 0    1   2   3   4    5  6  7  8   9
----| -----------------------------------
2000| 95   138 121 97  67   70 57 87 102 100
2001| 130  165 121 62  84   64 44 72 161 103
2002| 233  229 88  117 93   65 32 53 159 112
2003| 224  205 105 146 147  57 26 56 291 130
2004| 237  239 84  237 156  63 30 55 256 85
```

## 14.3 Advanced Queries

Q-SQL queries tend to get complicated because many `update`, `select` and `delete` statements are strung together on a single line. This complication can be removed by keeping the steps short and re-assigning to a variable between each step. There are cases however, where the q-SQL statement is confusing because the query has employed a powerful, though not often used function. We will finish our discussion on q-SQL by mentioning a few of these techniques.

### Selecting Specific Rows

Every q-SQL query has a virtual column `i` which can be used to refer to the row number. We now have a way to limit a query to a subset of rows based on their row number. To select rows 5 through 10 from the table, we can add a `where` clause referencing the column `i`.

```
q)select from t where i within 5 10
id date       price
-------------------------
0  2000.01.06 97.507
0  2000.01.07 98.71857
0  2000.01.08 98.8496
0  2000.01.09 99.71328
0  2000.01.10 99.36008
0  2000.01.11 99.32935
```

The column `i` in a q-SQL statement always refers to the row number. If we create our own column called `i`, q-SQL will ignore it completely (and thankfully not create a new column called `i`);

```
q)select i from ([]i:1 2)
x
-
0
1
```

The automatic `i` variable works for tables that are in memory or splayed on disk. This also includes each partition of a partitioned or segmented database. But to limit a query to specific rows across partitions, the index must be specified by using the `.Q.ind` operator. Our CEP engine creates a partitioned database by saving each day's data to a new dated directory. We can load the whole table by using the `\l` system command. To obtain specific rows we can then pass the table name and row numbers to the `.Q.ind` function.

```
q)\l qdb
q).Q.ind[trades;8 88]
date       id ts tp  time
--------------------------------------------------
2015.03.06 0  2  110 2015.03.06D13:14:41.908191000
```

```
2015.03.06 2  2  10  2015.03.06D13:14:49.808191000
```

Section 15.2 [211] discusses the concept of partitioned tables in more detail.

In-memory and splayed tables have more choices for customizing query results. To limit the results to the first n rows we can pass a single integer to the `select` statement.

```
q) select [5] from t
id date       price
--------------------
0  2000.01.01 100
0  2000.01.02 100.0632
0  2000.01.03 100.122
0  2000.01.04 99.74749
0  2000.01.05 98.30914
```

Passing a negative number returns the last n rows. Using this augmented version of `select` prevents q from having to allocate memory for the whole result set, only for us to truncate it later.

We can also pass a pair of integers to obtain a window of rows. The first integer is the initial row number, while the second integer is the number of rows to return.

```
q) select [5 5] from t
id date       price
--------------------
0  2000.01.06 97.507
0  2000.01.07 98.71857
0  2000.01.08 98.8496
0  2000.01.09 99.71328
0  2000.01.10 99.36008
```

The `select` statement has a few more variants. Instead of using the `xasc` and `xdesc` to sort a table after it has been created, we can specify which comparison operation to use at the time of table selection. Using this technique is useful when the sorting criteria is not an existing column in the table. We can, for example, sort by absolute price.[2]

```
q) select [< abs price] from t
id date       price
--------------------
6  2004.05.21 20.27205
6  2004.05.20 20.33403
6  2004.03.05 20.39991
6  2004.05.17 20.50209
6  2004.05.19 20.60917
..
```

---

[2] Q uses the underlying k language to parse and evaluate the sort expression. We therefore need to use the < and > operator for ascending and descending comparisons instead of the `iasc` and `idesc` operators.

To sort by multiple columns, we need to apply the < operator to a table of data instead of a single vector. To sort descending by date but ascending by ID, we can apply a custom comparison.

```
q)select[>([]date;neg id)] from t
id date       price
----------------------
0  2004.12.31 236.6237
1  2004.12.31 238.8049
2  2004.12.31 83.98941
3  2004.12.31 237.1457
4  2004.12.31 156.202
..
```

---

**Q Tip 14.10** Use `select` parameters to create custom sorting criteria

---

Using `xasc` and `xdesc` allows us to sort one or more rows in ascending or descending order. To mix both ascending and descending we must use the operators in tandem. This also requires all data needed for sorting exist in the table. A more flexible approach is to pass the custom sorting criteria as the first argument to `select`. This allows us to sort the table in any order we desire, including by the result of a calculation.

The two `select` arguments can even be combined.

```
q)select[5 5;>([]date;neg id)] from t
id date       price
----------------------
5  2004.12.31 62.66625
6  2004.12.31 30.19218
7  2004.12.31 54.75438
8  2004.12.31 256.1006
9  2004.12.31 84.82361
```

As we have seen, these extra parameters to `select` can be specified independently or in unison, depending on our need. These features are most handy when generating reports.

There are cases where we need to limit a q-SQL statement to a set of rows that depends on the table's data. Suppose, for example, we wanted to select only the rows where the security reached its highest value. One approach would be to sort the table by price and then pick the last row by ID.

```
q)select by id from `price xasc t
id| date       price
--| -------------------
0 | 2003.02.02 277.2975
1 | 2004.11.04 295.7552
2 | 2000.11.20 160.3264
3 | 2004.12.10 260.548
4 | 2004.06.17 187.6586
```

..

It is possible to achieve the same result much more efficiently. Instead of sorting the table, we can use
the `fby` operator.

```
q) select from t where 0=(rank;neg price) fby id
id date        price
---------------------
0  2003.02.02  277.2975
1  2004.11.04  295.7552
2  2000.11.20  160.3264
3  2004.12.10  260.548
4  2004.06.17  187.6586
..
```

This example used two new operators: `rank` and `fby`. The `rank` operator provides the ordinal ranking
of a list where the smallest value receives a rank of 0. It is also possible to rank values between a min
and max using the `xrank` operator. This, of course, leaves open the possibility of duplicate rankings
if there are more values in the list than ranking bins. This allows data to be grouped into percentiles,
deciles, quintiles or any other ntile.

```
q) 5 xrank til 10
0 0 1 1 2 2 3 3 4 4
```

The second new operator `fby` computes an aggregate statistic specified by the left operand over a set
of data grouped by the right operand. This syntax requires explaining. The left operand is a list with
the aggregate function as the first element and the data to operate over as the second. Similar to sorting
by multiple columns, grouping by more than one column requires a table to be specified as the right
operand. For example, to find the rows where each symbol achieved the maximum price per year we can
group by `id` and `date.year`.

```
q) select from t where 0=(rank;neg price) fby ([]id;date.year)
id date        price
---------------------
0  2000.10.02  113.1773
0  2001.10.14  189.1566
0  2002.11.10  239.5073
0  2003.02.02  277.2975
0  2004.09.10  269.6843
..
```

## Using q-SQL on Dictionaries

Q-SQL is not limited to tables. It also works on dictionaries. This is useful in CEP engines where new
events are typically passed as dictionaries. A new quote may arrive with bid and ask quote sizes and
prices.

```
q)show d:`id`bs`bp`ap`as`time!(0;20;100f;101f;80;0D09:05)
id  | 0
bs  | 20
bp  | 100f
ap  | 101f
as  | 80
time| 0D09:05:00.000000000
```

We can use q-SQL to add a new field to the dictionary that is a function of the other fields, just as if it was a table.

```
q)update mp:(bs;as) wavg (ap;bp) from d
id  | 0
bs  | 20
bp  | 100f
ap  | 101f
as  | 80
time| 0D09:05:00.000000000
mp  | 100.2
```

Again, this syntax adds no new functionality to the language, but does make it more convenient. There are some caveats to using q-SQL on dictionaries. A dictionary is equivalent to a single row of a table, and as such, the `where` and `by` clauses have no meaning. Including a `where` clause will throw a `` `type `` error, while the `by` clause is silently ignored. Just as table column names are stored as a list of symbols, a dictionary's key must also be a symbol vector for q-SQL to work.

Recall that namespaces are actually dictionaries whose keys are symbols. We can combine q-SQL's ability to modify data in-place and its ability to be used with dictionaries to delete values from namespaces - including the global namespace.

```
q)delete t from `.
`.
```

Attempting to access this variable now throws an error.

```
q)t
't
```

To delete all values from the global namespace, we can drop the variable name specification.

```
delete from `.
`.
```

## 14.4   Joining Datasets

Joining different (potentially disparate) datasets is one of q's most powerful features. Regardless of the original data format, joining the data becomes a trivial task once it has been imported into kdb+ (and q makes importing trivial as well). The ease of joining data allows us to answer questions we may have considered, but never attempted to answer because the effort was thought too hard. The combination of q and vast stores of data (potentially stored in a kdb+ database) allows us to ask questions, and quickly verify their answers. When an answer remains beyond our reach, it is typically because we are missing a vital piece of information, and not because we lack the machine power or algorithms to analyze the problem.

Having data and q at our disposal quickly ends conversations that begin with "I wonder ...", or end with "If only we knew ...". As a colleague once said, "Q allows you to code at the speed of thought". In fact, once you have begun using your new found powers to quickly answer the backlog of important questions, the hardest problem will be asking the next right question.

We have covered how to import data from both text files and kdb+ databases. We also have many standard q operators under our belt. And given the proper dataset, we can query, analyze, and summarize the data with .util.pivot [184]. We can now focus on pulling the different datasets together with each of q's join operators: lj, pj, uj, ij, ej, aj and wj.

### Exact Joins

Exact joins are used when an identifier (or list of identifiers) exists that uniquely identifies data in two tables. There are five joins used for exact matches: lj, pj, uj, ij and ej. The choice of which one to use depends on how we want to handle missing or duplicate matches. The left join operator lj is used when we want to add matching columns to an existing table but do not want the resulting table to increase or decrease in length. If data is missing from the right operand, the new column will contain null values. This is also the most efficient operator because the original table does not grow or reduce in size. Joining a table with static reference data is a typical use of lj. We can join the CEP engine's price table with the table loaded from ref.txt.

```
q)price lj ref
id| px  time                           ts    qs   vol  rfr
--| --------------------------------------------------------
0 | 110 2015.03.06D14:47:40.274138000 0.05  30   0.35 0.01
1 | 80  2015.03.06D14:47:40.274138000 0.05  50   0.25 0.01
2 | 10  2015.03.06D14:47:40.274138000 0.01  100  0.12 0.01
3 | 5   2015.03.06D14:47:40.274138000 0.01  300  0.09 0.01
4 | 2   2015.03.06D14:47:39.674138000 0.005 1000 0.5  0.01
```

Given two tables, lj will take each row of the left operand and append all the columns from the right operand for rows with a matching key. We do not often need all the columns from the join table, however. Since joining columns involves copying data, it is much better to select the columns we want before performing the join. For example, we can limit the join to only the tick size column `ts`. But to do so, we must also include the primary key. The `select` statement returns an unkeyed table, so we must re-apply the key.

```
q)price lj 1!select id,ts from ref
id| px       time                       ts
--| -----------------------------------------
0 | 109.6128 2015.03.06D15:15:44.450830000 0.05
1 | 79.74883 2015.03.06D15:15:45.050830000 0.05
2 | 9.996609 2015.03.06D15:15:45.050830000 0.01
3 | 4.999271 2015.03.06D15:15:44.450830000 0.01
4 | 1.992611 2015.03.06D15:15:44.950830000 0.005
```

The `select` statement also offers us the ability to rename the columns if the left and right operands to `lj` do not have matching column names. If we do not need to rename any columns, though, we can use a shorter notation to `select` a few columns. And in this case, there is no need to re-apply the key.

```
q)price lj (1#`ts)#/:ref
id| px       time                       ts
--| -----------------------------------------
0 | 109.6128 2015.03.06D15:15:44.450830000 0.05
1 | 79.74883 2015.03.06D15:15:45.050830000 0.05
2 | 9.996609 2015.03.06D15:15:45.050830000 0.01
3 | 4.999271 2015.03.06D15:15:44.450830000 0.01
4 | 1.992611 2015.03.06D15:15:44.950830000 0.005
```

The `#/:` operator leaves the table's key in-place and takes "#" the requested fields from each row of the right table. Although it uses the `each` notation, it is optimized to pick just the requested columns from the table instead of splitting the table into a list of dictionaries, taking the same field from each row and recombining the results into a table.

Q determines which rows belong together by using the primary key of the right operand. Since our table had a single column primary key, only one column is used for the mapping. If the table had more columns, each of those columns must exist in the left operand in order for the join to succeed. If no matching rows are found, null values are returned.

Joining these two small datasets will be fast regardless of how we have organized the data. Once the datasets become large, however, the join speed depends on how quickly q can find the correct row of the right table for every row of the left table. The performance of a table join depends critically on how fast each matching row can be found. Without any attributes on the first keyed column, matches are found by sequentially searching each row until equality is found. For large tables, this can take a long time. Everything we covered in Section 8.2 [97] about attributes is even more important for table joins.

When queries and joins are slow, it is often due to missing attributes. Attributes are expensive to add, so q does not create them by default. In addition, when elements are removed from a list its attribute is dropped as well. This is not an obvious, or popular, choice. Sorted lists, for example remain sorted even after removing elements. The problem occurs with the other attributes that maintain internal hash tables:

`u, `p and `g.  Building these hash tables is expensive, and removing elements can cause memory reallocation accompanied by erratic performance delays.  It is therefore left to the developer to determine when to add attributes.  Remember that each column of a table is itself a list, and any operation that deletes rows from a table, removes items from the underlying lists.  Since table attributes can be easily lost, careful attention must be paid to operations that drop them.

Only the upsert and compound assignment operators have the ability to preserve attributes.  All other operations return copies of the data structure, and thus lose the attribute, even if the attribute is still valid. In addition, only inserting new records to a list (or new rows to a table) can preserve attributes.  If a new element is added to a list with the ", :" compound assignment operator or the upsert operator, the attribute will be preserved if the list is sorted or unique and the new attribute does not invalidate the attribute.  The attribute will also be preserved if the list has the group attribute `g.  Compound assignments of tables with the partition attribute `p are rarely performed, and therefore do not preserve attributes.

The plus join pj operator behaves exactly like the left join operator, except that all columns that exist in both tables are added together, with missing entries filled with 0.  This implies that the pj operator requires all non-key columns of the right operand to be numeric.  We will use the pj operator in Section 17.1 [235] to compute the amount of time it takes to run a single function, excluding its children.

The inner join ij operator is very similar to the left join lj except that the number of rows in the resulting table depends on the existence, or lack there-of, of common keys.  Instead of returning null values for rows where no matching key is found in the right table, inner join ij removes the row from the resulting table.  This also implies that any attributes that may have existed on the left table before the join, will be removed from the resulting table.

We can see how this behaves by limiting the rows of the reference table to only those with even ids.

```
q)price ij select from ref where 0=i mod 2
id| px  time                         ts    qs   vol  rfr
--| ---------------------------------------------------------
0 | 110 2015.03.06D21:34:53.517425000 0.05  30   0.35 0.01
2 | 10  2015.03.06D21:34:53.917425000 0.01  100  0.12 0.01
4 | 2   2015.03.06D21:34:53.817425000 0.005 1000 0.5  0.01
```

In contrast to the inner join ij operator, where only the data for matching rows is returned, the union join uj operator returns data for rows that exist in either the left or right tables.  If a matching key is found, the data is aligned.  If not, null values are substituted.  As the name implies, a union join is the *union* of data from both tables.  The tables may both be keyed or unkeyed.  If they are both keyed, then matching rows are properly joined, and unmatched rows from the right table are appended to the end.  If neither table has a key, then the right table is appended to the left table, with nulls properly substituted. It is not possible to perform a union join if only one table is keyed and the other is not.  Remember that performance for the join can be improved by adding appropriate attributes to the first column of both keyed tables.

We can see how the uj operator introduces extra rows and null data, by joining the same tables but with uj instead of ij.

```
q)price uj ref upsert (5;1f;.001;5000;.25;.01)
id| px  time                          ts    qs   vol  rfr
--| ----------------------------------------------------------
0 | 110 2015.03.06D21:34:53.517425000 0.05  30   0.35 0.01
1 | 80  2015.03.06D21:34:53.917425000 0.05  50   0.25 0.01
2 | 10  2015.03.06D21:34:53.917425000 0.01  100  0.12 0.01
3 | 5   2015.03.06D21:34:53.517425000 0.01  300  0.09 0.01
4 | 2   2015.03.06D21:34:53.817425000 0.005 1000 0.5  0.01
5 | 1                                 0.001 5000 0.25 0.01
```

So far, all joins have required a primary key to determine which columns should be used to determine matching rows. A primary key indicates a uniqueness of values in a single column, or multiple columns for a composite key. Equi join `ej` allows us to join two tables where there is no primary key on either table, but yet we wish to specify a set of columns to use for the join. Based on the list of columns defined as the first parameter, the `ej` operator returns all rows of the second table that match the first table. If the columns we designate describe a primary key with unique elements, the result will be the same as an inner join `ij`.

```
q)ej[`id;price;ref]
id px  time                          ts    qs   vol  rfr
------------------------------------------------------------
0  110 2015.03.06D22:41:38.250133000 0.05  30   0.35 0.01
1  80  2015.03.06D22:41:38.750133000 0.05  50   0.25 0.01
2  10  2015.03.06D22:41:38.750133000 0.01  100  0.12 0.01
3  5   2015.03.06D22:41:38.250133000 0.01  300  0.09 0.01
4  2   2015.03.06D22:41:38.250133000 0.005 1000 0.5  0.01
```

For cases where the table has multiple rows with the same matching criteria, the result will have more rows than the equivalent inner join. If, for example, we want to find all the trades that occurred at the full quote size, we can join the `prices` and `trades` table with the `ej` operator, using the trade's ID, price and size as the key. We will, of course, need to pick between the bid and ask side. In this example, we find all the trade and quote times for all possible occurrences of a trade occurring at the bid prices. Since trades do not occur at the same time as quote updates in our simulated data, we will need to use our own judgment as to which of the many matches are real.

```
q)dt:2015.03.06
q)t:select id,ts,tp,ttime:time from trades where date = dt
q)q:select id,ts:bs,tp:bp,qtime:time from quotes where date = dt
q)ej[`id`ts`tp;t] q
id ts tp ttime              qtime
----------------------------------------------------
1  13 80 0D13:14:32.908191000 0D13:14:43.408191000
1  13 80 0D13:14:32.908191000 0D13:14:53.908191000
1  13 80 0D13:14:32.908191000 0D13:14:54.508191000
1  12 80 0D13:14:34.108191000 0D13:14:36.808191000
1  12 80 0D13:14:34.108191000 0D13:14:40.408191000
```

..

These are contrived examples because most joins involve at least one primary key. If a table has a set of columns that defines the primary key, it is much better to key the table with the "!" or xkey operators. A join using the lj and ij operators is much faster than the equivalent ej join.

## Asof Joins

Exact joins can be used when tables need to be joined by ID, date, symbol or any other integral value. But when analysis extends to a continuous process like time, we must use asof joins. Kdb+'s asof join aj and window join wj are very powerful tools for analyzing time series data. In fact, the asof join aj operator is one case where q provides unparalleled functionality. The ease and speed with which these joins can be performed is nothing but astonishing.

The typical use of the asof join occurs when you want to know the state of the world when a specific event happened. If the timestamps in both tables are synchronized, the aj operator can give you a precise answer. If, however, the timestamps are not synchronized, wj must be used to calculate an approximate estimate.

There are many places where asof joins can be used. Compliance or regulator reports provide a never ending source of opportunities for reporting *what happened*. Determining whether a sell order should be marked *sell long* or *sell short* depends on the position at the time an order is sent to the market. If we have access to a continuous feed of positions and order states we can use either the aj or wj operator to determine how the order should have been marked. Similarly, if we have recorded every trade and quote in the market, we can join the order table with the trade and quote tables to see if the sell orders violated any up tick rules that may exist in a particular market.

Using our quotes and trades tables we can find the prevailing best bid and offer for each trade.

```
q)\l qdb
q)dt:2015.03.06
q)t:select from trades where date = dt
q)aj[`id`time;t]select from quotes where date = dt
date          id ts tp    time                        bs bp  ap     as
---------------------------------------------------------------------------
2015.03.06 0  10 110      2015.03.06D14:35:17.907669000 28 110 110.05 19
2015.03.06 0  6  110      2015.03.06D14:35:19.107669000 15 110 110.05 10
2015.03.06 0  3  110      2015.03.06D14:35:20.307669000 6  110 110.05 12
2015.03.06 0  6  110      2015.03.06D14:35:21.507669000 12 110 110.05 24
2015.03.06 0  15 110.05   2015.03.06D14:35:22.707669000 6  110 110.05 18
..
```

Unlike left, plus, inner and union join, asof join does not require the tables to be keyed. The columns used for joining are passed as the first argument to aj. As always, the join columns must exist in both tables. The last specified join column must be the temporal column. It need not be called time, and in fact it can be any data type, but must represent the column used to demarcate the continuous process that needs to be matched. All asof joins use the binary search algorithm to find the proper rows to join. For this to work properly, the temporal column must be sorted in ascending order. Nothing guarantees or enforces this, so if the data is not sorted properly you will get wrong results.

All non-temporal join columns are used to find an exact match to narrow the rows before performing the binary search. It is within the narrowed set of rows that the temporal column must be sorted - not the whole column. If for example the table is partitioned by ID, the temporal column must be sorted within each ID partition.

The final table will include the all columns from the right operand except the columns used to perform the match. The values for the non-temporal columns will obviously be the same. But the values in temporal, will differ between the left and right operands. There are two ways to obtain the time values from the left operand. The first is to use the `aj0` operator which has the same syntax as the `aj` operator but returns the time from the right operand.

```
q)aj0[`id`time;t]select from quotes where date = dt
date       id ts tp    time                    bs bp  ap     as
--------------------------------------------------------------------
2015.03.06 0  10 110    2015.03.06D14:35:17.607669000 28 110 110.05 19
2015.03.06 0  6  110    2015.03.06D14:35:18.507669000 15 110 110.05 10
2015.03.06 0  3  110    2015.03.06D14:35:20.307669000 6  110 110.05 12
2015.03.06 0  6  110    2015.03.06D14:35:21.207669000 12 110 110.05 24
2015.03.06 0  15 110.05 2015.03.06D14:35:22.107669000 6  110 110.05 18
..
```

The second way to obtain the same information is to add a copy of the time column to left operand before performing the join.

```
q)aj[`id`time;t]select id,time,qtime:time,bp,ap from quotes where date = dt
date       id ts tp    time                    qtime
--------------------------------------------------------------------
2015.03.06 0  10 110    2015.03.06D14:35:17.907669000 2015.03.06D14:35:17.6..
2015.03.06 0  6  110    2015.03.06D14:35:19.107669000 2015.03.06D14:35:18.5..
2015.03.06 0  3  110    2015.03.06D14:35:20.307669000 2015.03.06D14:35:20.3..
2015.03.06 0  6  110    2015.03.06D14:35:21.507669000 2015.03.06D14:35:21.2..
2015.03.06 0  15 110.05 2015.03.06D14:35:22.707669000 2015.03.06D14:35:22.1..
..
```

This second method has the advantage of removing any doubt to what the time in the table refers to.

Performance of the asof join is very sensitive to how fast the exact match can be performed. Matching on more than two columns (such as ID and date) can slow the join down considerably. After the first column is matched, any attribute on the second column will be lost, resulting in a linear search. Instead of performing a 3-column asof join,

```
q)t:select from trades
q)aj[`date`id`time;t]select from quotes
```

```
date        id ts tp    time                    bs bp  ap     as
----------------------------------------------------------------------
2015.03.06 0  10 110    2015.03.06D14:35:17.907669000 28 110 110.05 19
2015.03.06 0  6  110    2015.03.06D14:35:19.107669000 15 110 110.05 10
2015.03.06 0  3  110    2015.03.06D14:35:20.307669000 6  110 110.05 12
2015.03.06 0  6  110    2015.03.06D14:35:21.507669000 12 110 110.05 24
2015.03.06 0  15 110.05 2015.03.06D14:35:22.707669000 6  110 110.05 18
..
```

it is much more efficient to join each date individually and merge the results. This increases the performance of the join for two reasons. Firstly, there is no need to load the quotes across multiple days into memory. The number of quotes is typically a large multiple of the number of trades. And secondly, the attributes within each quote partition are preserved.

```
q)t:select from trades
q)g:t group t`date
q)raze {aj[`id`time;y]select from quotes where date=x}'[key g;g]
date        id ts tp    time                    bs bp  ap     as
----------------------------------------------------------------------
2015.03.06 0  10 110    2015.03.06D14:35:17.907669000 28 110 110.05 19
2015.03.06 0  6  110    2015.03.06D14:35:19.107669000 15 110 110.05 10
2015.03.06 0  3  110    2015.03.06D14:35:20.307669000 6  110 110.05 12
2015.03.06 0  6  110    2015.03.06D14:35:21.507669000 12 110 110.05 24
2015.03.06 0  15 110.05 2015.03.06D14:35:22.707669000 6  110 110.05 18
..
```

Joining with a table that is lacking a `p or `g attribute on the first exact match column will lead to extremely slow joins. In the best case, this will take minutes if not hours to complete, in the worst case it will crash your machine. There are three ways to safeguard against this situation and two ways to recover. To prevent this from happening, we can follow Q Tip 11.10 [152] and start the kdb+ process with the −w command line argument to limit the amount of memory the process can allocate. Once the memory limit is reached, the process will crash with a `wsfull error. Another way to protect the machine from crashing is by adding a time limit for each query. The −t command line argument accepts the number of milliseconds each client query can take before the query is interrupted. And finally, if we are running on Linux, it is possible to configure the Out Of Memory Killer (OOM Killer) to kill our process before our process kills the machine.

Once a query has started, we have three ways to stop it. Using a Unix IPC signal, we can wait for the running query to end, interrupt the query, or kill the process. The SIGTERM(15) signal allows the current thread to complete and then calls the .z.exit callback before exiting. Although it will not stop a long-running query, it does provide a clean method for terminating a kdb+ process. The SIGINT(2) signal will interrupt the current thread of execution, if possible, and then call the .z.exit callback as well. If the process can not be interrupted, our only alternative is to kill the process immediately by issuing the SIGKILL(9) signal. Sending q the SIGINT and SIGKILL signals should only be used as a last resort. Neither signal allows a clean completion of the active query.

Again, as we discussed in Section 8.2 [97], applying proper attributes is critical for good join performance. While `kdb+`'s optimizations can typically compensate for missing attributes when using `lj`, `pj`, `ij` and `uj`, both `aj` and `wj` are unforgiving.

The validity of an asof join depends on the precision and synchronization of timestamps. Timestamps can be trusted when they are generated on the same machine. But clocks on two machines may not be synchronized. It is possible to synchronize clocks across machines, but achieving a high level of precision is expensive. Unsynchronized data provides an imprecise picture of what actually happened. In these cases it is useful to compare datasets with summary values computed over a window of time. The `wj` operator does exactly this. It allows us to choose a window of time and summarizing function to de-fuzz the data within that window. The `wj` operator can be considered a generalized version of the `aj` operator. The window of `aj` only goes back in time, while `wj` also allows forward looking windows. And while the `aj` operator only chooses the last value found in the window, the `wj` operator can compute the average, median or any other function to summarize the window.

Performing a window join is complex, and as such, has many arguments to define the exact operation to perform. To make it easier to manage, there are two assumptions about the data that must be true. Firstly, in addition to the time column, there can only be a single column which uniquely identifies a record. And secondly, the table **must** be sorted first by the identifier and then by time with the partition attribute `` `p `` on the identifier column. Other joins allow the data to be unpartitioned as long as a `` `g `` attribute is placed on the identifier column. The `wj` operator, however, does **not** allow this. The query will execute, but the results will be meaningless. For this reason it is not possible to use the `wj` operator across multiple ids on a real-time database like our in-memory `trades` or `quotes` tables. It is meant to be used on an historical database where data has been sorted within partitioned sections. We can load the data saved by our CEP engine to use the use `wj` operator.

```
q)dt:2015.03.06
q)t:delete date from select from trades where date = dt
q)q:delete date from select from quotes where date = dt
q)wj[t.time+/:-0D00:00:01 0D; `id`time;t] (q; (avg; `bp); (avg; `ap))
id ts tp     time                          bp     ap
----------------------------------------------------------------
0  13 110    2015.03.06D13:14:32.308191000 109.95 110
0  13 110    2015.03.06D13:14:33.508191000 109.95 110
0  13 110    2015.03.06D13:14:34.708191000 109.95 110
0  1  109.95 2015.03.06D13:14:35.908191000 109.95 110
0  3  110    2015.03.06D13:14:37.108191000 109.95 110
. .
```

The first argument of the `wj` operator is a pair of lists of times indicating the start and end time for each window's calculation. The second argument is a symbol list of the columns used for joining: first the identifier and then the temporal column. The third argument is the trade table. The last argument is a list of parameters specifying the source and definition of the summarizing functions. The first element of the list is the table to join (i.e.: the quote table). All the remaining elements are pairs of values indicating the aggregation operator and the aggregation column. In the previous example we joined the trade table with the average bid and ask price for a window of 1 second back.

Looking forward in time is generally a bad practice when attempting to reproduce a realistic simulation of historical events. But due to the fuzziness of timestamps, you may decide to include points slightly in the future. In addition, estimating market impact requires us to examine data at windows of time in the future. Unlike `aj`, `wj` allows this. This query averages the quote prices from one second prior to one second after the trade.

```
q)wj[t.time+/:-1 1*0D00:00:01;`id`time;t](q;(avg;`bp);(avg;`ap))
id ts tp    time                           bp     ap
------------------------------------------------------------
0  13 110   2015.03.06D13:14:32.308191000 109.95 110
0  13 110   2015.03.06D13:14:33.508191000 109.95 110
0  13 110   2015.03.06D13:14:34.708191000 109.95 110
0  1  109.95 2015.03.06D13:14:35.908191000 109.95 110
0  3  110   2015.03.06D13:14:37.108191000 109.95 110
..
```

For each window, there are two types of questions that can be asked: what was the state of the world and what changed. The `wj` operator considers the initial value within the window to be the prevailing values that existed before the window started. It answers questions about the state of the world - what was the average quote during the window. If we wanted to know the average trade price within the window, however, we would only want to consider trades that occurred within the window, and not consider the prevailing trade prices before the window started. Q has provided the `wj1` operator for this type of query. All parameters are the same, but the join does not consider events outside the window. To see the average trade price for the five second before each trade we can join the `trades` table with itself.

```
q)wj1[t.time+/:-0D00:00:05 0D;`id`time;t](t;(avg;`tp))
id ts tp       time
------------------------------------------------
0  13 110      2015.03.06D13:14:32.308191000
0  13 110      2015.03.06D13:14:33.508191000
0  13 110      2015.03.06D13:14:34.708191000
0  1  109.9875 2015.03.06D13:14:35.908191000
0  3  109.99   2015.03.06D13:14:37.108191000
..
```

The new average `tp` column was written over the original value, so we have lost the ability to compare values. To ensure both columns are returned, we need to rename the column in either the original trade table or the table we perform the join on. In this example we rename the `tp` column to `atp` and modify the aggregation query as well.

```
q)w:t.time+/:-0D00:00:05 0D
q)wj1[w;`id`time;t;(`id`ts`atp xcol t;(avg;`atp))]
id ts tp    time                           atp
------------------------------------------------------
0  13 110   2015.03.06D13:14:32.308191000 110
0  13 110   2015.03.06D13:14:33.508191000 110
0  13 110   2015.03.06D13:14:34.708191000 110
```

```
0  1  109.95 2015.03.06D13:14:35.908191000 109.9875
0  3  110    2015.03.06D13:14:37.108191000 109.99
..
```

Due to its implementation, the `wj` operator can only work with integer temporal values. This means that the `datetime` and any other float value can not be used with `wj` or `wjl`.

## Joins for Dictionaries

The most popular joins are `lj` for exact joins and `aj` for asof joins. These two joins have variants that work for dictionaries as well. Joining a dictionary with a table comes in handy when writing a CEP engine. Single events can arrive as dictionaries and will then need to be merged with existing data for analysis. In `.md.updp` `[140]` we obtained a dictionary p from the `price` table and a dictionary r from the `ref` table.

```
p:`price id;
r:`ref id;
```

Instead of storing two separate dictionaries, it would have also been possible to use the dictionary left join operator `","` to join the data to the existing dictionary. The security identifier was passed as an argument to the function, so we can initialize a dictionary containing just the ID.

```
q)id:0
q)show d:((1#`id)!1#id)
id| 0
```

We can then join the dictionary with the `ref` and `price` tables.

```
q)d,:ref
q)show d,:price
id  | 0
px  | 109.9787
ts  | 0.05
qs  | 30
vol | 0.35
rfr | 0.01
time| 2015.03.06D20:16:29.223662000
```

With all data in a single dictionary, we can then compute the price that corresponds to the next step in our random walk.

```
q)z:.stat.norminv rand 1f
q)tm:.z.P
q)select px*.stat.gbm[vol;rfr;(tm-time)%365D06;z],time:tm from d
px  | 104.6652
time| 2015.03.06D21:03:07.210198000
```

---

**Q Tip 14.11** Use dictionary joins for performance

---

Dictionaries are light-weight self-describing data structures well suited for CEP engines. Promoting dictionaries to single row tables merely to use `lj` and `aj` will slow the engine down. But `lj` and `aj` are actually built on more fundamental operators that can be used with dictionaries: native left join `","` and `asof`.

We have seen how the `","` operator, and the more efficient compound assignment version `",:"`, work like the `lj` operator to join a dictionary with either another dictionary or a table. The asof join operator `aj` also has a corresponding operator that works for dictionaries and tables: `asof`. The syntax for using the `asof` operator is similar to that of indexing into a step function as mentioned in the section called "Step Function" [111]. In our example, the left operand is the quote table, while the right operand is the dictionary or table representing the trade or trades that need to be matched. Every field in the dictionary (or column in the table) will be used to search through the quote table to find the rows depicting the state of the world `asof` the requested time. Since the right operand specifies the exact key to use for the search, there is no need to pass a third argument indicating the join columns. We can use `asof` to find the quote for an ID at a specific time in the past.

```
q)\l qdb
q)dt:2015.03.06
q)q:select from quotes where date = dt
q)q asof `id`time!(0;.z.P-0D06)
date| 2015.03.06
bs  | 4
bp  | 109.95
ap  | 110f
as  | 26
```

To recover the fields in the original dictionary we need to save them into a variable, and prepend them to the results of `asof`.

```
q)k,q asof k:`id`time!(0;.z.P-0D06)
id  | 0
time| 2015.03.08D08:56:06.224448000
date| 2015.03.06
bs  | 4
bp  | 109.95
ap  | 110f
as  | 26
```

Exact and asof joins are an integral component in data analysis. Q brings the power of SQL-like joins to the flexibility of a scripting language. Once you experience the power of an *asof* join, you will wonder how you ever survived without it. Extending these joins to dictionaries allows us to use the same functionality in CEP engines. With all these tools at your disposal you will only be limited by the amount of data you have. Chapter 15 [201] discusses the different methods data can be stored and written to disk.

# Big Data

> "Big data" is high-volume, high-velocity and high-variety information assets that demand cost-effective, innovative forms of information processing for enhanced insight and decision making.

> — Gartner *The Importance of 'Big Data': A Definition (2012)*

Our CEP engine generates approximately 3,000 records per minute. Running the engine for a whole day would only generate 4 million records. If we merely increase the number of ids from 5 to 5,000 our database would have close to 4 billion records. As the number of records increase, we can no longer keep a full days worth of data in memory. We have to make decisions about how to store the data to, and retrieve it from, disk. If we were to run the engine over many days, perhaps years, the amount of recorded data would inevitably surpass the space available on a single disk. Again, decisions must be made about how to split the data across disks. And once data is stored on multiple disks, we must finally make decisions on how to efficiently access and analyze the data. It is at this point that we have entered the realm of Big Data. Data becomes "big" when it exceeds the capacity of conventional tools.

Once we realize we have got Big Data, we need to find the right Very Large Database (VLDB) to hold it. A typical VLDB stores hundreds of millions, if not billions, of records per day. It can cover from many months to years of data. With this much data, it becomes vital to logically partition the data so that it can be systematically queried, and potentially loaded into memory, partition by partition. Given the constraints on memory and disk space, partitioning the data serves two purposes. Firstly, it ensures each partition is small enough to allow typical queries to fit into memory. And secondly, it allows queries within each partition to be executed concurrently. Kdb+ provides the ability to partition data by closely integrating itself with the file system. This allows us to use standard operating system tools to manage many aspects of the database.

## 15.1   Partitioning by Column

The first level of partitioning that kdb+ allows is called **splaying**. Splayed tables provide efficient access to specific columns by saving them each in separate files. We can create a splayed table by adding a trailing path separator to the file name when writing the table to disk.

```
q) `:prices/ set prices
`:prices/
```

### Memory Mapped Tables

The above command will create a directory called prices and add four files: one for each column and an auxiliary file named .d. We can list the contents of the directory with the key operator.

```
q) key `:prices
`s#`.d`id`px`time
```

We can then load the table back into memory and save it into any variable we want.

```
q) p:get `:prices/
```

Although the table looks normal when displayed on the terminal, it has actually been mapped into memory, queried, and unmapped.

```
q) p
id px       time
---------------------------------------
0  110.0032 2015.03.06D20:16:23.623662000
1  80.00902 2015.03.06D20:16:23.623662000
2  9.999783 2015.03.06D20:16:23.623662000
3  5.000181 2015.03.06D20:16:23.623662000
4  1.999962 2015.03.06D20:16:23.623662000
..
```

Adding a trailing path separator causes kdb+ to use deferred mapping. We can see that kdb+ has only created a structure with column names and a path used to locate the files.

```
q) 0N!p;
+`id`px`time!`:prices/
```

We can even confirm that nothing has been mapped into memory by displaying the memory usage.

```
q) .Q.w[] `mmap
0
```

Dropping the trailing path separator maps the memory immediately.

```
q)p:get `:prices
q).Q.w[]`mmap
18832
```

The .d file is used to specify the order in which the columns should appear in the table. We can easily remove, add, or delete columns to the table by modifying the contents of the .d file. The .d file is a simple vector that can be loaded, modified and saved again.

```
q)get `:prices/.d
`id`px`time
```

Since each column is a file, they can also be loaded, modified and saved independently.

```
q)get `:prices/px
110.0007 80.00185 9.999956 5.000037 1.999992 9.999969 80.00211 10.00004 80...
```

## Table Schemas

With this simple layout, changing the table schema merely requires adding, removing, or renaming files in the directory and updating the .d file to contain the proper column names. There are no special commands for system administrators to learn. A splayed table is just a bunch of kdb+ lists stored on disk.

We can, for example, reverse the table's column order by modifying the .d file.

```
q)`:prices/.d set reverse get `:prices/.d
`:prices/.d
q)get `:prices/
time                       px        id
----------------------------------------
2015.03.06D20:16:23.623662000 110.0032   0
2015.03.06D20:16:23.623662000 80.00902   1
2015.03.06D20:16:23.623662000 9.999783   2
2015.03.06D20:16:23.623662000 5.000181   3
2015.03.06D20:16:23.623662000 1.999962   4
..
```

We can even delete a column from the table without deleting the data from disk.

```
q)`:prices/.d set get[`:prices/.d] except `px
`:prices/.d
q)get `:prices/
time                       id
-----------------------------
```

```
2015.03.06D20:16:23.623662000 0
2015.03.06D20:16:23.623662000 1
2015.03.06D20:16:23.623662000 2
2015.03.06D20:16:23.623662000 3
2015.03.06D20:16:23.623662000 4
..
```

Let's revert the table to its original layout.

```
q) `:prices/.d set `id`px`time
`:prices/.d
```

When we perform a q-SQL query on the table, only the columns that we request are copied into memory.

```
q) 0N!select id,px from p;
+`id`px!(`g#0 1 2 3 4 2 1 2 1 2 1 2 1 2 1 2 1 0 2 3 1 4 2 1 2 1 2 1 2 1 2 1..
```

This allows us to query a table that has more data than our machine has physical memory. The columns are only loaded on-demand and released when no longer used. Care must be taken when loading a splayed table. The trailing path separator not only indicates we want to splay the table when saving to disk, it also indicates we should load each column on demand. If we remove the trailing path separator when loading the table, the whole table will be loaded into memory at once. Instead of seeing the columns mapped to a directory, we would see the actual data.

```
q) 0N!get `:prices;
+`id`px`time!(`g#0 1 2 3 4 2 1 2 1 2 1 2 1 2 1 2 1 0 2 3 1 4 ..
```

## Enumeration

It is, unfortunately, not always this easy to save and load splayed tables. Our example so far has used purely numeric data. This allows the values to be efficiently stored as vectors of data. But there are cases when a table can, or must, include symbols. Symbols are a popular alternative to numeric security IDs. We can mimic this use case by converting each of the numeric ids to symbols.

```
q) show prices:update `foo`bar`baz`qux`quux id from prices
id   px       time
-----------------------------------------
foo  110.0046 2015.03.06D09:23:04.937339000
bar  80.01269 2015.03.06D09:23:04.937339000
baz  9.999695 2015.03.06D09:23:04.937339000
qux  5.000255 2015.03.06D09:23:04.937339000
quux 1.999947 2015.03.06D09:23:04.937339000
..
```

Kdb+ will no longer allow us to splay this table.

```
q)`:prices/ set prices
k){$[@x;.[x;();:;y];-19!((,y),x)]}
'type
```

To be fair, it is actually possible to write and read a vector of symbols to disk. We could write our own `splay` function to write the `.d` file and each of the columns.

**.util.splay**

```
q)splay:{@[x;`.d,c;:;enlist[c],y c:cols y]}
```

We can now splay the table to disk and even load it back into memory.

```
q).util.splay[`:prices/] prices
`:prices/
q)get `:prices
id   px       time
-------------------------------------------
foo  110.0032 2015.03.06D20:16:23.623662000
bar  80.00902 2015.03.06D20:16:23.623662000
baz  9.999783 2015.03.06D20:16:23.623662000
qux  5.000181 2015.03.06D20:16:23.623662000
quux 1.999962 2015.03.06D20:16:23.623662000
..
```

Q prevents us from doing this by default to prevent us from making a terrible design choice. Each unique symbol is stored in memory a single time. But when written to disk, each occurrence of each symbol is recorded. This obviously causes the size of the data to explode. In addition, since each symbol is a different length, Q must load the entire column into memory before it can access a subset of the values. To permit efficient storage and random access, we must first **enumerate** the data. Enumerated values are stored as fixed width integers. This not only saves memory when storing the data on disk, it also permits random access to the values. To understand this process, let's first see how kdb+ splays character vectors.

A list of character vectors is not stored in contiguous memory yet q allows efficient random access to the values like any other data type.

```
q)`:prices/ set update string id from prices
`:prices/
q)get `:prices
id      px       time
-------------------------------------------
"foo"   110.0032 2015.03.06D20:16:23.623662000
"bar"   80.00902 2015.03.06D20:16:23.623662000
"baz"   9.999783 2015.03.06D20:16:23.623662000
"qux"   5.000181 2015.03.06D20:16:23.623662000
"quux"  1.999962 2015.03.06D20:16:23.623662000
..
```

If we examine the contents of the directory, we see an extra file `id#` in addition to the original `id` file.

```
q)key `:prices
`s#`.d`id`id#`px`time
```

All character vectors columns are stored in two separate files. The special file ending in "#" contains a single list of all the character vectors joined together. We can look inside this file by using the `read0` operator which can read standard text. The q interpreter will not parse the "#" character as part of a file name, so we must build the file name as a character vector and cast it to a symbol.

```
q)read0 `$":prices/id#"
"foobarbazquxquuxbazbarbazbarbazbarbazbarbazbarbazbarfoobazquxbarquuxbazbar..
```

The `id` file contains a list of offsets into the `id#` file. Loading the column directly automatically merges the two files and generates a list of character vectors.

```
q)get `:prices/id
"foo"
"bar"
"baz"
"qux"
"quux"
"baz"
"bar"
..
```

Storing character vectors in one file, and offsets in another is an important concept. The list of offsets stored in the `id` file are all equal length. This allows us to randomly access the data without having to first load the whole file into memory. In order to enable this same efficient access for a column of symbols, we are required to create the auxiliary file with the list of character vectors ourselves.

Symbols are treated differently than character vectors because they are typically repeated often. Whereas character vector columns do not have many repeated values, symbol columns do. Recall that every unique symbol in memory points to a single location. If we saved a column of symbols as a column of character vectors, we would explode the memory footprint and lose the ability to use random access to query the data. We can mirror the same small memory footprint when saving the data to disk by only saving a distinct set of symbols into one file, and a list of offsets in another. The process of mapping symbols to offsets, both in memory and on disk, is called **enumeration**.

Enumeration involves the indirection of data through a pointer to another variable. The internal workings of in-memory symbols are conceptually identical to enumeration. The stored value is a pointer to the actual data. The memory reduction benefits of enumeration are maximized when the enumerated values are repeated many times throughout our dataset.

For enumeration to work, we need to know where to look for our enumerated value. If the values are stored in a variable, we need to record the name of the variable and the offset to use when accessing the enumerated value.

To see how q does this, we will first make a list of symbols.

```
q)id:`foo`bar`baz
```

If we know the variable name and the index that we want, we can create our own enumerated values by using the familiar "!" operator with a symbol as the left operand.

```
q)`id!0 1 2
`id$`foo`bar`baz
```

As you see, q indexed into the variable id and returned the value corresponding to the elements we requested. The data is stored as a list of integers, but allows us to treat it as a list symbols.

Due to the tight coupling of the integers and the id list, we must be very careful not to reorder any elements. This would invalidate any existing enumerations. Appending new values to the end would not cause problems, however.

If, on the other hand, we have symbols and want to enumerate them, we can use the cast operator "$".

```
q)`id$`foo`bar`baz
`id$`foo`bar`baz
```

Although it still looks like a symbol, the resulting enumeration is actually a list of integers. We can see the underlying enumerated values by casting the values to integers.

```
q)"i"$`id$`foo`bar`baz
0 1 2i
```

It is not possible to enumerate a value with the cast operator "$" if the value does not exist in the enumeration list.

```
q)`id$`qux`quux
'cast
```

To do this, we need to use the find operator "?". The "?" operator searches this list and returns the index for each of the right operands. If the value is not found, q will append the missing value to the list and return its index. This allows us to enumerate any list of symbols with a single command.

```
q) `id?`foo`bar`baz`qux`quux
`id$`foo`bar`baz`qux`quux
```

We can even enumerate table columns.

```
q)update `id?id from prices
```

This is exactly what we need to save our symbols to disk. We need the list of unique symbols stored in one file, and the list of enumerated values in another. Instead of enumerating the column and then saving the variable id to disk, q allows us to perform both steps with a single command. Passing a file as the left operand of "?" causes q to lock the file on disk, read the complete file into a global variable with the same name, enumerate the right operand against the global variable, append new symbols to the file, and finally close (and therefore unlock) the file. This is the only case where q locks files. This is important because enumerations are often shared between processes.

After we enumerate the symbol identifiers,

```
prices:update `:id?id from prices
```

we can splay the table to disk.

```
q)`:prices/ set prices
`:prices/
```

Enumerating tables is so fundamental to database administration, q has a builtin operator for it. `.Q.en` provides us with an optimized tool for enumerating tables.

## Unenumerating a Table

Before we can use `.Q.en` to enumerate the `prices` table, we need to unenumerate the `id` column that we just enumerated. This can be done with the `get` (or `value`) operator.

```
q)prices:update get id from prices
```

Looking at the `id` column, we can see that the values are no longer enumerated.

```
q)prices`id
`foo`bar`baz`qux`quux`baz`bar`baz`bar`baz`bar`baz`bar`baz`bar`baz`bar`foo`b..
```

It is useful to have a function that unenumerates an entire table.

**.util.unenum**

```
unenum:{@[x;where (type each flip x) within 20 76;get]}
```

The function takes an unkeyed table as its only parameter. It begins by flipping the table into a dictionary of lists. It then finds which lists have a type within the allocated range of enumerations (20 through 76). Having obtained this list, it applies the `get` operator to each of those columns and returns the unenumerated table.

```
q).util.unenum prices
id    px        time
----------------------------------------
foo   110.0007  2015.03.06D03:24:13.630336000
bar   80.00185  2015.03.06D03:24:13.630336000
baz   9.999956  2015.03.06D03:24:13.630336000
qux   5.000037  2015.03.06D03:24:13.630336000
quux  1.999992  2015.03.06D03:24:13.630336000
..
```

## The sym File

The `.Q.en` operator searches a table for all columns with symbols. Then, instead of enumerating each column separately, `.Q.en` obtains the distinct list of symbols in the table and enumerates them into a file named `sym` with a single call to `"?"`. As a final step, each column in the table is enumerated against the newly populated global variable `sym`. To use `.Q.en` to enumerate our `prices` table, we pass the path to a directory where the `sym` file will be created and the unkeyed table. The following command places the `sym` file in the current directory.

```
q)prices:.Q.en[`:.;prices]
```

The `sym` variable is now populated and mirrored on disk to a file also named `sym`. We can see the `id` column has been enumerated.

```
q)prices`id
`sym$`foo`bar`baz`qux`quux`baz`bar`baz`bar`baz`bar`baz`bar`baz`bar`baz`bar`..
```

It is important to remember that the enumeration variable must be loaded before attempting to use the splayed table. If we delete the `sym` variable, we can see that `kdb+` is unable convert the enumerations into symbols.

```
q)delete sym from `.
`.
q)prices
id px       time
------------------------------------------
0  110.0032 2015.03.06D20:16:23.623662000
1  80.00902 2015.03.06D20:16:23.623662000
2  9.999783 2015.03.06D20:16:23.623662000
3  5.000181 2015.03.06D20:16:23.623662000
4  1.999962 2015.03.06D20:16:23.623662000
..
```

Once the `sym` variable is restored, the enumerations are complete.

```
q)sym:get `:sym
q)prices
id   px       time
------------------------------------------
foo  110.0032 2015.03.06D20:16:23.623662000
bar  80.00902 2015.03.06D20:16:23.623662000
baz  9.999783 2015.03.06D20:16:23.623662000
qux  5.000181 2015.03.06D20:16:23.623662000
quux 1.999962 2015.03.06D20:16:23.623662000
..
```

Loading a file from disk, and storing the data into a variable with the same name is a common operation. The `load` operator will automatically do this for us. We can either specify the file handle which specifies the path to the `sym` file,

```
q)load `:sym
`sym
```

or just the symbol if the file exists in the current working directory.

```
q)load `sym
`sym
```

The corresponding `save` operator saves the data in a variable to a file in the current working directory with the same name,

```
q)save `sym
`:sym
```

or to a different directory as long as the file component of the path matches the variable name.

```
q)save `:../sym
`:../sym
```

Q treats each enumeration as a different type. As previously mentioned, enumerations range from type 20h through 76h. Starting a fresh q instance, we can see that the first enumeration is not given the type 20h, but in fact 21h.

```
q)type `id?``
21h
```

This is because q treats the `sym` enumeration special and it will always get the enumerated type of 20h.

```
q)type x:`sym?``
20h
```

It is typically sufficient to use a single enumeration. This not only prevents repetition between enumerations, it also makes comparisons faster. When enumerations of the same type are compared, only the enumerated integer values are needed. But in order to compare an enumeration with a symbol, the enumeration must first be converted back to a symbol. And if two different enumerations are compared, they must both be converted to symbols before comparing.

The last example was specifically chosen to demonstrate that null symbols are never added to the enumeration vector. Even though we enumerated two null symbols, the `sym` vector is still empty.

```
q)sym
`symbol$()
```

This is because null symbols are enumerated to the null integer `0Ni` which automatically returns the null symbol when used to index into a symbol vector. If we delete the `sym` vector again, we can see the actual enumerated values.

```
q)delete sym from `.
`.
q)x
`sym!0N 0Ni
```

Splaying is perfect in cases where a table has many columns and there is a reasonable upper bound on the number of rows. But if the number of rows increases on a daily, weekly, or monthly basis, we risk the possibility that the columns outgrow our available memory. At this point, we would need to partition the data by rows as well.

## 15.2   Partitioning by Row

As we keep adding rows, there will inevitably be a day when we are unable to load the table because even a single column is too big to fit into memory. To prevent this we need to split the table into logical row-based partitions. Kdb+ allows us to pick the level of partitioning: date, month, year, or custom integer value. Using a date partition is by far the most common choice. If our data is not too big and only arrives on a monthly or annual basis, these too can be used. Though occasionally requested, it is not possible to partition on symbol. Instead, we can manage the mapping between symbol and integer ourselves, and partition the data by integer. As we will see in the section called "Partitioning Across Symbols" [216] we can also get around this by creating multiple partitions per date, each partition holding data for a subset of symbols.

### Virtual Column

Each table in our `qdb` database starts with a `date` column. But where did this column come from? When we load a partitioned or segmented database, `kdb+` sets many global variables to make querying partitioned tables as seamless as possible. Some important variables include `.Q.pt` which holds the names of each partitioned table, `.Q.pf` has the name of the virtual column, `.Q.pd` is the directory location of each partition, `.Q.pv` is the list of partition values, and `.Q.pn` is a lazily populated list of table counts. In the process of loading these variables, the virtual column is defined. Since our table is partitioned by date, there now exists a global variable called `date` which has all the dates loaded from the partitioned database. The variable is used to define the domain for the partitioned query.

If we are not interested in the whole range of dates in the database, we can limit all queries to a known list of partitions by calling the `.Q.view` operator. This internal q operator allows us to limit the visible partitions to the list of values passed as its only argument. We can, for example, limit the `date` vector to a single day.

```
.Q.view 2015.03.06
```

The `date` vector has now been trimmed.

```
q)date
,2015.03.06
```

To revert the list to its original length, we can call `.Q.view` with no arguments.

```
q).Q.view[]
```

Splitting the partitions across directories is quite flexible. But we have added one more layer of indirection which adds processing overhead. We now turn our attention to improving the performance of querying a partitioned database.

## Partitions

Since our CEP server generates thousands of rows per day, it partitions the data by date. In reality, a partition is just a directory with splayed tables. The `.md.dump` [142] function calls `.Q.dpft` which creates the daily partition and splays each table into that directory. Splitting data across dates makes the administration of the data quite flexible. For fast access, we can place recent partitions (say one year's worth of data) on fast and possibly expensive drives. For older data, we can migrate those directories to slower, older, and cheaper drives. Since each partition directory can contain multiple tables, we refer to this as a partitioned database, and not a partitioned table. There are two ways to load a database. The first is to start q with the database directory as the first argument.

```
$ q qdb
```

Any binary files (lists, dictionaries, tables, etc) found in the database directory are loaded first. This is where any enumeration files are loaded. Kdb+ then loads any splayed tables and the partitioned directories last. The enumerated columns can now be used. Any q scripts (files ending in `.q`) in the directory will be loaded last. This is our chance to define views, build custom data structures and provide functions for clients to use.

The second way to load a database is to use the `\l` system command.

```
q)\l qdb
```

After the database is loaded, the current directory will be changed to database root directory. All tables are assumed to be located relative to the current directory. If we change the directory with the `\cd` system command or with the `system` operator, all queries for data in the partitioned tables will fail. This also means that only one partitioned database can be loaded at a time. Once the database is loaded, it will not automatically recognize newly added partitions. This allows us to add new partitions without breaking any running kdb+ servers. To force kdb+ to refresh its list of partitions, we can reload the current directory.

```
\l .
```

We can now query the partitioned database.

```
q)prices
date       id px      time
---------------------------------------------------------
2015.03.06 0  110     2015.03.06D13:14:31.108191000
2015.03.06 0  109.9993 2015.03.06D13:14:31.808191000
2015.03.06 0  109.9932 2015.03.06D13:14:32.508191000
2015.03.06 0  109.984  2015.03.06D13:14:33.208191000
```

In addition to the `id`, `px`, and `tm` columns, we now have a `date` column. This is the virtual column that corresponds to the partition directory. Kdb+ will always add this extra column, so it is important to remove the column when we save the partition with `.Q.dpft`. Even though the actual dates come from the directory name, the column label `date` is the result of some dark magic. Deep in `q.k`, the operator `.Q.L` counts the number of characters in the directory name. Ten characters results in a column named `date`, seven characters results in a `month` title, four characters is `year` and anything else will be called `int` (just make sure your integer does not have four, seven or ten digits). As mentioned, `date` partitions are the most common.

Splayed tables can be queried efficiently because each column is mapped into memory directly from disk. There is no need to copy the data into memory until a selection of the data is performed. Querying a partitioned database adds a layer of indirection which allows the dataset to grow, but also slows down queries because each partition must be mapped in and out of memory. Splayed tables can handle upwards of 1-2 billions records. It is much better to have a single large splayed table than to have a partitioned table with small partitions.

Querying across partitions is much slower than querying within a partition. It is thus important to limit the search space to the exact partitions we need before restricting the query on any other criteria. When querying a partitioned database, the `where` clause should always start with the virtual column: `date`, `month`, `year` or `int`. For example, we can query the `prices` table for the last two days. Remember that the global variable `date` contains a list of all the available partitions. We can use it to limit the selected rows.

```
q)select from prices where date in -2#date
```

If we want to further restrict the query, we can add additional clauses at the end.

```
q)select from prices where date in -2#date, id in 2 3 4
```

As the size of each partition continues to grow, there comes a point where we will only be able to load a single partition into memory. In order to query across multiple partitions, we must write a function to process a single partition, and later merge the results. We may, for example, want to compare the volume differential between trades occurring on the bid and ask prices. This could give us an indication on future movements in the price of each security. To compute this statistic we need a function that selects the trades for a single day, joins the data with the quote prices, and categorizes the trades as bid initiated volume `bv` or ask initiated volume `av`. It is also possible for trades to occur between the bid

and ask. In order to correctly classify all the traded volume, we should also return the total volume t v
for each security.

**.util.bav**

```
bav:{[t;q;dt]
  r:select id,time,tp,ts from t where date=dt;
  r:aj['id'time;r] select id,time,bp,ap from q where date=dt;
  r:update bv:ts*tp<=bp,av:ts*tp>=ap from r;
  r:0!select date:dt,sum bv,sum av,tv:sum ts by id from r;
  r}
```

We can now call the **b**id **a**sk **v**olume function bav on each date in the database and raze the results to
obtain a single table.

```
q)raze .util.bav[trades;quotes] each date
date        id bv   av   tv
-----------------------------------
2015.03.06 0  61   95   156
2015.03.06 1  302  283  585
2015.03.06 2  318  453  771
2015.03.06 3  564  304  868
2015.03.06 4  1299 1221 2520
..
```

## 15.3   Segmenting the Partitions

Sequentially querying each partition adds delays into the total query time. Accessing a partition requires
kdb+ to map required columns, and then load the requested data from disk. The speed of this query is
often constrained by the time it takes to load the data from disk. If we store partitions across multiple
physical disks, we can improve query performance by allowing each partition query to be performed in
parallel. The results of each simultaneous query can then be merged and returned as a single result. This
technique is quite common for Very Large Databases and is referred to as map-reduce.

### Map-reduce

A single query is first *mapped* onto different partitions. This query may actually be different from the
original request. The *mapped* queries can be performed simultaneously which enables considerable
performance gains. The results of these queries are then *reduced* by perhaps another query to form the
results that the original query requested.

In our last example we split the query across each partition. This was, in fact, an example of *mapping* our
query. We did not, however, *reduce* it. To demonstrate the full map-reduce algorithm, we can summarize
the bid-ask volume statistic as a number between -1 and 1 indicating the buying or selling pressure.

```
q)t:raze .util.bav[trades;quotes] each date
q)select pressure:avg (av-bv)%tv by id from t
id| pressure
--| ----------
0 | 0.4304029
1 | -0.01338217
2 | -0.1371477
3 | -0.6454406
4 | 0.07924577
```

We can improve the performance of the *map* routine by querying each partition in parallel. The `peach` operator is a parallel version of `each`.

```
t:raze .util.bav[trades;quotes] peach date
```

By default, `peach` runs sequentially like `each`. We can enable parallel processing by using the `-s` command line argument to start q with multiple slaves.

```
$ q -s 4
```

And we can then confirm how many slaves are running with the `\s` system command.

```
q)\s
4i
```

To improve performance on partitioned tables, `kdb+` has implemented the map-reduce algorithm for many native functions. For example, to `count` the total number of rows in a partitioned table, `kdb+` first simultaneously counts the rows of each partition. After this *map* stage, it *reduces* the intermediate results by `sum`-ing the result from each partition. A slightly more complicated *map-reduce* computation is needed for the `avg` operator. In this case, the *map* phase keeps track of two values: the `sum` and `count` of each partition. In the *reduce* phase, it `sums` each partition's `sum` and divides the total by the `sum` of each `count`.

The list of operators that have been augmented to use *map-reduce* over partitioned tables can be found in the `.Q.a0` internal variable. This list includes: `count`, `first`, `last`, `sum`, `prd`, `min`, `max`, `all`, `any`, `distinct`, `avg`, `wsum`, `wavg`, `var`, `dev`, `cov`, `cor`, `svar`, `sdev` and `scov`.

Older versions of q used the *map-reduce* algorithm to compute the median across partitions as the median of medians. This may approximate the true median of the values, but the algorithm is not accurate. Starting in `kdb+` 3.0, q no longer allows the `med` operator to be used on partitioned tables.

## Multiple Disks

Running multiple slaves solves problems faster by using more RAM and CPU resources. But the benefits are limited if we are attempting to query data from a single disk. Our bottleneck has been moved from the CPU to the disk. To ensure each slave has unencumbered disk access, we must evenly distribute our partitions across different physical drives. Kdb+ has made this easy by allowing us to specify a list of directories (preferably located on different physical drives), that contain multiple partitions. This file, named par.txt, is usually accompanied by the enumeration file sym. Unlike a partitioned database, a segmented database does not have the partitions directly below the database root directory. They exist on other physical drives in directories which are listed in par.txt. When a segmented database is loaded, kdb+ will read the contents of par.txt and search each of the listed directories for partitions. For best performance, partitions that are typically queried simultaneously should be evenly distributed between the drives. Using a round-robin allocation for a date-based partition, for example, would allow a query against a range of dates to be efficiently executed in parallel.

---

**Q Tip 15.1** Use par.txt to spread data over multiple physical disks

---

Kdb+ attempts to make this easier by transparently picking an appropriate drive within the .Q.dpft function. The algorithm used to pick a physical drive based on the partition's value is performed in the .Q.par operator. This function can be used to determine the path for a specific partition. If we add a new drive to increase performance, the partitions will unfortunately need to be redistributed. Although we benefit from storing partitions across multiple drives, we must still keep small tables, splayed or not, and q scripts under the database root directory alongside par.txt.

## Partitioning Across Symbols

There comes a time when the database has so much data, that even a single partition may not fit within memory. Prior to kdb+ 3.0, a single file, and therefore column, was limited to 2 billion records. Even though kdb+ has since removed this upper limit, continuously increasing the size of a table will inevitably prevent it from being loaded into memory. In fact, even though there is no longer a 2 billion record limit within kdb+, if we are using the 32-bit version of q, we will still run into limitations imposed by the architecture.

To surmount these limitations, we have one last method of splitting tables across directories. Instead of using par.txt to segment partitions across disks, we can also use it to segment each partition. When a q-SQL query requests a table from a specific partitioned field, each segment listed within par.txt will be checked for matching partitions. The complete set of segments are stored in the internal variable .Q.P. And the partitions located within each segment are stored in .Q.D. Once the complete query is executed, perhaps with further constraints, the results from each partition are concatenated together. Segmenting these partitions across multiple drives will of course increase performance, but is not necessary.

Instead of segmenting dates with the par.txt file, we can actually segment across symbols. When q detects a par.txt file it performs the same query on each directory in the file and merges the results. This allows us to manage a different set of symbols within different CEP engines and merge the results with the par.txt. The same partitions will appear in each segment, but the data will reflect a different set of symbol. Querying for a specific date will return the merged datasets from each entry in par.txt. Each of the tables typically have the partition attribute `p applied to the identifier column. When merging the result set from multiple tables, q will retain the partition attribute if the combined table has not invalidated it. This is one case where an attribute is retained without using compound assignment.

```
q)(`p#1 1 2 2 3 3),(`p#4 4 5 5 6 6)
`p#1 1 2 2 3 3 4 4 5 5 6 6
```

## 15.4  Compressing Tables

As our dataset becomes larger, we will at some point use all available disk space and be faced with the difficult choice of either purchasing more space or deleting old datasets. Kdb+ offers a third option. If we are willing to pay the overhead of compressing data when writing to disk, and uncompressing it when reading it back, kdb+ provides us with two compression algorithms: the kdb+ proprietary IPC algorithm, and the ubiquitous GZIP algorithm. The kdb+ algorithm requires no external libraries and offers no choice of compression level. The GZIP algorithm requires the GZIP library but allows us to choose the level of compression (at the expense of performance). Both algorithms allow us to choose the compression block size. A higher block size will allow better compression but may also reduce the performance when reading a subset of the data from disk.

### Compressing Files

Given an uncompressed table on disk, we can compress it by applying the -19! operator to each column. Although this column by column (file by file) interface requires us to inspect and compress each column, it provides us the flexibility to compress each column with a different compression level, or not at all - providing faster access to more frequently used columns. We can, for example, compress a single file using a maximum block size of 20, the GZIP algorithm and its maximum compression level.

```
q)f:`:qdb/2015.03.06/prices/px
q)-19!(f;/tmp/x;20;2;9)
`:/tmp/x
system "mv /tmp/x ",1_string f
```

---

**Q Tip 15.2** Use an intermediate file during compression

---

The first two parameters of the -19! operator are the source and destination files. For ease of use, they can be the same file. But for faster compression the two files should exist on different physical drives. In addition, using separate files allows us to recover from an error during compression. The third parameter indicates the logical block size for each compression unit. The parameter is a power of 2 between 12 and 20 - where 12 indicates 4KB and 20 corresponds to 1MB. The larger the block size, the better the compression algorithm. But large block sizes also result in an increase in the minimum disk access when performing small queries. The fourth parameter indicates the compression algorithm. We can use 1 for `kdb+`'s IPC algorithm, or 2 to use the GZIP library. The final parameter indicates the level of compression to use with the GZIP algorithm. It has no effect if we use the `kdb+` IPC algorithm.

To make this process a bit more intuitive, the `set` operator can also accept the same arguments. The target file and all the compression parameters can be passed as the left operand, while the source file remains on the right.

```
q)(f;20;2;9) set f
`:qdb/2015.03.06/prices/px
```

To check if a file has been compressed, and if so, what parameters were used for compression, we can use the `-21!` operator.

```
q)-21!f
compressedLength  | 4301
uncompressedLength| 5608
algorithm         | 2i
logicalBlockSize  | 20i
zipLevel          | 9i
```

We can then uncompress the file by loading it into memory and saving it without compression parameters.

```
q)f set get f
`:qdb/2015.03.06/prices/px
```

The file no longer has compression statistics, so `-21!` returns an empty dictionary.

```
q)0N!-21!f;
(`symbol$())!()
```

## Compressing by Default

If this level of granularity is not needed, we can alternatively set the `.z.zd` system variable with our desired **z**ip **d**efaults and all future extensionless files written to disk will be compressed with the specified parameters. Files with an extension are assumed to contain text and are therefore not compressed.

```
q).z.zd:20 2 9
q)f set get f
`:qdb/2015.03.06/prices/px
```

To clear the compression configuration we can use the `\x` system command and `.z.zd` will be cleared.

```
q)\x .z.zd
q).z.zd
'.z.zd
```

## Compressing a Directory Tree

The benefits of compression are never appreciated until you run out of disk space or receive the bill for the used space. It is at this point that we need to compress the whole database. Unfortunately, we can not just compress the files using a standard compression tool. Compressed `kdb+` files have meta information stored within the file and must therefore be compressed from within q. Given the right tools, however, this is not a hard task. It may take a long time, but the process is straightforward. At first glance we may be tempted to write a function that recurses into each directory and compresses each file and sub-directory along the way. This approach does not generalize well to other problems. If, on the other hand, we write a function that creates a list of files within a directory, we can then use that list in many other ways. We can even filter the list before applying our compression function.

**.util.tree**

```
tree:{$[x~k:key x;x;11h=type k;raze (.z.s ` sv x,) each k;()]}
```

The `tree` function accepts a file path as its only parameter and returns all the files found within the directory or any sub-directory. It first checks the return value of the `key` operator. When used on a file path, the `key` operator returns one of three things. If the path is an existing file, `key` returns the file, letting you know it exists. If the path is a directory, the contents of the directory are returned as a list of symbols (which has a type of 11h). And if the path does not exist, an empty list, with a type of 0h, is returned.

If the result of `key` is a file, our `tree` function will return the file itself. If the result is a list of symbols, it will recursively call `tree` on each sub-directory and `raze` the results. In all other cases it returns the empty list. As we will see in <traverse>, the `tree` function can also be used to traverse a namespace or directory.

**Q Tip 15.3** Use `.z.s` to make recursive function calls

It is possible to call `tree` directly from within `tree`, but q offers a more portable way of implementing recursion : `.z.s`. The `.z.s` system variable always contains a reference to the currently executing function. It does not exist from the standard q) prompt because there is no executing function.

```
q).z.s
'nyi
```

But we can see how it gets set by forcing an error within a function.

```
q){a+b}[]
{a+b}
'b
```

Q suspends execution and allows us to inspect the current environment. We can now display `.z.s`.

```
q)).z.s
{a+b}
```

As this example demonstrates, it is preferable to use `.z.s` instead of the actual function name because it continues to work even when the function is copied to another name, or even used anonymously.

Returning to the `tree` function we see that `.z.s` is called for each of the files and the results are razed before being returned to ensure the result is a single list of files. Following Q Tip 9.1 [111], this implementation uses a set of parentheses to create a composition instead of braces to create an anonymous function.

Using the `tree` function, we can compress every file in our database.

```
q).z.zd:20 2 9
q){x set get x} each .util.tree `:qdb
`:qdb/2015.03.06/prices/.d`:qdb/2015.03.06/prices/id`:qdb/2015.03.06/prices..
```

Alternatively, we can filter out specific files. In this example, we exclude any file ending in `.d`.

```
q){x set get x} each {x where not x like "*.d"} .util.tree `:qdb
`:qdb/2015.03.06/prices/id`:qdb/2015.03.06/prices/px`:qdb/2015.03.06/prices..
```

## Regular Expressions

The `like` operator is capable of handling a simplified regular expression syntax. The wildcard `"*"` matches an arbitrary sequence of characters. It can appear once or twice within an expression. But if it appears twice, it must be at the beginning and end.

```
q)"qtips" like "*tip*"
1b
```

The wildcard `"?"` matches a single arbitrary character, and can appear any number of times.

```
q)`qtips like "qt??s"
1b
```

The character sequence brackets `"[]"` can contain a list or range of characters - optionally negated with the `"^"` character.

```
q)`qtips`ktips like "[^a-pr-z]tips"
10b
```

## Remote File Systems

Market data compresses well: symbols, sizes and prices frequently repeat themselves. Both of the available compression algorithms significantly reduce the size of market data, often achieving compression ratios greater than 5:1. With this level compression it is also important to consider disk read access performance.

The performance degradation due to compression critically depends on how much time it takes to read the larger dataset versus how much time it takes to decompress the smaller dataset. If our machine's CPU is fast compared to the speed of disk read access, it is conceivable that compressing the data can actually increase the performance of reading data from our kdb+ database.

---

**Q Tip 15.4** Compress data to improve query performance from remote file systems

---

This is often the case with remote file systems. Reading data over a remote file system significantly decreases the speed of data access. Compressing a kdb+ database over a remote filesystem allows the compressed file to be transported over the network, and then expanded locally for processing. Remote file systems such as NFS are a popular means of sharing a single kdb+ database with multiple clients. In this setup, compressing data not only reduces the disk usage, but also increases data access performance.

## 15.5 Mapped Data

When partitioned and segmented databases are queried, the columns are mapped into memory, queried, and then unmapped. This action does not result in any lasting memory allocation. We can query a splayed (and partitioned in this case) table and see how the memory mapped from disk does not increase. The 5th element of the \w system call is still zero.

```
q)\l qdb
q)select from prices where date=first date;
q)\w
113760 67108864 67108864 0 0 2147483648
```

But if we store the results into a variable, the data is mapped into memory until it is no longer needed. If, for example, we only need a subset of the table in memory, the requested rows are copied into RAM and the table is unmapped. For a very large table, this can be an expensive operation. It is best to leave large tables mapped to disk, and use operators such as lj and aj to merge only selected rows with existing in-memory tables. We can see that taking a single row from the table t, copies the data into RAM (thus increasing the first element of the \w system call, and unmaps the table (setting the 5th element back to 0).

```
q)t:select from prices where date=first date
q)\w
119776 67108864 67108864 0 17096 2147483648
q)t:1#t
q)\w
115808 67108864 67108864 0 0 2147483648
```

Constant mapping and unmapping columns can decrease performance for a database that uses the same tables from the same partitions. As of `kdb+` 3.1, tables in a partitioned and segmented databases can be permanently mapped into memory with the `.Q.MAP` operator. We can see how the mapped memory increases once we call `.Q.MAP`.

```
q).Q.MAP[]
q)\w
116992 67108864 67108864 0 45520 2147483648
```

## 15.6  Grid Computing

With a little coding, it is possible to turn `kdb+` into a grid computing platform where the master and each slave in the cluster are q processes. An example implementation can be found in `mserve.q` located in the Kx Example Repository [example] [266]. Kdb+ 3.1 introduced support to make this configuration even easier.

### Negative Slave Count

By starting `kdb+` with a negative slave count we can use a multi-process instead of multi-threaded implementation of the `peach` operator. Marshaling between the processes is managed by `kdb+`, but connectivity is left to us. This allows us to choose between running each slave on the same host to achieve minimum network latency, and spreading the slaves across hosts to access maximum computing resources. Running slaves on multiple machines also lets us scale our grid by adding or removing nodes based on demand.

When a positive slave count is specified, q starts a new thread for each slave. Specifying a negative count simply informs q that we will provide a list of network handles with which it will delegate computation. To determine the list of network handles, q accesses the `.z.pd` system variable. It is up to us to open and manage the state of these handles.

As an example, we can start a master process pointing to our qdb database.

```
$ q qdb -p 5000 -s -4
KDB+ 3.2 2015.03.04 Copyright (C) 1993-2015 Kx Systems
m32/ 4()core 2048MB nick nicks-macbook.local 192.168.1.103 NONEXPIRE
```

Following the example from `mserve.q`, we can then start the slave processes from within q.

```
q)(system "q . -p ",) each string p:system["p"]+1+til neg system"s"
```

We can now open network handles to each of the slaves by calling `hopen` on the ports saved in the variable p and save the result into the `.z.pd` system variable.

```
q).z.pd:`u#hopen each p
```

To ensure we have not specified the same handle twice, q requires that the network handle list returned from the .z.pd system variable have the unique attribute `u applied.

## Multi-process `peach`

From this point on, all calls to the `peach` operator with an argument of more than one element, will be delegated to the slave processes. This includes implicit calls to the `peach` operator that occur in the implementation of q-SQL. Calling `peach` with an atom or single element list will not, however, be delegated to a slave. The function will be executed in the master. To confirm that we are indeed querying data from the slave processes, we can obtain the process ID for each partition.

```
q)select pid:.z.i by date from trades
date       | pid
-----------| -----
2015.03.03| 52436
2015.03.04| 52438
2015.03.05| 52440
2015.03.06| 52436
```

Executing `peach` with a single partition will execute in the master.

```
q)select pid:.z.i by date from trades where date=2015.03.06
date       | pid
-----------| -----
2015.03.06| 52434
```

Notice that the query for each partition was allocated to the slaves in the order we opened and assigned their network handles to the .z.pd system variable. Once this initial allocation is made, however, further processing is allocated to the next free slave. Unlike multi-threaded `peach`, multi-process `peach` can dynamically assign jobs depending on how busy the processes are. In the case of uneven workloads between partitions, this implementation allows for an improved allocation of work over the multi-threaded implementation of `peach`.

When q needs to access the network handles, it uses a pair of brackets to call .z.pd as if it were a niladic function.

```
.z.pd[]
```

This allows .z.pd to contain either an array or a function. If a function is used, it should confirm a connection exists to each of the slaves and reopen any that have closed.

## Slave Layout

Distributing computations across process and/or hosts requires that the same dataset be available from each slave. When the slaves are on different hosts, we either need a separate copy of the data on each host, or the servers need to be mounted on a network file system to access the single source of data.

A networked file system can add considerable delay to data access. It is therefore recommended that for maximum performance, each slave should run on the same server. The difference between running a single q process with multi-threaded slaves versus running multiple slave processes is subtle. Using `.Q.MAP` with multiple processes allows each processes to share the same memory pages instead of allocating new ones. This brings the multi-process setup on par with the multi-threaded configuration. The advantage of using multiple processes lies with the fact that a q process started with slaves requires the lock to be used when accessing or modifying certain data structures such as reference counts. Locks are used when q is started with multiple slaves or in multi-threaded input queue mode discussed in Section 11.2 [143]. A single-threaded q process runs faster because it does not need to lock data structures.

In addition, the main thread of a q process can perform certain operations faster than its threaded slaves. For example, if we start a q process with two slave threads, and count the distinct symbols in a vector, performing this calculation with `peach` is actually slower than `each`.

```
$ q -s 2
KDB+ 3.2 2015.03.04 Copyright (C) 1993-2015 Kx Systems
m32/ 4()core 2048MB nick nicks-macbook.local 192.168.1.103 NONEXPIRE
q)v:1000000?`8
q)\t  {count distinct v} each 0 1
25
q)\t  {count distinct v} peach 0 1
121
```

This chapter has covered many options we have when choosing how to set up our database. But storing data is not the end goal. Data exists to be analyzed. The next chapter discusses the different ways we have of accessing data from a `kdb+` server.

# Chapter 16

# Remotely Accessing Data

It is a capital mistake to theorize before one has data. Insensibly one begins to twist facts to suit theories, instead of theories to suit facts.

— Sir Arthur Conan Doyle *Sherlock Holmes*

We have built a CEP engine and stored intra-day price, quote and trade data. We have learned how to partition the data to allow the database to efficiently grow with increased volumes of data. We have also learned how to query the data with q-SQL. But to actually benefit from data, we need to analyze it. And that often means extracting the data from kdb+ into other systems. Kdb+ provides three different methods for accessing and extracting data.

- Q to q (native IPC)

- Binary protocol (C/C++/C#/Java/...)

- Text-based protocols (HTTP GET/POST and JSON)

## 16.1   q to q

Q makes Inter-Process Communication (IPC) extremely easy. To open a connection from one kdb+ process to another, we can use the hopen operator. To demonstrate this communication we can first start the CEP engine on port 5001 and have the timer run every 100 milliseconds.

```
$ q cep.q -p 5001 -t 100
```

Then we start a new q session and open a connection to the CEP engine.

```
$ q
q)h:hopen `::5001
```

With the network handle h, we can send both synchronous and asynchronous messages. A positive network handle causes all communication to be synchronous. The operation will not return until the message has reached its destination, and a response has been received, or an error is reported. Using a negative network handle, on the other hand, sends an asynchronous message. The operation returns immediately, perhaps even before the message has been sent to the network. Passing the generic null : : to the network handle will block the process until all previously sent asynchronous messages have been flushed to the network: h[] or h(::). To guarantee delivery, a synchronous message must be sent. The simplest way to perform this is with an empty character vector: h"".

Synchronous communication is used to query q databases and obtain snapshots from CEP engines. We can send the request in one of three ways. A simple character vector with our desired command can be passed to the network handle.

```
q)h"select avg px by id from prices"
id| px
--| --------
0 | 109.9824
1 | 80.0027
2 | 10.00018
3 | 4.999995
4 | 1.999363
```

We can also send an atom or list of values which will be evaluated by the remote connection.

```
q)h(`prices;0)
id  | 0
px  | 110f
time| 2015.03.06D16:30:28.416867000
```

And finally, we can even send our own custom function, along with parameters, to the server for evaluation.

```
q)f:{aj[`id`time;trades]quotes}
q)h(f;`)
id ts tp   time                       bs bp     ap    as
--------------------------------------------------------------
1  2  80.05 2015.03.06D16:30:29.016867000 3  80     80.05 20
2  59 9.99  2015.03.06D16:30:29.516867000 71 9.99   10    9
0  13 110   2015.03.06D16:30:29.616867000 13 109.95 110   28
1  2  80    2015.03.06D16:30:29.616867000 3  80     80.05 37
1  13 80    2015.03.06D16:30:30.216867000 42 80     80.05 18
..
```

## Subscriptions

Asynchronous messages are often used to send messages as fast as possible without needing an acknowledgment that the message arrived safely. Another use is to send a subscription request where we expect multiple responses at an unknown time in the future. As a client, we can add a timer entry to the CEP's timer that sends us the contents of the price table every 10 seconds. First we define a table to hold our copy of the data, and a callback function upd that will be called by the remote timer. The kdb+ tickerplant application [tick] [266] has set the standard of calling the callback upd. The function should accept two arguments: a table name and the new values for that table. These two arguments make writing callback routines effortless. If we define upd as upsert then every time our callback is called the new data will be inserted into our table.

```
price:1!flip `id`px`time!"jfp"$\:()
upd:upsert
```

## Insert

The kdb+ tickerplant defines upd as insert, which is an optimized, but limited, version of upsert. It only accepts one or more records, not dictionaries or tables, and only updates global variables. Unlike the upsert operator, the return value of insert is the row number of the inserted values.

```
q)`price insert (0 1;100 101f;2#.z.P)
0 1
```

Finally, the insert operator throws an error when attempting to insert a duplicate key into a keyed table. This is in contrast to upsert which can both **up**date and **ins**ert rows.

## Asynchronous Messages

Next, we define a **p**ublish **f**unction pf that will be called by the timer to send the price table to us. In order to send the data to us, it requires access to the network handle corresponding to our TCP connection. This information, found in the .z.w system variable, will be bound to the pf function before we use it as a timer function. When publishing the response, the function negates the network handle to use asynchronous communication. This is done for two reasons. The first reason is that the CEP engine does not actually need confirmation that the client has received the data. The second reason is that the CEP engine needs to operate as efficiently as possible. Sending the message asynchronously allows the CEP engine to continue processing its own messages while the data is sent over the network.

```
pf:{[w;tm]neg[w](`upd;`price;price)}
```

Since we want the data to arrive every 10 seconds, we will use the .timer.until [129] function to repeatedly call our publish function pf. We will also specify the end time as midnight which can be achieved by casting the next date to a timestamp. We use parse tree notation to create a list containing the **until f**unction and its first two parameters. The third parameter, which will be the publish function pf can only be added to the list after .z.w is available.

```
uf:(`.timer.until;0D00:00:10;"p"$1+.z.D)
```

The final function f will combine the **until f**unction uf and the publish function pf when it executes within in the context of the CEP engine. During its execution, the client handle .z.w will be obtained and bound to the publish function pf, which will then be attached to the parse tree **until f**unction uf, which will finally be added to the timer.

```
f:{[uf;pf].timer.add[`timer.job;`cb;uf,pf[.z.w];.z.P]}
```

We can now add our timer entry and observe as the data in our own copy of the price table is updated every 10 seconds.

```
h(f;uf;pf)
```

## 16.2   Binary Protocol

The communication between two kdb+ sessions can be one of two formats. The original binary protocol, or the newer compressed protocol. After the release of kdb+ 2.6, kdb+ processes and the C API are capable of sending compressed messages. The initial handshake between a kdb+ server and a client (either another kdb+ session or a client using an implementation of the native protocol), includes a declaration of its capabilities. If the client was not written to handle the compressed format, the uncompressed format will be used. For increased performance, messages between processes on the same host, and message that do not compress to less than half the original size will be sent uncompressed.

Kdb+ 2.6 also introduced the timestamp and timespan data types. Using the compressed protocol enables the transmission of these types as well. When the server reverts to using the uncompressed protocol, the new types can not be sent.

Once the compressed format has been locally decompressed, converting the stream of bytes into usable data types is exactly the same in both formats. Implementations of the self-describing binary protocol [ipc] [267] can be found in the Kx C repository [crepo] [266]. The Java kx/c.java, C# c.cs and javascript c.js API all implement the decompression logic. The compression algorithm, however, has not been published.

The C API can be used in two ways. Clients can use the C header file k.h, along with the object file c.o located in platform specific sub-directory of the Kx q repository [qrepo] [266], to communicate with kdb+ servers. The Cookbook section on the Kx wiki [cookbook] [266] has examples on how to communicate with a kdb+ server in the *Interfacing with C* section. There are also examples for many other languages and programs.

In addition to allowing remote access to data, the C API also enables us to embed custom functions into a running kdb+ process. By compiling a dynamically loaded library, new features can be added to the q environment. This allows the use of statistical libraries such as LAPACK, enabling communication with other applications such as R, and implementing serializing/deserializing algorithms for third party network protocols. A few examples of extending q functionality with C libraries can also be found in the cookbook section of the Kx wiki [cookbook] [266] under the section *Extending With C*.

## 16.3 HTTP Access

Once a kdb+ server has been started, and a port opened, the kdb+ process can be remotely queried. Without resorting to any programming, the HTTP interface is the easiest to use. Typing the server name and port as the URL will access kdb+'s builtin web server. In this example, we loaded the cep.q script on port 5001.

**http://localhost:5001/**

```
c       |opt def                   doc
handle  |---------------------------------------------------
p       |     ()                   ()
price   |ref `:ref.csv             "file with reference data"
prices  |eod 0D23:59:00.000000000  "time for end of day event"
prof    |db  `:db                  "end of day dump location"
quote   |log 2                     "log level"
quotes  |
ref     |
trade   |
trades  |
```

In addition to accessing data by using the provided web interface, we can also query the kdb+ server programatically. We can see that kdb+ has implemented routines to return results in five formats by looking in the .h namespace: JSON, CSV, TXT, XML and XLS.

```
q).h.tx
json| k){$[10=abs t:@x;s@,/{$[x in r:"\t\n\r\"\\";"\\","tnr\"\\"r?x;x]}'x;9..
csv | k){.q.csv 0:x}
txt | k){"\t"0:x}
xml | k){g:{(#*y)#'(,,"<",x),y,,,"</",x:($x),">"};(,"<R>"),(,/'+g[`r]@,/(!x..
xls | k){ex eb es[`Sheet1]x}
```

Speadsheet applications often have facilities to import data from external sources. The easiest way to import data from kdb+ is using the CSV or TXT formats which produce comma and tab delimited result sets.

```
$ curl http://localhost:5001/q.csv?ref
id,px,ts,qs,vol,rfr
```

```
0,110,0.05,30,0.35,0.01
1,80,0.05,50,0.25,0.01
2,10,0.01,100,0.12,0.01
3,5,0.01,300,0.09,0.01
4,2,0.005,1000,0.5,0.01
```

The query can be the name of a table, or any q expression that results in a table. When used as the datasource for a pivot table or pivot chart, the combination of a q database and customizable spreadsheet can be very powerful.

The other formats can be accessed by replacing the csv on the URL with any of the other extensions. As can be seen in the following example, q returns the query with a valid HTTP header informing clients of the encoding.

```
$ curl -i http://localhost:5001/q.txt?ref
HTTP/1.1 200 OK
Content-Type: text/plain
Connection: close
Content-Length: 138

id      px      ts      qs      vol     rfr
0       110     0.05    30      0.35    0.01
1       80      0.05    50      0.25    0.01
2       10      0.01    100     0.12    0.01
3       5       0.01    300     0.09    0.01
4       2       0.005   1000    0.5     0.01
```

The .z.ph function is used to respond to HTTP GET requests. Similarly, the .z.pp function is used for POST requests. Kdb+ provides a default implementation for .z.ph. As you have seen, it provides a web server implementation and access to tables in four formats.

```
q).z.ph
k){x:uh$[@x;x;*x];$[~#x;hy['htm]fram[$.z.f;x]("?";"?",*x@<x:$(."\\v"),."\\b..
  "?"=*x;@[{hp jx[0j]R::1_x};x;he];"?"in x;@[{hy[t]@`/:tx[t:`$-3#n#x]@.(1+n..
  #r:@[1::;`$":",p:HOME,"/",x;""];hy[`$last@"."\:x]"c"$r;hn["404 Not Found"..
```

The utility functions used in this definition are located in the .h namespace and, like everything in q.k, are written in k. Though not documented, the functions can be used to implement your own .z.pg and/or .z.pp event handlers.

```
q).h
    | ::
htc | k){,/("<";x;y;"</";x:($x),">")}
hta | k){,/("<";$x;,/" ",'($!y),'"=",'{$[10h=@x;"\"",x,"\"";$x]}'. y;">")}
htac| k){,/(hta[x]y;z;"</";$x;">")}
ha  | k){htac['a;(,`href)!,x]y}
hb  | k){htac['a;`target`href!`v,,x]y}
```

```
pre | k){htc['pre]@'/:x}
..
```

If the URL used to query the `kdb+` server specifies a file before the "?" character, it is assumed to be a file located in the directory specified by the `.h.HOME` variable. If a file with the given name is found, it is returned to the client like a standard web server. An error is produced if the file can not be located. The `.h.HOME` variable is set to "html" by default. If it is set to a relative path, the directory will be searched relative to `$QHOME`. If for nothing else, a `favicon.ico` file can be placed in this directory to allow web browsers to display an icon along with the server's URL. More advanced uses of the `.h.HOME` directory allow placing web pages that generate reports and/or graphs of the database's data.

The websocket protocol is also capable of communicating with the `kdb+` database using text messages. The distinguishing feature of the websocket protocol is its ability to send and receive asynchronous messages. This allows a single query to trigger a stream of results. This is useful for generating graphs that dynamically change based on events published by the `kdb+` database. The `.z.ws` system variable can be used to define how the `kdb+` server should respond to websocket queries. The default implementation is to echo the query to the client.

When using a synchronous protocol like HTTP POST or GET, large datasets can most efficiently be returned in CSV or TXT formats. The column headers are listed once, and the uniform data follows. But when an asynchronous protocol like web sockets is used, each returned value must be self-describing. XML is one of the most popular self-describing formats. But it is also very verbose. The JSON format is also self-describing, but is more human readable and compact than XML. As of `kdb+` 3.2, functions to convert between `kdb+` data-structures and the JSON format are available in the `.j` namespace. We can see how a dictionary can be transformed from q to JSON,[1]

```
q)-1 j:.j.j first 0!ref;
{"id":0,"px":110,"ts":0.05,"qs":30,"vol":0.35,"rfr":0.01}
```

and back again.

```
q).j.k j
id | 0
px | 110
ts | 0.05
qs | 30
vol| 0.35
rfr| 0.01
```

Text based interfaces are convenient for small datasets. For larger datasets, or more efficient access to the `kdb+` database, the native binary protocol should be used.

---

[1] We used the -1 file handle instead of the `show` operator to display the JSON character vector in order to see the contents of the character vector instead of the character vector itself, which includes enclosing quotes and internal backslashes.

## 16.4   Qcon Binary

The q prompt is best used for writing new code and analyzing data. But a running kdb+ server does not permit access to its REPL interface. To simulate this interface from a client connection, Kx has provided the qcon binary. The qcon binary can be found in the original q repository [qrepo] [266] under the platform specific sub-directory.

To open a new qcon connection, we must specify the host (unless the process is on the current machine), the port, and optionally the user and password - all separated by colons. The syntax for qcon's command line argument is the same as hopen's except it does not need the leading handle identifier: `:.

```
$ ./qcon -h
qcon host:port[:usr:pwd]
```

The qcon application makes a new connection to the kdb+ server for each request. It reads the response and then immediately closes the connection. The connection is not persistent. This is important because qcon connections will never appear in the list of active TCP connections displayed with the .z.W operator. If a connection request fails, the qcon processes will exit. Typing a double backslash "\\" will also exit the qcon process. Not to worry, the kdb+ server will not exit. If you do want to force the kdb+ server to exit, the exit 0 operation will still work. For most use cases, the qcon interface is a drop-in replacement for the q) prompt. One important difference is that qcon connections can not change directories with the \d system command. In addition, although .z.w returns 0 from the q) prompt, attempting to use this variable from the qcon binary will return the handle for the transient TCP connection created for each request. Even though the qcon process continues to run between queries, the connection to the server, and potentially the value of .z.w, will change with every request.

The number of rows and columns displayed by qcon queries is governed by the server's \c system setting. Sometimes, however, the results seen from the client are truncated. This is because the amount of data transferred between the server and client is limited by the network. The qcon binary was written to make a single attempt to read data from the network. It then closes the TCP connection. If the full response requires two or more calls to read data from the network, the displayed results will be incomplete. The displayed text, therefore, depends on the network connectivity between server and client. The amount of data transmitted between any two machines is limited by the Maximum Transmission Unit or MTU. The actual MTU is the minimum MTU between the kdb+ server and your qcon process. This upper limit on the amount of data that can be transferred has a strange effect on qcon. Increasing the number of columns with the \c system command has the paradoxical effect of reducing the number of rows displayed. Just as confusing is that the number of rows returned depends on how many significant digits are displayed for each floating point number. As more characters are required to represent each value in a table, fewer values can be displayed. Aside from this limitation, qcon is a great tool to manage kdb+ servers.

This completes our discussion on Big Data. While kdb+ is often advertised as a high performance data processing platform, not enough attention is given to the flexibility and efficiency of the q programming language. The next chapter combines a few more q features, such as reflection and parallel execution, to create a profiler library, derivative pricing library, and histogram charting library. The amount of code needed to implement each of these libraries is astonishingly small. To achieve this level of succinctness it is important to use proper data structures. Once the data structures are chosen, q's internal library of operators make light work of implementing our libraries.

# Chapter 17

# Advanced Techniques

> Functional programming is like describing your problem to a mathematician. Imperative programming is like giving instructions to an idiot.
>
> — arcus *#scheme on Freenode*

In addition to the q language, Kx System's most popular offering is `kdb+tick`. It includes the tickerplant (tp), realtime database (rdb), historical database (hdb) and q library to subscribe to realtime updates. The q scripts needed to run these servers, and a brief introduction on how to use them, can now be found on the Kx wiki [tick] [266] and downloaded for free. For a look back in time at the origins of the current tickerplant architecture, we can read "High Volume Transaction Processing Without Concurrency Control, Two Phase Commit SQL, or C++" by Arthur Whitney, Dennis Shasha, and Stevan Apter [hpts] [267]. But q can be used for much more than recording and analyzing tick data.

In this chapter we will discuss how the performance of a CEP engine can be analyzed by using q's reflection features to build a function profiler. We will also present two ways to compute the price of simple equity options. The first approach demonstrates the use of parallel programming to implement Monte Carlo simulation. The second approach uses the tools built throughout the book to implement the Black-Scholes-Merton model and compute implied volatilities. And finally, to wrap things up, we use functional programming techniques to create a histogram charting library that allows for multiple bucketing and charting algorithms.

## 17.1 Profiling q Functions

Q operators are highly optimized for vector calculations. When writing a CEP engine, however, many computations are atomic. The performance of a CEP engine depends not only on how long each function takes, but also what percent of the time is spent in each function. It is possible to use the \t system command to time individual calls to a function, but this will not provide a complete picture of a dynamic system that reacts to complex events. To obtain a clear picture of the dynamics of a CEP engine we must record the time each function begins and ends. In addition, we need knowledge of the function call graph: how much time is spent in the current function versus how much time is spent in each of child function. Although q does not provide a builtin profiler, the language is transparent enough to allow us to build our own.

We begin by defining an events table to store the function ID, parent ID, function name and elapsed time.

```
prof.events:flip `id`pid`func`time!"jjsn"$\:()
```

To keep track of the parent-child relationship between functions we must create global variables to hold function and its parent ids. We begin by initializing them to 0.

```
pid:id:0
```

## Timing Functions

Modifying the execution of a function to record statistics such as the execution begin and end time is known as instrumentation. The first step in instrumenting a function is to create a utility function that records the execution time as well as the ID, parent ID, and function's name.

**.prof.time**

```
time:{[n;f;a]
 s:.z.p;
 id:.prof.id+:1;
 pid:.prof.pid;
 .prof.pid:id;
 r:f . a;
 .prof.pid:pid;
 `prof.events upsert (id;pid;n;.z.p-s);
 r}
```

The time function accepts a function **n**ame, a **f**unction to call, and the **a**rguments to call it with. It begins by saving the start time in the variable s. Each function profiled increments the global identifier id. To keep track of the current id we copy the value to a local variable. We are now the parent function for any functions that get called by this function. To record this fact, we first save our parent id into pid for later use, and set the global pid variable to our id.

With the global values safely incremented and stored, the next line calls the original function and saves the result in r. Now that the execution of any child function is complete, we can reset the global pid to our parent id for profiling any functions that may run after the current function. The time function finishes by recording the id, pid, function name and the time spent executing the profiled function to a global table prof.events. The last line returns the results from the profiled function.

## Instrumenting Functions

Q functions are first class objects, and as such, they can be evaluated, passed as parameters, and even inspected. The get operator provides metadata about each q function.

```
q)get {x+y}
0x7978410003
`x`y
`symbol$()
,`
"{x+y}"
```

The first returned element is the function's bytecode representation. The next item is a list of parameter names used by the function. The third and fourth elements are lists of the local and global variables used within the function. The first item of the global variables list is actually the directory in which the function was defined. If there are any constants used in the function, they are listed until finally the last reported element is the text of the function itself.

To instrument a function, we must replace the definition with a call to time, while ensuring the interface remains the same. The instr function accepts the **n**ame of a function to profile.

**.prof.instr**

```
instr:{[n]
 m:get f:get n;
 system "d .",string first m 3;
 n set (')[.prof.time[n;f];enlist];
 system "d .";
 n}
```

It uses the get operator to extract the function definition from the name and saves it in f. It then calls get again to obtain the metadata which it saves in m. The third line of the function uses the fourth field of the function's metadata to change the directory to where the function was defined. All variable and function references are relative to the directory in which they are defined. To ensure function's behavior is unchanged, we must enter to the directory of its definition before redefining it. Once this is done, the last line of the function changes back to the root directory.

The instrumentation occurs in the fourth line of the instr function. We can determine how many parameters the function expects by checking the second field of the metadata. But we do not actually need to know this number. The time function accepts the function's arguments as a single list. What we need is a way to turn a list of function parameters into a single list. The enlist operator can do this. In fact, it is not even limited to 8 arguments.

```
q)enlist[0;1;2;3;4;5;6;7;8;9;10]
0 1 2 3 4 5 6 7 8 9 10
```

The fourth line of instr creates a composition of .prof.time with enlist so that all parameters passed to the composition are converted into a single list and passed as the last parameter of .prof.

time. We have implicitly made compositions in the past by stringing a list of functions together that end with a dyadic operator. The `instr` function explicitly creates a composition using the `'[;]` operator.[1]

```
q)'[{x};{x+y}]
{x}{x+y}
```

As an example of `.prof.instr`'s usage, we can now instrument `.util.rnd`,

```
q).prof.instr`.util.rnd
`.util.rnd
```

see that its definition has changed,

```
q).util.rnd
{[n;f;a]
 s:.z.p;
 id:.prof.id+:1;
 pid:.prof.pid;
 .prof.pid:id;
 r:f . a;
 .prof.pid:pid;
 `prof.events upsert (id;pid;n;.z.p-s);
 r}[`.util.rnd;{x*"j"$y%x}]enlist
```

but its behavior has not.

```
q).util.rnd[.01] 1%3
0.33
```

Checking the `prof.events` table shows the event was recorded.

```
q)prof.events
id pid func      time
-------------------------------------
1  0   .util.rnd 0D00:00:00.000013000
```

## Traversing the Directory Tree

To instrument every function in every directory, we first need to find all the directories. Each directory is a dictionary mapping variable names to their definition. The `key` operator gives us the name of all variables within the directory. For the special case where the directory name is null, q returns all the directory names.

---

[1] We must place the "'" within parentheses to prevent q from interpreting set ' as a call to set each.

```
q)key `
`q`Q`h`j`o`util`stat`sim`timer`log`md`opt`hist`deriv`prof
```

We are typically interested in profiling our own code, and not that of the q language or the profiler itself. So we can exclude q, Q, h, j, o, and prof from the list of directories to inspect. Once we find the complete list of directories, we must join the name with the parent directory, just as if we were building a file path. Similar to the technique we used in .util.tree [219], we build a composition so we only have to each over the list a single time.

**.prof.dirs**

```
dirs:{(` sv x,) each key[x] except `q`Q`h`j`o`prof}
```

In fact, we can reuse the .util.tree [219] function on these directories to find all the variables located within them.

```
q).util.tree each .prof.dirs`
`.util.`.util.use`.util.wday`.util.rng`.util.rnd`.util.randrng`.util.sattr`..
`.stat.`.stat.pctile`.stat.u12`.stat.skew`.stat.kurt`.stat.bm`.stat.gbm`.st..
`.sim.`.sim.path`.sim.genp`.sim.tickrnd`.sim.delay`.sim.filter`.sim.genq`.s..
`.timer.`.timer.merge`.timer.add`.timer.run`.timer.loop`.timer.until
`.log.`.log.h`.log.lvl`.log.unit`.log.mult`.log.mem`.log.hdr`.log.msg`.log...
`.md.`.md.updp`.md.updq`.md.updt`.md.dump
`.opt.`.opt.config`.opt.getopt`.opt.wrap`.opt.usage
..
```

In addition to the directories we created to hold our code, we can also profile any function located within the root directory. For this we must add the directory named `. to our list.

```
q).util.tree `.
`..sym`..timer.`..timer.job`..prices`..trades`..quotes`..prof.`..prof.event..
```

But not all the variables are functions. And not all functions can be profiled. Only lambdas, which have type 100h, allow us to modify their structure. We must therefore build a filtering function to include only variables with type 100h.

**.prof.lambdas**

```
lambdas:{x where 100h=(type get@) each x}
```

The instrall function pulls together the these two functions and .util.tree [219] to profile all interesting functions.

**.prof.instrall**

```
instrall:{instr each lambdas raze .util.tree each `.,dirs`}
```

## Profile Statistics

We can now start q, instrument all the functions and start the CEP engine. We will set the log level to 0 so logging does not interfere with our profiling.

```
$ q cep.q -log 0
```

Instrumenting all the functions returns a list of each function instrumented.

```
q).prof.instrall`
`..genu`..main`.util.use`.util.wday`.util.rng`.util.rnd`.util.randrng`.util..
```

And finally we set the timer to 100 ms to start the engine.

```
q)\t 100
```

We can see that the profiler has begun to record events.

```
q)prof.events
id pid func        time
----------------------------------------
3  2   .md.updt    0D00:00:00.000018000
2  1   .timer.until 0D00:00:00.000053000
4  1   .timer.merge 0D00:00:00.000080000
1  0   .timer.run  0D00:00:00.000204000
7  6   .md.updt    0D00:00:00.000011000
..
```

With the parent/child relationship documented, it is possible to generate a report that lists how much time each function took exclusive of its children. This will show us which functions deserve our attention the most.

### .prof.stats

```
stats:{[e]
 e:e pj select neg sum time,nc:count i by id:pid from e;
 s:select sum time*1e-6,n:count i,avg nc by func from e;
 s:update timepc:time%n from s;
 s:`pct xdesc update pct:100f*time%sum time from s;
 s}
```

This stats function takes the events table as its argument. The first line computes the time spent in each function, exclusive of any children. We start by computing the statistics for each parent id pid. This is the total time spent in each of the child functions. We rename the column from pid to id so we can then subtract these values from their actual parent function. We also add the nc column which counts how many child functions were called for each parent. The final step is to use the plus join pj operator to subtract (or add the negative of) the child values from their parent's statistics. The pj operator behaves just like `lj` but instead of overwriting existing values in the left table with new values from the right table, the two values are added. In the case of missing values from the left table, the default value of 0 will be used.

---
**Q Tip 17.1** Embrace automatically generated column names
---

To keep q-SQL statements short, it is important to leverage q's default naming rules. By placing operators in the proper order, q will automatically assign the results on top of an existing column. There is therefore no need to use the assignment operator to save the results. As a general rule, the name will be taken from the last token in the q-SQL command. As an exception to that rule, the operators +,-,*,%,& and | use the first token (which is their left operand). If the token is not a valid name, like the automatic variable `i`, the operators stored in `.Q.res` or the `.q` directory, or a literal like 1e-6, the name will become x. If the name already exists in the table, Q will append a number, starting with 1, to distinguish the column.

---
**Q Tip 17.2** Delete unused columns before adding new ones
---

Reusing columns also makes the code more efficient. Memory must be allocated with each new column. By assigning values on top of an existing column we limit the amount of memory needed by the function. Deleting unused columns before adding new columns will also make the code more efficient. Deleted memory is returned to a memory pool for reuse. When the data type of a new column is the same size as one just deleted, the required memory can be quickly acquired from the pool without having to allocate new memory or coalesce smaller chunks.

The `stats` function summarizes each function by name, and not `id`. The second line sums the time values, computes the total number of calls, and the average number of children for each function. At today's computer speeds, the execution time varies from fractions of a millisecond to multiple milliseconds. Displaying time values in nanoseconds would result in very large reported values. To display the elapsed values in milliseconds, the function multiplies each time (stored in nanoseconds) by 1e-6. The next line computes the amount of time each function takes per call. The final line of the function converts to, and sorts by, the percentage of time taken for each function.

The final report displays the elapsed **time** exclusive of children, the **n**umber of calls to the function, the average **n**umber of **c**hildren, the average **time** **p**er **c**all and the total **percent**age of time spent in each function.

```
q).prof.stats prof.events
func         | time     n      nc timepc     pct
-------------| ---------------------------------------
.timer.merge| 1590.278 25553 0  0.06223449 19.18796
.timer.run  | 1378.854 25553 2  0.05396055 16.63696
.md.updp    | 1246.257 16400 2  0.07599128 15.03708
.md.updq    | 841.354  6178  1  0.1361855  10.1516
.stat.horner| 690.185  49200 0  0.01402815 8.327628
..
```

Nearly 35 percent of the time is spent manipulating the timer, and not actually doing any "real" work. Building a better timer utility would thus be beneficial.

As the profiler continues to accumulate events, the report takes longer and longer to run. Even if the underlying data has not changed, we will have to wait the same amount of time each time the report is run. This report is a perfect candidate to be turned into a view.

Functions and q-SQL statements re-execute their definition each time they are called - even if none of their arguments have changed. One way to reduce computational overhead and increase the speed of execution is to use views. A view keeps track of its arguments and only re-executes the body when any of the arguments have changed and the view is actually accessed.

## Declaring a View

Declaring a view is similar to assigning a variable. But instead of using a single colon ":", we use a double colon ::. Assigning a variable with a double colon within a function performs a global assignment. Doing the same thing outside of any function creates a view. View definitions should not end with a semicolon. Ending the definition with a semicolon will cause the view to evaluate to null. Views are used for their return values, not their side effects. A view returning a null value would therefore be useless.

We can now save the results of .prof.stats [240] into a view.

```
prof.rpt::.prof.stats prof.events
```

Once a view is created, we can use the \b system command to see which views are defined. Since we defined the view in the prof namespace, we must query it specifically.

```
q)\b prof
,`rpt
```

Remember that, as we mentioned in Section 5.4 [59], directories can not contain views. If we attempted to define the view within the .prof directory, the statement would be evaluated a single time and the results saved as a table, and not a view.

```
.prof.rpt::.prof.stats prof.events
```

To see the difference we must check the view's definition. Although we can access a function's definitions simply by referencing the variable containing its value, accessing a view's definition is slightly more complicated. By construction, views are supposed to behave like variables and their definitions are hidden. To access the view's definition, we must use the view's name to index into its base namespace.

While prof.rpt remains a view,

```
q)prof`rpt
.prof.stats prof.events
```

`.prof.rpt` is now a table.

```
q).prof`rpt
func| time n nc timepc pct
----| --------------------
```

The body of a view is only executed after it is referenced. The next time we access the view it will only be re-evaluated if any of the variables in its definition have changed. We can see the list of views scheduled for re-evaluation by using the \B system command.

```
q)\B prof
,`rpt
```

Once we evaluate the view, it is removed from the results of \B.

```
q)prof.rpt
func| time n nc timepc pct
----| --------------------
q)\B prof
`symbol$()
```

If we then instrument all the functions and start the timer, the view will be flagged as dirty and scheduled to be re-evaluated the next time we request its value.

```
q).prof.instrall`
`..genu`..main`.util.use`.util.wday`.util.rng`.util.rnd`.util.randrng`.util..
q)\t 100
q)\B prof
,`rpt
```

It is actually possible to see how q keeps track of the inter-variable dependencies. The `.z.b` system variable contains a mapping from each variable to a list of views that depend on it. When any variable is modified, kdb+ checks this map, and marks any dependent views dirty. It would then check the map again (and again) to see if a change in this view would result in another view needing to be updated. In this way, it is possible to add to the chain of inter-variable dependencies without having to change existing code. In our case, we can see that every time `prof.events` is modified, `prof.rpt` will be marked as dirty.

```
q).z.b
prof.events| prof.rpt
```

Like functions, we can access metadata relating to views. The data stored for views includes its current value, functional form, dependencies and textual representation.

```
q)get prof`rpt
(+(,`func)!,`symbol$())!+`time`n`nc`timepc`pct!(`float$();`long$();`float$(..
(`.prof.stats;`prof.events)
```

```
, `prof.events
".prof.stats prof.events"
```

Views do not offer an advantage in historical databases. The dependency tracking is superfluous because the data never changes. Derived tables can be generated when the server starts. Views are useful for derived datasets where there is a mismatch in the update and query frequency. For real-time servers, processes where the contents of each table changes throughout the day, views provide a great way to reduce both processing resources and code complexity. Instead of modifying the publisher to update all sets of derived statistics, views can be added without having to change upstream logic.

---

**Q Tip 17.3** Factor long view definitions into separate functions

---

It is important to remember that only variables explicitly mentioned in the view definition are tracked by kdb+. A view will not be marked dirty if a variable changes but is only referenced from within a function. This reinforces the need for writing functions that do not access global variables, but only operate on their arguments. It is thus advisable to factor view definitions into a function with arguments and a simple view declaration that calls the function. This allows the function to be tested independently of the view's definition. A single view can be split into multiple views if the parameter list grows too long.

Now that we have generated the prof.rpt view, we can directly access the table, ignoring the complex query that created it. If we access prof.rpt after new rows are added to prof.events, the query will be re-run. But if prof.events is exactly the same as the last time we accessed prof.rpt, the view will return the cached results.

```
q)prof.rpt::.prof.stats prof.events
prof.rpt
func         | time      n     nc timepc     pct
-------------| -----------------------------------------
.timer.merge| 1590.278  25553 0  0.06223449  19.18796
.timer.run  | 1378.854  25553 2  0.05396055  16.63696
.md.updp    | 1246.257  16400 2  0.07599128  15.03708
.md.updq    | 841.354   6178  1  0.1361855   10.1516
.stat.horner| 690.185   49200 0  0.01402815  8.327628
..
```

## 17.2   Derivative Pricing

Kdb+ is a single threaded process by default. To increase performance we either need to spread computations across multiple kdb+ processes or take advantage of q's ability to delegate computations to multiple threads. In the section called "Partitions" [212] we saw how to increase performance by using peach to query multiple partitions simultaneously. In this section we will cover two more ways to improve computational performance.

To make the use case more tangible, we will develop functions to price European options. We will first use a brute force method called Monte Carlo simulation then introduce a more elegant closed form solution using the Black-Scholes-Merton model.

A European option is a financial derivative that gives the holder the right, but not the obligation, to buy or sell a security on a specific date, known as the expiration or maturity date, for a specific price, known as the strike price. If the contract gives the owner the right to buy the security, it is called a Call option while the contract giving the owner the right to sell the security is called a Put option.

## Monte Carlo Simulation

Monte Carlo simulation is a general purpose tool that can be used to compute the value of many derivative instruments to within a specified confidence interval. Using Monte Carlo simulation to value an option is based on the principle that averaging an instrument's payoff over many independent price paths produces a value which tends to the exact value as the number of simulations increases. Unfortunately, the precision does not grow linearly with the number of paths - the improvement is proportional to the square root on the number of paths. Monte Carlo simulation is easy to implement, but hard to implement efficiently.

Using the functions we have already introduced, implementing Monte Carlo simulation is very simple. The function must accept all the parameters required to generate a price path with the `.stat.gbm` [63] function: the security's standard deviation $s$, growth rate $r$, and time steps to maturity $t$. In addition, it must accept the current security price $S$, the derivative's payoff function $pf$ and the number of independent paths to simulate $n$.

**.deriv.mc**

```
mc:{[S;s;r;t;pf;n]
 z:.stat.norminv n?/:count[t]#1f;
 f:S*.stat.gbm[s;r;deltas[first t;t]] z;
 v:pf[f]*exp neg r*last t;
 v}
```

The first line of the function generates a matrix of normal random variables $z$. Then second line computes the elapsed time between each simulation step and passes the result to the `.stat.gbm` [63] function. The result is a matrix of forward prices for the security. The last line of the function calls the payoff function $pf$ passed in as a parameter to the function. After computing the payoff at expiration, it is then discounted to the present value $v$.

We passed the complete security path to the payoff function in case the payoff depends on the exact path the security took. We can now define a few payoff functions. The European option compares the last price on each path with the strike price $k$. The function must handle both Put and Call options. The first parameter is a boolean indicating if the option is a call. The next parameter is the strike price $k$. The final parameter is a list of forward prices generated from `.stat.gbm` [63].

**.deriv.eu**

```
eu:{[c;k;f]0f|$[c;last[f]-k;k-last f]}
```

A Call option's payoff is the difference between the final price and the strike price floored at 0. The Put option's payoff is exactly the opposite. It returns the difference between the strike price and the final security price, floored at 0.

We can now generate many paths and compute the present value of each payoff. In this example, we will price a Call option with a strike price of 90 on a security with current price at 100, standard deviation of .2, and growth rate of .03.

```
q)c:1b;S:100;k:90;s:.2;r:.03
```

The option will expire in 1 year and we will assume there are 252 business days in the year. And finally, we will generate 10000 paths to average over.

```
q)t:til[252]%251;n:10000
```

We can now use the mc function to view the present values of the final payoffs.

```
q).util.use '.deriv;
q)mc[S;s;r;t;eu[c;k];n]
23.34801 12.38778 23.97196 47.88279 12.7648 17.36042 26.33101 0 10.69967 0 ..
```

To compute the option price we average all the values.

```
q)avg mc[S;s;r;t;eu[c;k];n]
15.23515
```

But using Monte Carlo simulation to price options is an inexact process. There is always an uncertainty with every computation. It is important to report this uncertainty along with the estimate. The mcstat function computes statistics for the Monte Carlo results. It returns three values, the **e**xpected **v**alue (which is the best estimate of the option's value), the **err**or of the estimate (to within 2 standard deviations), and the **n**umber of data points averaged.

**.deriv.mcstat**

```
mcstat:{`ev`err`n!(avg x;1.96*sdev[x]%sqrt n;n:count x)}
```

Using the mcstat function gives us a better picture of our result.

```
q)mcstat mc[S;s;r;t;eu[c;k];n]
ev | 15.63627
err| 0.3379061
n  | 10000
```

With 10,000 simulations we have determined the value of the option as `15.58 +-.33`. This is not very precise, thus demonstrating the problem with Monte Carlo simulation. To improve the precision of our estimate, we can increase the number of paths.

```
q)mcstat mc[S;s;r;t;eu[c;k];2*n]
ev | 15.51418
err| 0.2356573
n  | 20000
```

But each time we increase the number of paths, the matrix of data grows as well. We can not keep increasing the number of paths because we will quickly run out of memory. Instead, we can call `mc` many times successively. To do this we use the `each` operator to call `mc` multiple times and then we recombine the results by calling `raze` before computing the statistics with `.deriv.mcstat`.

```
q)mcstat raze mc[S;s;r;t;eu[c;k]] each 20#n
ev | 15.46422
err| 0.07441876
n  | 200000
```

## Parallel Execution

As we increase the number of paths, computing the final price takes longer and longer. To make this process run quicker, we can run the simulations in parallel. By starting q with multiple slaves and replacing `each` with `peach` q will run multiple paths simultaneously.

```
$ q qtips.q -s 4 -w 400
q).util.use `.deriv;
q)c:1b;S:100;k:90;s:.2;r:.03
q)t:til[252]%251;n:10000
q)mcstat raze mc[S;s;r;t;eu[c;k]] peach 100#n
ev | 15.43258
err| 0.03325139
n  | 1000000
```

---

**Q Tip 17.4** Use `peach` to run computations in parallel

---

All updates in q occur in the main thread. But by starting multiple slave threads with the `-s` command line argument, we can use the `peach` operator to compute values in parallel before being joining together in the main thread.

When q starts, it checks how many cores are on the machine, and how many are licensed to be run simultaneously. This information is printed in the startup banner. The free version allows full use of all system cores. In addition to checking the banner, you can also check how many cores are on your system by displaying the `.z.c` system variable. For example, my laptop has four cores.

```
q).z.c
4i
```

If we now start q with 4 slaves and limit the memory to 400 Mb, we can compare execution times between serial execution with `each` and parallel execution with `peach`. The `peach` operator (or parallel each) assigns jobs to each slave, and recombines the results when all slaves have finished. We can see that the results are returned more than twice as fast.

```
$ q qtips.q -s 4 -w 400
q).util.use `.deriv;
q)c:1b;S:100;k:90;s:.2;r:.03
q)t:til[252]%251;n:10000
q)\t mcstat raze mc[S;s;r;t;eu[c;k]] each 20#n
4761
q)\t mcstat raze mc[S;s;r;t;eu[c;k]] peach 20#n
1742
```

Functional programming lends itself nicely to parallel programming because functions and data are stored separately. This design makes it easy to switch from serial to parallel computation. When a function has no side effects, the order of computation no longer matters. Instead of computing the function on each element of a single list, a long list can be split into smaller lists, and processed independently. The results can then be reassembled into the original order. When no slaves are used, `peach` performs exactly like `each`.

Q creates a new thread for each slave specified using the -s command line parameter. Once created, each slave has read-only access to all global variables (including function definitions), but manages its own memory. For optimal performance, `kdb+` does not lock data structures, so all inter-thread communication must be done with pipes. Once a slave computation is complete, the results are returned to the main thread by serializing the data into a self-describing binary message [ipc] [267] and writing it to a pipe. The main thread reads the message from the internal pipe and deserializes it. It then combines the results with those from each of the other slaves. This process is also known in parallel computing as the fork-join model.

The self-describing binary messages format used to transfer data from a slave to the main thread is also used by `kdb+` to communicate between q processes and with clients. The time required to serialize a large dataset can far exceed any speed improvements obtained by using parallel execution. The benefits of using `peach` are maximized when it is used with a function that has high computational overhead or IO, but only returns a small result. This is, in fact, the exact case with our implementation of Monte Carlo simulation.

Slave local memory management also means that the workspace limit we provided on the command line is a per-slave limit. Be careful when running process in multiple slaves, a conservative workspace limit can easily be rendered useless by starting too many slaves.

We resorted to using `each` because the computation we were performing began to take too much memory. Given enough memory, computing a single vector computation is preferred to **each**ing a function over a list. There are three reasons using a single vector computation is faster than using `each`. Firstly, every function call in `q` must determine the type of its arguments. Q is an interpreted language and type checking happens at runtime, not compile time. This runtime overhead makes it very important to perform as much work as possible with every single function call. We can see the performance degradation this causes by performing the same number of computations, but instead of running 20 rounds of 10000 paths, we run 20000 rounds of 10 paths.

```
q)\t mcstat raze mc[S;s;r;t;eu[c;k]] each 20000#10
15911
```

When `mc` is called on a vector, every operator checks the type once and then does the actual mathematical processing. Using `each`, however, forces the types to be checked on each call.

A second reason **each**ing is slow is that calling `each` causes more memory to be allocated, copied, and then destroyed. When we call a function over each element of a vector, the elements must be promoted to a proper `k` object before being used as a function parameter. When we are done performing these computations, the results are joined with the `raze` operator. After the results are copied to a memory-efficient vector, the intermediate results and parameters are destroyed.

Finally, running algorithms on vectors of data allows `q` to use hardware intrinsics to speed up computations. Modern CPUs can actually perform multiple computations in parallel. This is known as Single Instruction Multiple Data or SIMD. Chip manufacturers continuously increase the number of bytes that can be used for a single SIMD calculation. Each generation of computer chip has allowed more and more computations to be performed in parallel. Using vectors allows code to run faster by upgrading to new hardware. Kx periodically releases new versions of the `q` binary to take advantage of the new SIMD instruction sets.

## Path Dependent Payoffs

We designed the `mc` function to accept the payoff function `pf` as an argument. This allows the library user to extend the functionality without having to duplicate code. Writing functions that accept functions as parameters is a hallmark of functional programming. In addition to the `eu` payoff function that only depends on the final security price, we can also create payoff functions that depend on the path the security takes on its way to expiration. For example, the payoff of an Asian option depends on averaging some prices the security had reached. The decision on when and how frequently the prices should be averaged varies between options. For simplicity, we will assume the payoff depends on the average of all prices along the path.

**.deriv.as**

```
as:{[c;k;f]0f|$[c;avg[f]-k;k-avg f]}
```

Asian options are worth less than their European equivalent because the process of averaging effectively reduces the volatility of the security.

```
q)mcstat raze mc[S;s;r;t;as[c;k]] peach 20#n
ev | 12.00835
err| 0.04524092
n  | 200000
```

Another popular variant of European options is the Lookback option. The holder of this option has the right to look back at the whole security path and pick the optimal price to use when exercising the option. For a Call option, the holder would pick the maximum price ever reached along the path. Conversely, a Put option holder would pick the minimum price ever reached. Again, the decision on when and how frequently the prices can be observed depends on the actual option. But for simplicity, we will use all points along the path.

**.deriv.lb**

```
lb:{[c;k;f]0f|$[c;max[f]-k;k-min f]}
```

Lookback options are worth more than their European equivalent because the ability to look back effectively increases the volatility of the security.

```
q)mcstat raze mc[S;s;r;t;lb[c;k]] peach 20#n
ev | 27.1987
err| 0.06589128
n  | 200000
```

Finally, to make things even more exotic, we can mix each of these payoff structures with barrier features. Barrier options either cease or begin to exist once the security has broken through a predefined barrier. When an option ceases to exist once the security goes above a barrier, the option is known as an Up and Out or a Knock Out Barrier option. If it begins to exist once the barrier is breached, it is known as an Up and In or Knock In Barrier option. Similarly, there are Down and Out and Down and In Barrier options for the cases when an option ceases or begins to exist when the security has breached a lower barrier. By once again writing a function that accepts functions as parameters we can implement all four barrier payoffs with the introduction of only one function.

```
bo:{[bf;pf;f]bf[f]*pf f}
```

The barrier option function bo accepts a barrier function bf, the original option payoff function pf and all the future prices f. The results of the payoff function are multiplied by the results of the barrier function. If the barrier function results in a false value, the final path value will be set to 0. In all other cases, it will continue to be the result of the pf function.

For example, we can compute the value of an Up and In Barrier option on the European Call we previously used. If we specify the barrier function bf as any 120<=, the option will exist when any price along the path reaches 120 or above.

```
q)mcstat raze mc[S;s;r;t;bo[any 120<=]eu[c;k]] peach 20#n
ev | 11.41564
```

```
err| 0.07980763
n  | 200000
```

The Up and Out option is worth less.

```
q)mcstat raze mc[S;s;r;t;bo[all 120>]eu[c;k]] peach 20#n
ev | 3.990454
err| 0.02974377
n  | 200000
```

It is known that the combination of an Up and In Barrier option and an Up and Out Barrier option is equal to the equivalent European option. It is good to see that the prices generated approximate this rule.

```
q)11.41564+3.990454
15.40609
q)mcstat raze mc[S;s;r;t;eu[c;k]] peach 20#n
ev | 15.40601
err| 0.07417285
n  | 200000
```

We now move on to computing the theoretical value of a European option.

## Black-Scholes-Merton

The Black-Scholes or Black-Scholes-Merton formula[2] is the most famous formula for computing the price of European option on a non dividend paying security. Given the same inputs as the Monte Carlo simulation, it can compute the theoretical price of the option. To implement the formula, we need to add one more function to our statistics library: the cumulative normal distribution. Where Monte Carlo simulation estimates the probability that an option will have a positive pay-out by simulation, the Black-Scholes-Merton formula uses the cumulative normal distribution to compute the same probability analytically.

The cumulative normal distribution `cnorm` is related to the error function, typically found in most statistical packages. Here we implement `erf` ourselves based on the polynomial approximation found in the "Handbook of Mathematical Functions" by Milton Abramowitz and Irene A. Stegun.[3] Once again, it uses the `.stat.horner` [47] function to evaluate the polynomial.

### .stat.erf

```
erf:{
 a:1.061405429 -1.453152027 1.421413741 -0.284496736 0.254829592;
```

---

[2] Black, Fischer & Scholes, Myron S, 1973."The Pricing of Options and Corporate Liabilities," Journal of Political Economy, University of Chicago Press, vol. 81(3), pages 637-54, May-June.

[3] Abramowitz, Milton; Stegun, Irene A., eds. (1965), "Chapter 7", *Handbook of Mathematical Functions with Formulas, Graphs, and Mathematical Tables*, New York: Dover, p. 297.

```
t:1f%1f+0.3275911*abs x;
t:1f-t*horner[a;t]*exp neg x*x;
x:t*1 -1f x<0f;
x}
```

The cumulative normal distribution is a simple shifting and rescaling of the `erf` function.

### .stat.cnorm

```
cnorm:{.5*1f+erf x%sqrt 2f}
```

The Black-Scholes-Merton equation can now be implemented in q.

### .deriv.bsm

```
bsm:{[S;k;r;t;c;s]
 x:(log[S%k]+rt:r*t)%ssrt:s*sqrt t;
 d1:ssrt+d2:x-.5*ssrt;
 n1:m*.stat.cnorm d1*m:-1 1f c;
 n2:exp[neg rt]*m*.stat.cnorm d2*m;
 p:(sn:S*n1)-kn:k*n2;
 g:n1%s*ssrt;
 v:sn*ssrt;
 th:neg (r*kn)+.5*v*s%t;
 rho:t*kn;
 d:`price`delta`gamma`vega`theta`rho;
 d!:(p;n1;g;sn*ssrt;th;rho);
 if[0h<type p;d:flip d];
 d}
```

In addition to calculating the price of the option, the `bsm` function returns the sensitivities to changes in the function parameters. To return multiple values and make the results convenient to interpret, the results are passed to the user in a dictionary.

```
q).deriv.bsm[S;k;r;last t;c;s]
price| 15.42923
delta| 0.7813624
gamma| 19.53406
vega | 15.62725
theta| -3.443935
rho  | 62.70701
```

The formulas for Put and Call options are considerably different, but the `bsm` function successfully computes both values without a single conditional statement. The differences between Put and Call prices are embedded in the variable m.

```
m:-1 1f c;
```

Q often treats booleans just like the integers 0 and 1. In this case, we used the boolean c to index into the array -1 1f. If we are evaluating a Call, c will be true (1b) and m will evaluate to 1f. The m variable will modify each of the equations to evaluate to the price of a Call. Similarly, when c is false (0b) and m will evaluate to -1f and the computed values will be Put prices.

The erf function uses the same technique to simplify calculations. Since the erf function is mirrored across the x and y-axis, the implementation computes the values for the absolute value of x. As the last step, the values are negated if x is less than 0.

Using this technique to implement conditional statements with mathematical calculations allows functions to be used for all data types, not just atoms or lists. To make the function atomic, the last line flips the dictionary and creates a table (which can be thought of as a list of dictionaries) if multiple prices were calculated.

For example, we can simultaneously compute the value of a Put and Call option by using a dictionary.[4]

```
q) .deriv.bsm[S;k;r;last t;'put'call!01b;s]
     | price    delta      gamma     vega      theta     rho
  --- | ---------------------------------------------------------------
put  | 2.769328 -0.2186376 -5.465939 -4.372751 1.176268 -24.63308
call | 15.42923 0.7813624  19.53406  15.62725  -3.443935 62.70701
```

---

**Q Tip 17.5** Use mathematical operations instead of conditionals

---

Using conditional operators like $[;;] and ?[;;] limits calculations to atoms and vectors respectively. Mathematical operators, however, can be used with any data type. This includes matrices, dictionaries and tables. Use mathematical operators to implement conditions statements and your functions will be much more generic.

## Brawn vs Brain

Even when a function has been perfectly optimized, it may still not be fast enough. Aside from re-implementing the function in C/C++, we have two choices. We can use more hardware to compute values simultaneously, or we can be smarter about how many computations we actually perform.

---

**Q Tip 17.6** Use .Q.fc to run an atomic function across multiple cores

---

The Black-Scholes-Merton formula involves many operations, and even though we have implemented it efficiently, it may still be too slow for our needs. Q offers two operators to help improve the speed of our code without having to change our algorithms. The first method uses more resources by splitting the algorithm over multiple cores. The *function cut* .Q.fc operator combines the performance benefits of vector algorithms with the horse power of multi-core processing. Instead of executing the function once

---

[4] The result is not actually a keyed table. Although the value of the dictionary is a table, the key is a simple vector.

for each element of its argument list, `.Q.fc` cuts the argument list into the same number of pieces as the `kdb+` process has slaves. Each slave process one list and the results are then combined.

For example, if we assign a projection of `.deriv.bsm` to `f` and a long list of security prices to `x`, we can then compare the performance boost gained from splitting the execution over multiple cores.

```
q)S:100;k:90;s:.2;r:.03;t:1;nt:365;n:10000
q)f:.deriv.bsm[;k;r;t;0b;s]
q)x:.01*1+200000?2000
q)\ts f x
108 23069280
q)\ts .Q.fc[f] x
71 4194656
```

Function cut `.Q.fc` is implemented using `peach` and is therefore subject to the same limitation that only monadic functions, compositions, or projections can be used.

---

**Q Tip 17.7** Use `.Q.fu` to speed up an atomic function applied to repeated values

---

The second operator that can give our function a boost in performance is *function unique* `.Q.fu`. Instead of using brawn to improve performance, it uses brains. This operator optimizes the execution time by only computing the results for the unique values in the list. The more repetition there is in our dataset, the more beneficial using `.Q.fu` becomes.

```
q)\ts .Q.fu[f] x
37 10486016
```

We can see, however, that the speed enhancement comes at the cost of using more memory. Grouping the security prices into unique lists must allocate memory. But this is a much faster operation than serializing and deserializing the data between the master `kdb+` process and its slaves.

## Implied Volatility

A security's volatility is an abstract concept, and one subject to much interpretation and disagreement. Among the inputs to option prices, the volatility is the most uncertain. But option prices are readily visible in the market. Since the price of an option is a strictly monotonically increasing function of its volatility, it is possible to derive the volatility that generates the observed price of an option. This is known as the option's implied volatility. A common approach to inverting a closed form analytic equation is to use the Newton-Raphson root finding algorithm.

The Newton-Raphson algorithm iteratively evaluates a function at different points until the algorithm converges upon a single point. Each new point is chosen by following a tangent line from the previous point to the x-axis. Given a well behaved function, and enough iterations, repeating this algorithm converges to a point on the x-axis. There is thus a clear requirement that we can find the slope of any point along the function. At each step we must evaluate x according to the function in question and also find its slope (or first derivative). Assuming we have a function f that produces both of these values, the Newton-Raphson algorithm can be implemented with the following function.

**.stat.nr**

```
nr:{[e;f;x]$[e>abs d:first[r]%last r:f x;x;x-d]}
```

Depending on the function, the Newton-Raphson algorithm can take many steps before it converges on a single value. This implementation allows the user to pass an error tolerance e that will cause the function to stop iterating once the next step changes less than the specified tolerance.

To demonstrate how the nr function works, we can find the roots of $x^2-2$. The algorithm requires a function that both evaluates the function and also returns its slope. In this case, the slope is $2x$.

```
f:{(-2+x*x;2*x)}
```

We can then use q's ability to repeatedly call a function until it produces two results that are exactly the same. By passing 0 for the error tolerance, we allow q to keep iterating until an exact solution is found.

```
q).stat.nr[0f;f]\[1f]
1 1.5 1.416667 1.414216 1.414214 1.414214
```

We can see that it converged to the square root of 2, which is exactly where the function passes through the x-axis.

To find the other root, we can start with a negative value.

```
q).stat.nr[0f;f]\[-1f]
-1 -1.5 -1.416667 -1.414216 -1.414214 -1.414214
```

If we are not interested in the path q takes to the final solution, we can use the over operator "/" instead of scan "\".

```
q).stat.nr[0f;f]/[-1f]
-1.414214
```

As with all other monadic operators, q has provided English words that correspond to these single character operators.

```
q).stat.nr[0f;f] scan 1f
1 1.5 1.416667 1.414216 1.414214 1.414214
q).stat.nr[0f;f] over 1f
1.414214
```

Inverting a function is closely related to finding its roots. If we subtract the y value from the original function, the resulting function will now have a root where f(x)=y. In our previous example we subtracted 2 from $x^2$ and the root was exactly at the square root of 2.

To generalize this we can create a new function `invert` that accepts four parameters. The first parameter will be a root finding function `rf`. The second parameter will be a function `f` that returns both `f(x)` and the slope `f'(x)`. The third parameter is the `y` value that needs inverting, and the final parameter `x` is the initial guess.

**.stat.invert**

```
invert:{[rf;f;y;x]rf[(neg y;0f)+f@]x}
```

To find the square root of 2 we can use `invert` with the `nr` root-finding algorithm.

```
q).stat.invert[.stat.nr[0f];{(x*x;2*x)};2]\[1f]
1 1.5 1.416667 1.414216 1.414214 1.414214
```

Using this same technique we can invert the Black-Scholes-Merton formula and compute the volatility that is implied by a specific option price. In order to use the Newton-Raphson algorithm, we need a monadic function that accepts a volatility and returns the option's price and slope with respect to volatility (or vega). We can create a projection of `bsm` that applies all parameters except the volatility. In addition, we need to extract just the price and vega from the returned dictionary. Instead of creating a new function with all the same parameters as `bsm`, we can create a composition.

```
pv:@[;`price`vega].deriv.bsm[S;k;r;last t;c;]@
```

It is also possible to build compositions without appending the trailing "@" by using the "'" operator.

```
pv:(')[@[;`price`vega];.deriv.bsm[S;k;r;last t;c;]]
```

Using either of these compositions to invert the option's price, we obtain the exact volatility used to price the option.

```
q).stat.invert[.stat.nr[0f];pv;15.42923]/[.1f]
0.2
```

If we look a bit closer, we can see that it took 245 iterations to stop iterating.

```
q)count .stat.invert[.stat.nr[0f];pv;15.42923]\[.1f]
246
```

To reduce this number, we can increase the error tolerance,

```
q)count .stat.invert[.stat.nr[.0001];pv;15.42923]\[.1f]
59
```

and can see that the value is still quite close.

```
q).stat.invert[.stat.nr[.0001];pv;15.42923]/[.1f]
0.1999477
```

---

**Q Tip 17.8** Use null, zero and positive/negative infinity as on/off switches

---

This is a good example where a numeric parameter can both parameterize a function and also serve as a boolean flag to turn the feature off. When the error tolerance is set to 0, the feature is completely disabled. In other cases, null or positive/negative infinity can also achieve the same results. In most languages, this type of parameterization is only possible with floating point numbers. But q provides null and positive/negative infinity values for all numeric and temporal types. This allows us to enable and disable parameters by providing null, 0, or positive/negative infinity. Use these features to simplify your code.

## 17.3  Histograms

Q provides a few basic operators for statistical analysis. For in-depth analysis and charting tools, we need to use more general purpose statistical software. But having the ability to create rudimentary histograms in q is often enough to continue research without having to change applications.

Combining many of the techniques we have already learned, we can create a function to generate histograms. Generating a histogram can be broken down into three parts: determining the number of bins needed for the histogram, grouping the data into each bin, and rendering the histogram. There is no single solution to determining the number of bins a histogram should have. Similarly, there is no single way to render a histogram. But given a function to determine the number of bins and another to render each bar, we can easily group data into bins. Let's begin there.

### Grouping Data

Assuming we have a binning function `bf` and our dataset `x`, we can group the data into bins with a `bgroup` function.

**.hist.bgroup**

```
bgroup:{[bf;x]
 b:nrng[bf x;min x;max x];
 g:group b bin x;
 g:b!x g til count b;
 g}
```

The first line uses the binning function `bf` to determine the optimal number of bins and generates a range of bins between the minimum and maximum values in the dataset. To demonstrate this process we can assume a simplistic binning function that uses the square root of the number of data elements.

**.hist.sqrtn**

```
sqrtn:{ceiling sqrt count x}
```

In addition, we must define the `nrng` function which generates the bins.

**.hist.nrng**

```
nrng:{[n;s;e]s+til[1+n]*(e-s)%n}
```

The `nrng` function accepts the number of bins in the range, followed by the starting and ending value.

```
q).hist.nrng[10;0;100]
0 10 20 30 40 50 60 70 80 90 100f
```

We can now generate the bins for a few random values.

```
q)bf:.hist.sqrtn
q)x:"f"$25?100
q)show b:.hist.nrng[bf x;min x;max x]
0 19.8 39.6 59.4 79.2 99
```

At this point, we use q's `bin` operator to determining which bin each of the values in our dataset belongs in. The operator assumes, but does not enforce, that our list of bins is sorted in ascending order. The result is a list of indices corresponding to the appropriate bin for each element.

```
q)b bin x
1 3 4 3 3 1 0 1 0 3 2 0 5 3 0 3 4 1 2 4 3 0 4 0 4
```

Our function then uses the `group` operator to group the results by bin. Unlike the by clause in q-SQL, the `group` operator does not sort the resulting dictionary by key, the order depends on the ordering of the bin's appearance within the dataset.

```
q)show g:group b bin x
1| 0 5 7 17
3| 1 3 4 9 13 15 20
4| 2 16 19 22 24
0| 6 8 11 14 21 23
2| 10 18
5| ,12
```

This is already looking like a horizontally oriented histogram. To clean it up, we need to sort the data by bin and convert the indices back to their original value. The last line of `bgroup` does exactly this.

```
q)b!x g til count b
0   | 14 0 2 12 7 0f
19.8| 37 30 37 28f
39.6| 45 44f
59.4| 79 63 74 62 62 76 62f
79.2| 97 93 87 90 89f
99  | ,99f
```

## Charting Data

We begin the processes of charting histograms by writing a generic charting function.

**.hist.chart**

```
chart:{[pf;w;d]
 n:"j"$(m&w)*n%m:max n:value d;
 d:d,'enlist each pf[w] each n;
 d}
```

The first parameter of the `chart` function is a plotting function `pf` that can plot a single value. The second parameter is the maximum width of the chart. The last parameter is a dictionary containing a mapping from x to y values.

The function begins by determining the scaled values `n` for each item in the dictionary - ensuring they are a fraction of the maximum width `w`. The second line applies the plotting function `pf` to generate the text for each value. The function is passed two parameters: the width `w` of the chart and the scaled value. Before the dictionary is returned, the text is appended to the original dictionary which now has both values and a graphic for each item in the dictionary.

To make the `chart` function usable, we need to provide a function that charts a single value. The `bar` function accepts an ASCII character used to plot each point, the width of the chart, and the number of characters in the bar.

**.hist.bar**

```
bar:{[c;w;n]w$n#c}
```

The function creates `n` instances of the character `c`, and then uses the cast operator "`$`" to right pad the character vector up to `w` characters.

```
q).hist.bar["*";30;10]
"**********                    "
```

We can now generate a histogram by charting the results of `bgroup`.

```
q).util.use `.hist
q)chart[bar"*";30] count each bgroup[sqrtn] .stat.bm 100?1f
-1.932808  | 3   "***                           "
-1.491141  | 6   "******                        "
-1.049473  | 18  "******************            "
-0.6078061 | 15  "***************               "
-0.1661388 | 20  "********************          "
0.2755286  | 14  "**************                "
0.7171959  | 12  "************                  "
1.158863   | 8   "********                      "
1.600531   | 2   "**                            "
2.042198   | 1   "*                             "
2.483865   | 1   "*                             "
```

The chart function was parameterized to accept a function that generates text for each value. This makes it easy to change how the chart is displayed. Instead of creating a bar chart, we can also generate a dot chart.

**.hist.dot**

```
dot:{[c;w;n]w$neg[n]$1#c}
```

The dot function left-pads a single character c up to n characters. It then right-pads the character vector up to w characters. We can now generate dot charts.

```
q)chart[dot"*";30] count each bgroup[sqrtn] .stat.bm 100?1f
-2.898934 | 2   "  *                                          "
-2.40191  | 3   "   *                                         "
-1.904885 | 5   "      *                                      "
-1.407861 | 10  "           *                                 "
-0.9108367| 20  "                     *                       "
-0.4138124| 21  "                      *                      "
0.08321189| 16  "                *                            "
0.5802362 | 11  "           *                                 "
1.07726   | 6   "      *                                      "
1.574285  | 5   "    *                                        "
2.071309  | 1   "*                                            "
```

## Alternate Bin Algorithms

Determining the bin width is a critical step in generating a histogram. To display histograms properly, the binning function bf must reduce the number of bins to a significant fraction of the number of data points, while still preserving the distribution's structure. There have been many attempts at improving this process. Sturges' rule[5], developed in 1926, has historically been the most popular.

**.hist.sturges**

```
sturges:{ceiling 1f+2f xlog count x}
```

Sturges' rule assumes normally distributed data and is perfect for our normally distributed random variates.

```
q)x:.stat.bm 100?1f
q)chart[bar"*";30] count each bgroup[sturges] x
-2.085927 | 5   "*****                          "
-1.507408 | 13  "*************                   "
-0.9288888| 24  "************************        "
-0.3503699| 22  "**********************          "
```

---

[5] Sturges, H. A. (1926). "The choice of a class interval". *Journal of the American Statistical Association*: 65–66.

```
0.2281491 | 14  "*************        "
0.806668  | 12  "************         "
1.385187  | 7   "*******             "
1.963706  | 2   "**                  "
2.542225  | 1   "*                   "
```

But the `sturges` method does not handle skewed data well. If we plot the distribution of stock prices for a security with 30% volatility after 7 years, we can see that the `sturges` method only produces 9 bins and almost all the data points are compressed into the first 2 bins.

```
q)p:.stat.gbm[.3;.05;7] x
q)chart[bar"*";30] count each bgroup[sturges] p
0.1977695| 58  "******************************"
1.146786 | 22  "***********          "
2.095803 | 10  "*****                "
3.044819 | 6   "***                  "
3.993836 | 1   "*                    "
4.942853 | 2   "*                    "
5.891869 | 0   "                     "
6.840886 | 0   "                     "
7.789903 | 1   "*                    "
```

Doane's rule[6], developed in 1976, is an adjustment to Struges' rule that accounts for skewed data. Using the skewness of the dataset reduces the chance that outliers cause the bins to be too wide, thus losing detail on the data's true distribution. The `nskew` function is used by `doane` to compute a normalized skew.

**.hist.nskew**

```
nskew:{[x].stat.skew[x]%sqrt 6f*(n-2)%(n+1)*3+n:count x}
```

**.hist.doane**

```
doane:{ceiling 1f+(2f xlog count x)+2f xlog 1f+abs nskew x}
```

We can see how the `doane` function produces a plot with many more bins. This allows us to see more details of the skewed distribution.

```
q)chart[bar"*";30] count each bgroup[doane] p
0.1977695| 42  "******************************"
0.8304473| 28  "********************* "
1.463125 | 10  "*******              "
2.095803 | 8   "******               "
2.728481 | 5   "****                 "
3.361158 | 3   "**                   "
```

---

[6] Doane DP (1976) Aesthetic frequency classification. *American Statistician*, 30: 181–183

```
3.993836 | 1   "*                                       "
4.626514 | 0   "                                        "
5.259192 | 2   "*                                       "
5.891869 | 0   "                                        "
6.524547 | 0   "                                        "
7.157225 | 0   "                                        "
7.789903 | 1   "*                                       "
```

Scott's rule[7], developed in 1979, also improved on Sturges by using the dataset's actual standard deviation to compute the bin widths. To convert from bin width to the number of bins, we introduce the **n**umber-from-**w**idth function `nw`.

**.hist.nw**

```
nw:{[w;x]ceiling (max[x]-min x)%w}
```

**.hist.scott**

```
scott:{nw[;x] 3.4908*sdev[x]*count[x] xexp -1f%3f}
```

The results are similar to `sturges` (including the mishandling of skewed data).

```
q)chart[bar"*";30] count each bgroup[scott] p
0.1977695| 58 "******************************"
1.146786 | 22 "***********
2.095803 | 10 "*****                                   "
3.044819 | 6  "***                                     "
3.993836 | 1  "*                                       "
4.942853 | 2  "*                                       "
5.891869 | 0  "                                        "
6.840886 | 0  "                                        "
7.789903 | 1  "*                                       "
```

Freedman-Diaconis' rule[8], developed in 1981, follows Doane's rule by handling skewed data. But instead of using the distribution's standard deviation and skew, it uses the more robust inter-quartile range. Using the `.stat.pctile` [12] function, an inter-quartile range function `iqr` can be easily developed by subtracting the third quartile from the first.

**.stat.iqr**

```
iqr:{(-) . pctile[.75 .25;x]}
```

**.hist.fd**

---

[7] Scott, David W. (1979). "On optimal and data-based histograms". *Biometrika* **66** (3): 605–610

[8] Freedman, David; Diaconis, P. (1981). "On the histogram as a density estimator: L2 theory". *Zeitschrift für Wahrscheinlichkeitstheorie und verwandte Gebiete* **57** (4): 453–476

```
fd:{nw[;x] 2*iqr[x]*count[x] xexp -1f%3f}
```

Plotting the same data again, but this time with the `fd` binning function produces many more bins, and displays much more detail.

```
q)chart[bar"*";30] count each bgroup[fd] p
0.1977695| 42 "******************************"
0.7400648| 23 "****************            "
1.28236  | 10 "*******                     "
1.824655 | 7  "*****                       "
2.36695  | 7  "*****                       "
2.909246 | 4  "***                         "
3.451541 | 3  "**                          "
3.993836 | 1  "*                           "
4.536131 | 0  "                            "
5.078427 | 1  "*                           "
5.620722 | 1  "*                           "
6.163017 | 0  "                            "
6.705312 | 0  "                            "
7.247608 | 0  "                            "
7.789903 | 1  "*                           "
```

Once we have settled on a combination of functions that generate histograms the way we like, we can create a composition of the functions to create a new function.

**.hist.fdhist**

```
fdist:chart[bar"*";30] count each bgroup[fd]@
```

Using the composition instead of the original function allows us to generate plots by simply supplying the data.

```
q)fdhist p
```

Because each of the charting components was written generically, we can use them to chart any dataset. For example, instead of plotting a histogram, we can plot the range of values that a European option takes as we vary the current security price.

```
q)c:1b;S:100;k:90;s:.2;r:.03
q)chart[bar"*";30] S!@[; `price] .deriv.bsm[;k;r;1;1b;s] S:50+5*til 15
50 | 0.01039141 "                            "
55 | 0.04874352 "                            "
60 | 0.1690701  "                            "
65 | 0.4635251  "                            "
70 | 1.05574    "*                           "
75 | 2.074917   "**                          "
80 | 3.624009   "***                         "
```

```
85  | 5.756847   "*****                          "
90  | 8.472052   "*******                        "
95  | 11.72187   "**********                     "
100| 15.42923   "**************                 "
105| 19.50565   "******************             "
110| 23.86513   "***********************        "
115| 28.43254   "*************************      "
120| 33.14715   "*******************************"
```

Properly factoring algorithms into reusable components requires experience with the problem at hand. Since we're not likely to factor the algorithm correctly on the first attempt, we often need to refactor code. It is easy, if not fun, to refactor q code. The language is so concise and expressive that trying different approaches requires minimal effort.

---

**Q Tip 17.9** Pursue the functional-vector solution

---

I hope you have enjoyed exploring the q language with me. The presented solutions embody two important coding paradigms: functional and vector programming. To use q efficiently requires a change in mindset. Instead of procedural programming, we need to think in terms of functions. And instead of loops, we must think in terms of vectors. From character vectors, byte arrays and the keys and values of dictionaries, to table columns and table column names, vectors permeate the q language. Algorithms are at the heart of q. Written once, each algorithm can be used with different data types. To achieve mastery of q we must develop functional algorithms that exploit q's functional-vector nature. As you continue your own journey with q, nurture your own functional-vector nature.

# Selected Web Resources

## Kx Systems Links

[1] [free] Kdb+ Download - http://kx.com/software-download.php. This site provides a free version of q language and kdb+ database. Only the 32-bit version is available and is thus limited by the system architecture to 4GB in-process memory.

[2] [downloads] Kx Downloads - http://downloads.kx.com/. This site provides access to the latest binaries from Kx. It is password protected and requires your login to be associated with a paying customer. Depending on your access rights, different downloads will be available. The full history of bug fixes and new feature additions can be found in each version's README.txt.

[3] [wiki] Kx Systems kdb+ Wiki - http://code.kx.com/wiki. This is the primary documentation site for kdb+ and q. It includes links for full function documentation, cookbooks, tutorials and more.

[4] [qref] The Q Reference - http://code.kx.com/wiki/Reference. This site includes links for the documentation of all functions.

[5] [qunref] The .Q Unreference - http://code.kx.com/wiki/DotQ. This site has many useful but unofficial functions located in the .Q namespace.

[6] [internal] Q Internal Functions - http://code.kx.com/wiki/Reference/-BangSymbolInternalFunction. This site documents each of the internal C functions accessible from q. Some functions have proven so useful that q operators, both official and unofficial (in the .Q namespace) have been created.

[7] [tolerance] Q Comparison Tolerance - http://code.kx.com/wiki/Cookbook/-ComparisonTolerance. This site documents how q implements comparison tolerance. It provides a concrete example and details which operators and data types use comparison tolerance.

[8] [syscmd] Q System Commands - http://code.kx.com/wiki/Reference/-SystemCommands. This site documents each of q's commands that display and modify system settings. Many of these commands have corresponding command line parameters.

[9] [cmdline] Q Command Line Options - http://code.kx.com/wiki/Reference/Cmdline. This site documents each of q's single letter command line arguments. Many of these commands have corresponding system commands to retrieve and set their values.

[10] [cookbook] Q Cookbook - http://code.kx.com/wiki/Cookbook. This site provides documentation, examples, and solutions for many common problems. Extending with C and Interfacing with C are good resources for understanding how native K objects are stored and manipulated.

[11] [svn] Kx Public Repository - http://code.kx.com/wsvn/code. This site includes code contributed by the Kx community.

[12] [qrepo] Kx Q Repository - http://kx.com/q/. This site includes links to many useful and interesting .q files. The stat.q file provides examples of commonly requested statistical functions not included with a kdb+ installation.

[13] [crepo] Kx Connectivity Resources - http://kx.com/q/c/. Whether you want to interface with a kdb+ server via C, C++, C# or JAVA, this site provides the necessary libraries you need. Specifically, k.h is needed to compile both standalone applications seeking to communicate with a kdb+ process and also to build a shared library that can be loaded at runtime.

[14] [example] Kx Example Repository - http://kx.com/q/e/. This site provides examples written in q. In addition to a few performance benchmarks, it includes an example implementation of Huffman coding huff.q and utilities to help import the popular CSV text format: csvguess.q and csvutil.q.

[15] [tick] Kdb+Tick - http://code.kx.com/wiki/Startingkdbplus/tick. The kdb+ tickerplant provides a fast and lightweight platform to record market data, store it in a real time database and save it for historical queries. This site provides an introduction to the setup and configuration of the kdb+ tickerplant.

[16] [listbox] Listbox Forum - http://www.listbox.com/member/archive/1080. A discussion forum available to licensed clients. The discussion typically involve more advanced techniques, new release bug reports and algorithm optimization requests.

[17] [google] Google Groups Forum - http://groups.google.com/d/forum/personal-kdbplus. A discussion forum available to everyone. Topics are typically relevant to most beginners.

[18] [drepo] Original Kx Documentation Repository - http://www.kx.com/q/d/. This directory includes many of the original documents created for learning the q language and

the kdb+ database. The files written by Arthur Whitney are considered abridged - not because they contain less information but because they contain less text. They are, in fact, a great source of knowledge.

[19] [cobj] Kx System's C Object File - http://kx.com/q/l64/c.o. This file is needed to compile standalone processes communicating with a kdb+ server. Links for other platforms are available as well.

[20] [ipc] Kdb+ IPC protocol - http://code.kx.com/wiki/Reference/ipcprotocol. This site documents Kdb+'s proprietary self-describing binary IPC protocol. Sample deserialization implementations can be found in the Kx Connectivity Resources repository http://kx.com/q/c/.

[21] [hpts] HPTS Presentation - http://www.cs.nyu.edu/faculty/shasha/papers/hpts.pdf. A paper written by Arthur Whitney, Dennis Shasha, and Stevan Apter detailing how a single threaded application written in C can achieve very high performance. The kdb+ database is based on this paper.

## Other K/Q Related Links

[22] [aplus] A+ Dev - http://www.aplusdev.org. The A+ (initially A) language was written by Arthur Whitney while he worked at Morgan Stanley.

[23] [jsoftware] JSoftware - http://www.jsoftware.com. A vector-based programming language with similar APL roots as Q.

[24] Incunabulum - http://www.jsoftware.com/jwiki/Essays/Incunabulum. The initial "one page in one day" interpreter that inspired the J programming language.

[25] [kparc] KPARC - http://kparc.com. K3 was the original language written by Arthur Whitney that was quickly adopted by the financial community. Rewritten as k4 and supplemented with q, it was rebranded as kdb+. Now in its fifth edition, k5 has ambitions to become an operating system and web development platform.

# List of Terms

**Adverb**

Adverbs are language constructs that modify verbs. The result of combining an adverb and a verb will be a new verb that performs a different but related operation. Q adverbs modify how a verb iterates over its arguments. There are six adverbs: each "'", each-prior "': ", scan "\", over "/ ", each-right "\:", and each-left "/:". The first four have monadic variants defined with names: each, prior, scan, and over. The "': " adverb is also used to define the peach adverb.

**Aggregate**

A function whose return value has fewer dimensions than its argument. A function that accepts a list and returns an atom, for example, is an aggregate. Similarly, a function that accepts a matrix and returns a vector would also be an aggregate.

**Attribute**

A flag attached to a list that indicates which method should be used when searching for elements. The available attributes are (in increasing complexity): **s**orted, **u**nique, **p**artitioned, and **g**rouped. The sorted attribute incurs no memory overhead, while the remaining attributes store additional metadata either in memory or on disk.

**Atom**

A single value - in contrast to a list of values.

**Atomic**

A function that returns an atom when called with an atom, and a list when called with a list. The return value for a given argument is always the same, regardless if it was called as an atom or a member of a list.

**Composition**

A function that is created by associating two other functions such that the application of the composition is equivalent to applying the two functions in succession.

**Dyad**

> A function that accepts two arguments. Such functions are referred to as dyadic. The name has its roots in mathematical theory and the APL language.

**Enumeration**

> A non-numerical dataset whose values are mapped to numbers to save memory (in process and on disk), and to increase the speed of comparison and data access.

**Intern**

> The process of converting a variable length character array into a pointer to a globally unique instance of that character vector. An interned character vectors is known as a symbol and benefits from the ability to perform equality tests by comparing pointer addresses instead of character vector comparison. See Symbol.

**Juxtaposition**

> The act of placing a list, dictionary, table (keyed or unkeyed), or function directly next to the indices, keys, or function parameters without the use of brackets.

**Lambda**

> An anonymous function that can be assigned, inspected and called. The term was originally used in the formal system in mathematics named *Lambda Calculus* and is often represented by the Greek letter $\lambda$.

**Monad**

> A function that accepts a single argument. Such functions are referred to as monadic. The name has its roots in mathematical theory and the APL language. Monadic functions in q may be called without any argument. In this case, the generic null (::) is passed instead.

**Nilad**

> A function that accepts no arguments. Such functions are referred to as niladic. The name has its roots in mathematical theory and the APL language. Niladic functions in q may be called with a single ignored argument.

**Noun**

> Nouns are language constructs that can be passed as arguments to verbs. Data, variables, functions, projections and compositions are all nouns. Q operators can be converted to into nouns by surrounding them with parentheses, or passing them as arguments to functions using bracket notation. In these cases, their evaluation is deferred.

**Partition**

> 1. A method of indexing a vector such that all equal values are grouped together. In kdb+, the symbol `p is used to denote that a vector is partitioned. The first column of an historical table is typically partitioned.

2. A method of structuring a Very Large Database (VLDB) such that reasonably sized chunks of data can be sequentially loaded into memory. This structure can also increase performance by allowing queries to partitions to be run in parallel. When `kdb+` loads a partitioned database, the subdirectories become a virtual column in each table of each partition.

## Projection

A function created by fixing (or binding) one or more arguments of another function. This new function can be assigned, inspected, called, and passed as an argument just like any lambda. Monadic functions can not be projected, as the function will be instantly called.

## REPL

An acronym for the read-eval-print-loop common in many interpreted programming languages.

## Segment

A method of allocating partitions in a Very Large Database (VLDB) across disks so that partitions commonly queried together are stored on separate physical disks. This increases query performance by allowing each segment's disk to be queried in parallel.

## Splay

A method of saving large tables such that each column is saved in a different file. This permits faster loading and querying when only a subset of the table's columns are needed.

## Symbol

A symbol is similar to a character vector. The one notable difference is that each symbol in `kdb+` points to the same address in memory. This reduces the memory footprint of `kdb+` processes, and also allows for faster equality testing by address instead of character comparisons. See Intern.

## Uniform

Like an atomic function, a uniform function returns an atom when called with an atom, and a list of equal length when called with a list. But when called with a list, the results depend on other elements within the list. The results are therefore not the same as calling the function individually on each element of the list.

## Vector

A list of uniform typed values.

## Verb

Verbs are language constructs that can be passed arguments using juxtaposition. User defined monadic functions and monadic q operators are verbs. Dyadic q operators are also verbs. To use a q dyadic operator as a noun, it must be surrounded by parentheses.

Appendix A

# Source Code

## A.1 Utilities

**util.q**

```
\d .util

/ import designated function or entire directory
use:{system["d"] upsert $[99h=type v:get x;v;(-1#` vs x)!1#v]}

/ return weekdays from list of dates
wday:{x where 1<x mod 7}

/ return a range of numbers between (s)tart and (e)nd
/ with specified (w)indow size
rng:{[w;s;e]s+w*til ceiling(e-s)%w}

/ round y to nearest x
rnd:{x*"j"$y%x}

/ generate (n) uniform random numbers between (s)tart and (e)nd
randrng:{[n;s;e]s+n?e-s}

/ automatically set attributes on first column of (t)able
sattr:{[t]
 c:first cols t;
 a:`g`u 1=n:count keys t;
 t:n!@[;c;a#]0!t;
 t}
```

```
/ rename columns of (t)able based on (d)ictionary
mapcol:{[d;t](c^d c:cols t) xcol t}

/ sort dictionary (or keyed table) by key
kasc:{$['s=attr k:key x;x;('s#k i)!value[x]i:iasc k]}

/ string implementation of pivot
/ pivot (c)olumns, (g)roup column, (d)ata column, (t)able
pivots:{[c;g;d;t]
 s:"exec (`$exec string asc distinct ",string[c]," from t)";
 s,:"#(`$string ",string[c],")!",string d;
 s,:" by ", ","," sv ":" sv'string flip 2#enlist g,();
 s,:" from t";
 p:eval @[parse s;1;:;t];
 p}

/ parse-tree implementation of pivot
/ pivot (c)olumns, (g)roup column, (d)ata column, (t)able
pivotp:{[c;g;d;t]
 u:`$string asc distinct t c;
 pf:{x#(`$string y)!z};
 p:?[t;();g!g,:();(pf;`u;c;d)];
 p}

/ q implementation of pivot
/ pivot (c)olumns, (g)roup column, (d)ata column, (t)able
pivotq:{[c;g;d;t]
 u:`$string asc distinct t c;
 p:asc[key p]#p:group (g,())#t;
 p:u#/:(`$string t c)[p]!'t[d] p;
 p}

/ keyed-(t)able implementation of pivot
/ last column of key are pivot columns
/ remaing columns of key are group by columns
/ last column of table is data
pivot:{[t]
 u:`$string asc distinct last f:flip key t;
 pf:{x#(`$string y)!z};
 p:?[t;();g!g:-1_ k;(pf;`u;last k:key f;last key flip value t)];
 p}

/ splay table to disk without enumerating sym columns
splay:{@[x;`.d,c;:;enlist[c],y c:cols y]}

/ generate a list of nodes(files or variables) within tree node
```

```
tree:{$[x~k:key x;x;11h=type k;raze (.z.s ` sv x,) each k;()]}
```

```
/ unenumerate any enumerated columns in table
unenum:{@[x;where (type each flip x) within 20 76;get]}
```

```
/ bid-ask volume (example HDB query)
/ (t)rade table, (q)uote table, (d)a(t)e
bav:{[t;q;dt]
 r:select id,time,tp,ts from t where date=dt;
 r:aj[`id`time;r] select id,time,bp,ap from q where date=dt;
 r:update bv:ts*tp<=bp,av:ts*tp>=ap from r;
 r:0!select date:dt,sum bv,sum av,tv:sum ts by id from r;
 r}
```

## A.2  Statistics

**stat.q**

```
\d .stat
```

```
/ percentile
pctile:{[p;x]x iasc[x] -1+ceiling p*count x}
```

```
/ 12 uniforms
u12:{-6f+sum x cut (12*x)?1f}
```

```
skew:{avg[x*x2]%sqrt m2*m2*m2:avg x2:x*x-:avg x}
kurt:{-3f+avg[x2*x2]%x*x:avg x2:x*x-:avg x}
```

```
/ box-muller
bm:{
 if[count[x] mod 2;'`length];
 x:2 0N#x;
 r:sqrt -2f*log first x;
 theta:2f*acos[-1f]*last x;
 x: r*cos theta;
 x,:r*sin theta;
 x}
```

```
/ geometric brownian motion
/ (s)igma, (r)ate, (t)ime, z:uniform random
/ user multiplies by (S)pot
gbm:{[s;r;t;z]exp (t*r-.5*s*s)+z*s*sqrt t}
```

```
/ inter quartile range
```

```
iqr:{(-) . pctile[.75 .25;x]}

/ auto correlation
ac:{x%first x:x{(y#x)$neg[y]#x}/:c-til c:count x-:avg x}

/ horner's method
/ x:coefficients, y:data
horner:{{z+y*x}[y]/[x]}

/ exponentially weighted moving average
/ x:decay rate, y:data
ewma:{first[y](1f-x)\x*y}

/ central region - normal inverse
cnorminv:{
 a:-25.44106049637 41.39119773534 -18.61500062529 2.50662823884;
 b: 3.13082909833 -21.06224101826 23.08336743743
   -8.47351093090 1;
 x*:horner[a;s]%horner[b] s:x*x-:.5;
 x}

/ tail region - normal inverse
tnorminv:{
 a:0.0000003960315187 0.0000002888167364 0.0000321767881768
   0.0003951896511919 0.0038405729373609 0.0276438810333863
   0.1607979714918209 0.9761690190917186 0.3374754822726147;
 x:horner[a] log neg log 1f-x;
 x}

/ beasley-springer-moro normal inverse approximation
norminv:{
 i:x<.5;
 x:?[i;1f-x;x];
 x:?[x<.92;cnorminv x;tnorminv x];
 x:?[i;neg x;x];
 x}

/ open high low close
ohlc:{`o`h`l`c!(first;max;min;last)@\:x}

/ count, min, max, median, standard deviation of x
summary:{`n`mn`mx`md`dv!(count;min;max;med;sdev)@\:x}

/ error function
erf:{
 a: 1.061405429 -1.453152027 1.421413741
   -0.284496736  0.254829592;
```

```
 t:1f%1f+0.3275911*abs x;
 t:1f-t*horner[a;t]*exp neg x*x;
 x:t*1 -1f x<0f;
 x}

/ cumulative normal
cnorm:{.5*1f+erf x%sqrt 2f}

/ newton-raphson
/ (e)rror tolerance, (f)unction
nr:{[e;f;x]$[e>abs d:first[r]%last r:f x;x;x-d]}

/ function inversion
/ (r)oot-finding (f)unction, (f)unction
invert:{[rf;f;y;x]rf[(neg y;0f)+f@]x}
```

## A.3 Simulation

### sim.q

```
\d .sim

/ generate simulated security paths
/ (s)igma, (r)ate, (t)ime
path:{[s;r;t]
 z:.stat.norminv count[t]?1f;
 p:prds .stat.gbm[s;r;deltas[first t;t]] z;
 p}

/ generate price path
/ security (id), (S)pot, (s)igma, (r)ate, (d)ate/(t)i(m)e
genp:{[id;S;s;r;dtm]
 t:abs type dtm;
 tm:("np" t in 12 14 15h)$dtm;
 p:S*path[s;r;tm%365D06];
 c:`id, `time`date[t=14h], `price;
 p:flip c!(id;dtm;p);
 p}

/ round price to nearest tick (up and down)
tickrnd:{if[99h=type x;x@:y];(y;x+y:x*floor y%x)}

/ randomly delay a timeseries
delay:{abs[type x]$x+next deltas[x]*count[x]?1f}
```

```
/ randomly throw away elements of list
filter:{y asc (neg"j"$x*n)?n:count y}

/ generate bid/ask quotes
/ (t)ick (s)ize, (q)uote (s)ize, (p)rice path
genq:{[ts;qs;p]
 q:p,'flip `bp`ap!tickrnd[ts] p `price;
 q:q,'flip `bs`as!1+count[p]?/:2#qs;
 q:`id`time`bs`bp`ap`as#q;
 q}

/ generate trade event
/ (b)id/ask flag, pct:percent fills
/ (b)id (s)ize, (b)id (p)rice, (a)sk (p)rice, (a)sk (s)izie
trd:{[b;pct;bs;bp;ap;as](ceiling pct*?[b;bs;as];?[b;bp;ap])}

/ generate trade event
/ (q)uote table and (pct) fill rate
gent:{[pct;q]
 q:filter[pct] raze (-1_@[;`time;delay] q@) each group q `id;
 t:q,' flip `ts`tp!trd[n?0b;(n:count q)?1f] . q `bs`bp`ap`as;
 t:`id`time`ts`tp#t;
 t}
```

## A.4  Timer

**timer.q**

```
/ timer jobs
timer.job:flip `name`func`time!"s*p"$\:()
timer.job,:(`;();0Wp)

\d .timer

/ merge record(y) into table(x) in reverse chronological order
merge:`time xdesc upsert

/ add new timer (f)unction with (n)ame and (t)i(m)e into (t)able
add:{[t;n;f;tm]
 r:(n;f;gtime tm);
 t:merge[t;$[0h>type tm;r;reverse flip r]];
 t}

/ run timer job at (i)ndex from (t)able and current time tm
run:{[t;i;tm]
```

```
 j:t i;
 t:.[t;();_;i];
 r:value (f:j `func),ltime tm;
 if[not null r;merge[t;(j `name;f;tm+r)]];
 t}

/ scan timer (t)able for runable jobs
loop:{[t;tm]
 while[tm>=last tms:t `time;t:run[t;-1+count tms;tm]];
 t}

/ helper function to generate repeating jobs
/ (d)elay, (e)nd (t)ime, (f)unction, tm:current time
until:{[d;et;f;tm]if[tm<et;@[value;f,tm;0N!];:d]}


.z.ts:loop`timer.job
```

## A.5  Logging

**log.q**

```
\d .log

h:-2                 / handle to print log
lvl:2                / log level
unit:"BKMGTP"        / memory unit character
mult:5 (1024*)\ 1    / memory multiplier

/ build memory string
mem:{@[string"i"$(3#x)%mult m;2;,;unit m:mult bin x 2]}

/ build log header
hdr:{string[(.z.D;.z.T)],mem system "w"}

/ build log message
msg:{if[x<=lvl;h " " sv hdr[],(y;$[10h=type z;z;-3!z])]}

/ user level functions to log messages
err:msg[0;"[E]"]
wrn:msg[1;"[W]"]
inf:msg[2;"[I]"]
dbg:msg[3;"[D]"]
trc:msg[4;"[T]"]
```

## A.6   Market Data

**md.q**

```
/ empty tables
ref:.util.sattr 1!flip `id`px`ts`qs`vol`rfr!"jffjff"$\:()
prices:.util.sattr flip `id`px`time!"jfp"$\:()
price:.util.sattr 1!prices
trades:.util.sattr flip `id`ts`tp`time!"jjfp"$\:()
trade:.util.sattr 1!trades
quotes:.util.sattr flip `id`bs`bp`ap`as`time!"jjffjp"$\:()
quote:.util.sattr 1!quotes

\d .md

/ update the current price for id
updp:{[id;tm]
 .log.dbg "updating price for ", string id;
 p:`price id;
 r:`ref id;
 z:.stat.norminv rand 1f;
 f:.stat.gbm[r `vol;r `rfr;(tm-p `time)%365D06;z];
 p:`id`px`time!(id;f*p `px;tm);
 `price`prices upsert\: p;
 }

/ update the current quote for id
updq:{[id;tm]
 .log.dbg "updating quote for ", string id;
 px:`price[id; `px];
 r:`ref id;
 q:`id`time!(id;tm);
 q,:`bp`ap!.sim.tickrnd[r `ts] px;
 q,:`bs`as!1+2?r `qs;
 `quote`quotes upsert\: q;
 }

/ update the current trade price for id
updt:{[id;tm]
 if[not id in key `quote;:(::)];
 .log.dbg "updating trade for ", string id;
 q:`quote id;
 t:`id`time!(id;tm);
 t,:`ts`tp!.sim.trd[rand 0b;rand 1f] . q `bs`bp`ap`as;
 `trade`trades upsert\: t;
 }
```

```
/ dump all md.q tables in partitioned database format
dump:{[db;tm]
 dt:"d"$tm;
 .log.inf "dumping tables in ", 1_ string ` sv db,`$string dt;
 0!/:`price`quote`trade;
 .Q.dpft[db;dt;`id] each`price`quote`trade`prices`quotes`trades;
 1!/:`price`quote`trade;
 }
```

## A.7 CEP Server

**cep.q**

```
\l qtips.q

c:.opt.config
c,:(`ref;`:ref.csv;"file with reference data")
c,:(`eod;0D23:59;"time for end of day event")
c,:(`db;`:db;"end of day dump location")
c,:(`debug;0b;"don't start engine")
c,:(`log;2;"log level")

/ utility function to generate until timer events
/ (e)nd (t)ime, ids, (d)uration, (f)unction
genu:{[et;ids;d;f]flip(`.timer.until;d;et;flip(f;ids))}

/ (p)arameter list, current (t)i(m)e
main:{[p;tm]
 r:("J FFJFF";1#",") 0: p `ref;
 `ref upsert `id`px`ts`qs`vol`rfr xcol r;
 `price upsert flip ((0!ref)`id`px),tm;
 tms:(n:count ids:key[ref]`id)#tm;
 u:genu[p `eod;ids];
 .timer.add[`timer.job;`updp;u[d:n?0D00:00:01;`.md.updp];tms];
 .timer.add[`timer.job;`updq;u[d+:n?0D00:00:01;`.md.updq];tms];
 .timer.add[`timer.job;`updt;u[d+:n?0D00:00:01;`.md.updt];tms];
 .timer.add[`timer.job;`dump;(`.md.dump;p `db);p[`eod]+"d"$tm];
 }

p:.opt.getopt[c;`ref`db] .z.x
if[`help in key p;-1 .opt.usage[1_c;.z.f];exit 1]
.log.lvl:p `log
if[not p`debug;main[p;.z.P]]
```

## A.8   Options

**opt.q**

```
\d .opt

/ empty getopt configuration
config:1#flip `opt`def`doc!"s**"$\:()

/ parse x according to (c)onfig and list of (h)syms
getopt:{[c;h;x]
 p:(!). c`opt`def;
 p:.Q.def[p] .Q.opt x;
 p:@[p;h;hsym];
 p}

/ wrap a list of (s)trings (l)eft and (r)ight text
wrap:{[l;r;s](max count each s)$s:l,/:s,\:r}

/ print usage according to (c)onfig and (f)ile
usage:{[c;f]
 u:enlist "usage: q ",(string f)," [option]...";
 a:wrap[(7#" "),"-";" "] string c `opt;
 a:a,'wrap["<";"> "] c `doc;
 a:a,'wrap["(";")"] -3!'c `def;
 u,:a;
 u}
```

## A.9   Network

**net.q**

```
/ table to hold active and inactive connection information
handle:.util.sattr 1!flip `h`active`user`host`address`time!"ibss*p"$\:()

/ record new client connection
.z.po:{[h]`handle upsert (h;1b;.z.u;.Q.host .z.a;"i"$0x0 vs .z.a;.z.P);}
.z.po 0i / simulate opening of 0

/ mark client connection as inactive
.z.pc:{[h]`handle upsert `h`active`time!(h;0b;.z.P);}

/ modify log header to include user, handle and host
\d .log
hdr:{string[(.z.D;.z.T;.z.u;.z.w;`handle . (.z.w;`host))],mem get"\\w"}
```

# A.10 Profiling

**prof.q**

```
/ empty events table
prof.events:flip `id`pid`func`time!"jjsn"$\:()

/ view of profile statistics report
prof.rpt::.prof.stats prof.events

\d .prof

pid:id:0

/ record timing of a (f)unction with (n)ame when called with (a)rgs
time:{[n;f;a]
 s:.z.p;
 id:.prof.id+:1;
 pid:.prof.pid;
 .prof.pid:id;
 r:f . a;
 .prof.pid:pid;
 `prof.events upsert (id;pid;n;.z.p-s);
 r}

/ instrument function (n)ame
instr:{[n]
 m:get f:get n;
 system "d .",string first m 3;
 n set (')[.prof.time[n;f];enlist];
 system "d .";
 n}

/ generate list of directories
dirs:{(` sv x,) each key[x] except `q`Q`h`j`o`prof}

/ generate list of profileable functions
lambdas:{x where 100h=(type get@) each x}

/ instrument all functions
instrall:{instr each lambdas raze .util.tree each `.,dirs`}

/ generate profile statistics report given an (e)vents table
stats:{[e]
 c:select sum time,nc:count i by id:pid from e;
 e:e pj update neg time from c;
 s:select sum time*1e-6,n:count i,avg nc by func from e;
```

```
s:update timepc:time%n from s;
s:`pct xdesc update pct:100f*time%sum time from s;
s}
```

## A.11  Derivative Pricing

**deriv.q**

```
\d .deriv

/ monte carlo
/ (S)pot, (s)igma, (r)ate, (t)ime,
/ (p)ayoff (f)unction, (n)umber of paths
mc:{[S;s;r;t;pf;n]
 z:.stat.bm n?/:count[t]#1f;
 f:S*prds .stat.gbm[s;r;deltas[first t;t]] z;
 v:pf[f]*exp neg r*last t;
 v}

/ monte carlo result statistics
/ (e)xpected (v)alue, (err)or, (n)umber of paths
mcstat:{`ev`err`n!(avg x;1.96*sdev[x]%sqrt n;n:count x)}

/ european option payoff
/ (c)all flag, stri(k)e, (f)uture prices
eu:{[c;k;f]0f|$[c;last[f]-k;k-last f]}

/ asian option payoff
/ (c)all flag, stri(k)e, (f)uture prices
as:{[c;k;f]0f|$[c;avg[f]-k;k-avg f]}

/ lookback payoff
/ (c)all flag, stri(k)e, (f)uture prices
lb:{[c;k;f]0f|$[c;max[f]-k;k-min f]}

/ barrier option
/ (b)arrier (f)unction, (p)ayoff (f)unction
/ (f)uture prices
bo:{[bf;pf;f]bf[f]*pf f}

/ black-scholes-merton
/ (S)pot, stri(k)e, (r)ate, (t)ime,
/ (c)all flag, (s)igma
bsm:{[S;k;r;t;c;s]
 x:(log[S%k]+rt:r*t)%ssrt:s*sqrt t;
```

```
d1:ssrt+d2:x-.5*ssrt;
n1:m*.stat.cnorm d1*m:-1 1f c;
n2:exp[neg rt]*m*.stat.cnorm d2*m;
p:(sn:S*n1)-kn:k*n2;
g:n1%s*ssrt;
v:sn*ssrt;
th:neg (r*kn)+.5*v*s%t;
rho:t*kn;
d:`price`delta`gamma`vega`theta`rho;
d!:(p;n1;g;sn*ssrt;th;rho);
if[0h<type p;d:flip d];
d}
```

## A.12   Histograms

**hist.q**

```
\d .hist

/ create range of n buckets between (s)tart and (e)nd
nrng:{[n;s;e]s+til[1+n]*(e-s)%n}

/ group data by a (b)inning (f)unction
bgroup:{[bf;x]
 b:nrng[bf x;min x;max x];
 g:group b bin x;
 g:b!x g til count b;
 g}

/ convert (w)indow size to number of buckets
nw:{[w;x]ceiling (max[x]-min x)%w}

/ square root bucket algorithm
sqrtn:{ceiling sqrt count x}

/ sturges' bucket algorithm
sturges:{ceiling 1f+2f xlog count x}

/ normalized skew used for doane
nskew:{[x].stat.skew[x]%sqrt 6f*(n-2)%(n+1)*3+n:count x}

/ doane's bucket algorithm
doane:{ceiling 1f+(2f xlog count x)+2f xlog 1f+abs nskew x}

/ scott's windowing algorithm
```

```
scott:{nw[;x] 3.4908*sdev[x]*count[x] xexp -1f%3f}

/freedman-diaconis windowing algorithm
fd:{nw[;x] 2f*.stat.iqr[x]*count[x] xexp -1f%3f}

/ bar-chart plotting function
/ (c)haracter, (w)indow size, (n)umber of points
bar:{[c;w;n]w$n#c}

/ dot-chart plotting function
/ (c)haracter, (w)indow size, (n)umber of points
dot:{[c;w;n]w$neg[n]$1#c}

/ use (p)lotting (f)unction to chart (d)ata with max (w)idth
chart:{[pf;w;d]
 n:"j"$(m&w)*n%m:max n:value d;
 d:d,'enlist each pf[w] each n;
 d}

/ example freedman-diaconis histogram composition
fdhist:chart[bar"*";30] count each bgroup[fd]@
```

## A.13   Q Tips

**qtips.q**

```
\l util.q
\l stat.q
\l sim.q
\l timer.q
\l log.q
\l md.q
\l opt.q
\l net.q
\l hist.q
\l deriv.q
\l prof.q
\l hist.q
```

# Index

# Acknowledgments

I would like to first and foremost thank my family. You have provided endless support and inspiration.

Thank you Attila Vrabecz for tearing my original draft to pieces. My understanding of q has proven unmatched to your encyclopedic knowledge of both k and q. The time you spent proofreading this book exceeded my expectations. Thank you Charles Skelton, for catching my exaggerations, assumptions and misunderstandings. Stevan Apter, Ye Tian, Winghang Chan, and Alexandre Beaulne, this book is vastly better because of your comments and suggestions. And to those I did not and cannot mention, thank you for being my enthusiast, disciplinarian, and sounding board. Of course, any errors that remain are my sole responsibility.

I would like to thank Kx Systems for their timely responses to all my questions, bug reports, and feature requests. And finally, I would like to acknowledge Tom Ferguson, who dared to say that q was better than Perl, and subsequently proved it to me.

# About the Author

Nick Psaris has been developing automated trading systems for over 15 years. After graduating Duke University with a degree in Physics and Chinese, he began his career in finance at Morgan Stanley in New York. He obtained his CFA charter in 2003, and a Masters in Computational Finance from the Tepper School of Business at Carnegie Mellon University in 2006. Nick then moved to Hong Kong and built an equity portfolio trading and backtesting system in q. After spending three years at Liquid Capital Markets Hong Kong building a high frequency automated market making system in q, he is now building an inventory optimization platform in q at a top tier American investment bank. Q Tips is based on his years of practical experience developing production trading systems in q.

5426202R00183

Printed in Germany
by Amazon Distribution
GmbH, Leipzig